NAZI JUSTIZ

NAZI JUSTIZ

Law of the Holocaust

RICHARD LAWRENCE MILLER

Westport, Connecticut
London

Library of Congress Cataloging-in-Publication Data

Miller, Richard Lawrence.
 Nazi justiz : law of the Holocaust / Richard Lawrence Miller.
  p. cm.
 Includes bibliographical references and index.
 ISBN 0–275–94912–5 (alk. paper)
 1. Jews—Legal status, laws, etc.—Germany—History. 2. National
socialism. 3. Holocaust, Jewish (1939–1945)—Germany. I. Title.
KK928.M55 1995
342.43'0873—dc20
[344.302873] 94–46176

British Library Cataloguing in Publication Data is available.

Library of Congress Catalog Card Number: 94–46176
ISBN: 0–275–94912–5

First published in 1995

Praeger Publishers, 88 Post Road West, Westport, CT 06881
An imprint of Greenwood Publishing Group, Inc.

Printed in the United States of America

The paper used in this book complies with the
Permanent Paper Standard issued by the National
Information Standards Organization (Z39.48–1984).

10 9 8 7 6 5 4 3 2 1

Copyright Acknowledgments

The author and publisher gratefully acknowledge permission for use of the following material:

From *The Destruction of the European Jews*, by Raul Hilberg (New York: Holmes & Meier Publishers, 1985). Copyright © 1985 by Raul Hilberg. Reprinted by permission of the publisher.

From *The Racial State*, by Michael Burleigh and Wolfgang Wipperman (New York: Cambridge University Press, 1991). Copyright © 1991 by Michael Burleigh and Wolfgang Wipperman. Reprinted with the permission of Cambridge University Press.

From *In Hitler's Germany* by Bernt Engelmann. English translation copyright © 1986 by Random House, Inc. Reprinted by permission of Pantheon Books, a division of Random House, Inc.

From *Blood and Banquets* by Bella Fromm. Copyright © 1990 by Carol Publishing Group. Published by arrangement with Carol Publishing Group. A Birch Lane Press Book.

From *Racial Hygiene* by Robert N. Proctor (Cambridge, MA: Harvard University Press, 1988). Reprinted with permission of Harvard University Press.

From *Voices from the Third Reich: An Oral History* edited by Johannes Steinhoff, Peter Pechel, and Dennis Showalter. Copyright © 1989 by Regnery Gateway, Inc. All Rights Reserved. Reprinted by special permission of Regnery Publishing, Inc., Washington, D.C.

From *Reaching for the Stars* by Nora Waln (Boston: Little, Brown, 1939). Reprinted by permission of the Estate of Nora Waln Osland-Hill, Buckshire, England.

From *A Nazi Childhood* by Winfried Weiss (Santa Barbara, CA: Capra Press, 1983). Reprinted with permission of Capra Press, Inc.

From *When Time Ran Out* by Frederic Zeller (Sag Harbor, NY: Permanent Press, 1989). Reprinted by permission of Permanent Press.

Every reasonable effort has been made to trace the owners of copyright materials in this book, but in some instances this has proven impossible. The author and publisher will be glad to receive information leading to more complete acknowledgments in subsequent printings of the book and in the meantime extend their apologies for any omissions.

CONTENTS

Apologia: THE SPIRIT OF LAWS

The spectacle of this new weapon—the legal arm of the anti-Jewish legislation of the Third Reich—used against a whole people, crushing not heads and bones but souls and spirits, is a new one. This approach is more subtle; it is endowed more with the aspect of permanence; it can be challenged with much greater difficulty; it does not lend itself easily to vivid dramatization and is hence less potent than cracked skulls or torn beards in arousing the horrified sympathy of foreign nations.

—Jacob R. Marcus, 1934[1]

This book seeks to view the Holocaust from the perspective of perpetrators. It seeks to show how decent and reasonable persons of high intelligence can cooperate to produce stupidity, brutality, and madness—yet be oblivious to what they are doing. Heinrich Himmler was deluded, but not lying, when he told SS colleagues in October 1943, "We have fulfilled this heavy task with love for our people, and we have not been damaged in the innermost of our being, our soul, our character."[2]

One of the most important, and least considered, aspects of the Holocaust is law. Nazis were fastidious about following legal requirements. A well-informed American declared in 1933 that the Nazi victory in the May *Reichstag* election, held after Hitler's accession to dictatorship, was "a legal victory, won under constitutional forms."[3] The Jewish-owned *Frankfurter Zeitung* newspaper agreed, "The movement has won power in a legal, democratic way."[4] Admittedly bureaucrats, lawyers, and judges followed specified procedures as they signed, stamped, and sealed documents authorizing actions by agents of the regime. The regime's obedience to legal forms strengthened its power. Upstanding citizens felt a moral obligation to submit to the law's authority; Thoreau's doctrine of civil disobedience was alien to the German public. Resistance was immoral. If any citizens felt unease about a particular policy, their pained consciences were salved via display of a suitably stamped document in pursuance to a decree. Nazis stacked their legal authorizations in a pile reaching to the moon—and Nuremberg Military Tribunal prosecutors gratefully used those authorizations to document Nazi crimes. Those prosecutors understood what escaped the American observer and the *Frankfurter Zeitung* in 1933.

Nuremberg tribunal prosecutors understood the spirit of laws. Law does not exist independently of persons who believe in it. During a Roman Catholic mass the faithful witness and participate in a miracle. A group of atheists could gather and mimic the proceedings, but the activity would no longer have meaning even though words and ceremony were duplicated in finest detail. Nazis were legal atheists; they did not believe in law. They duplicated the outward form but emptied legal ritual of meaning. The decrees, courts, and documents were no more valid than a mass celebrated by an atheist. Retaining the outward forms of law, however, made citizens feel comfortable: The old priests were gone, and the new ones spoke with a strange accent, but nonetheless they were adept with traditional words and ceremonies, and the congregation felt reassured. Even troubled members would not consider leaving the Church. What they did not realize was that the Church was gone. The community of believers remained, but had been hijacked by unbelieving persons garbed in priestly robes, who cynically exploited the congregation's beliefs in order to enslave the faithful.

Nuremberg prosecutors saw through all that. Elections do not demonstrate existence of democracy; they are a ritual of democracy and are meaningless when performed in other contexts. Court sessions are a ritual of law but mean nothing if conducted by persons who demolish the foundation upholding law. All that is left is rubble.

Nazis argued that law is neutral, a tool that can be used for any purpose. Nuremberg prosecutors countered that law cannot exist apart from its protection of individuals against excess by ruthless private and public agents. Defendants accused of crimes against humanity coolly produced decrees and permits in triplicate, and were genuinely shocked when prosecutors dismissed all those documents.

Although this book views the Holocaust from the angle used by perpetrators, it evaluates perpetrators with standards used by Nuremberg prosecutors. The Nuremberg Military Tribunal was not "victor's vengeance." It was an all too rare evocation of law's purpose, a purpose that opponents of democracy seek to obscure, deny, and forget. Nazis did not write and enforce laws. Nazis plotted and committed crimes.

This book not only documents how outward forms of law can be used to commit crimes. That documentation is part of a larger story, in which the Holocaust becomes a case study of a destruction process available for use against other victims—anytime, anywhere. In this interpretation mass killings of the Holocaust were but the climax of the final stage in the destruction process. That outcome was not incomprehensible. It was probable once the German public decided that ordinary productive people should be excluded from life in normal society. In his monumental work *The Destruction of the European Jews* Raul

Hilberg outlines the destruction process. The following outline is adapted from his.[5]

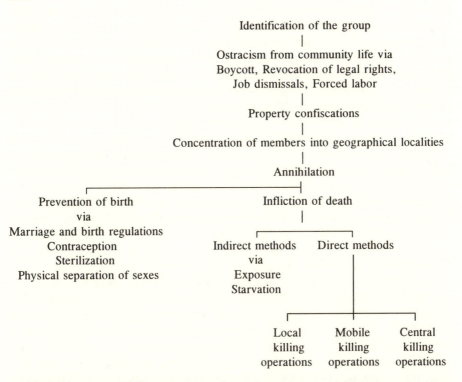

By definition a "process" is something that continues. If volatile chemicals are combined and produce a violent reaction we cannot stop the process until the ingredients are exhausted. To say, "this far, and no farther," is to ignore that a process—not a journey—is underway. And if we ignore what is happening, we cannot control what is happening. The only sure way to avoid fulfillment of a process is to stop feeding it, smother any violent reaction already underway, and abandon the disastrous experiment.

Most Germans did not believe the final steps would be taken. They saw each measure as a discrete event and failed to understand that each step prepared the way for the next. The SS journal *Das Schwarze Korps* noted in 1938, "What is radical today is moderate tomorrow."[6] In 1933 the Nazis had no plan to kill all the Jews, and even militants would have shrunk in horror from such a suggestion. Gradually, over the next decade, "reasonable people" found they had to become a little harsher. By 1943, the context of the war against Jews had escalated to the point where warriors could blandly pass bureaucratic memos back and forth about behavior that would have seemed unconscionable in 1933. What happened in the Third Reich could happen in any country holding the values of Western civilization. Not only could happen, but *will* happen if a country targets a group of ordinary people for exclusion from everyday life.

This book's examples of Nazi actions come mainly from Germany of the 1930s. That era is chosen because it was a time of peace. Measures we shall discuss were not taken in desperation as military reverses mounted. The measures were passed "lawfully" after due deliberation in a robust country of growing strength. Leaders who proposed and officials who implemented the measures saw themselves as dealing simply and firmly with a "problem" that seemed to grow worse no matter what was done. The steps they took had wide support from the news media and from law-abiding citizens.

At the time this book was written, the Holocaust was normally interpreted as a Jewish experience. Yes, other groups suffered from Nazi persecution, but scholars who concentrated on them were thought to miss the Holocaust's essence. This book argues, however, against interpreting the Holocaust as a Jewish experience—at least as the term "Jewish" is commonly understood in the 1990s. As we shall see, Nazis defined Jews by genealogy rather than religion, using the bogus concept of a Jewish "race." (Whenever this book uses Nazi terminology, quotation marks around the passage should be inferred even if they are not supplied.) In Nazi Germany a person did not have to practice Judaism in order to be a Jew; lifelong Christians could be Jews, be forced to wear the yellow star, be transported "to the east." Practitioners of Judaism were the primary victims, but Nazis classified as Jews many persons who were not considered such before or after the Third Reich. The number of those victims is unclear. As we shall see, about 1933 racial Jews may have numbered six million in Germany. From the beginning, they were subject to the same sanctions directed against the 600,000 persons who practiced Judaism. A Jew was a Jew. The impact on German society, however, was such that even Nazis shrank back; eventually new legal definitions of "Jew" allowed many of those millions to escape sanctions imposed on practitioners of Judaism. At first, however, the millions experienced the full force of the war on Jews. Those victims were neither more nor less blameless than practitioners of Judaism, members of Romany, or people who loved someone of the same gender. But the millions we speak of here, unlike gypsies and homosexuals, were attacked because Nazis considered them "Jews." Nazis were less interested in someone's religion than in someone's ancestors. Judaism was considered an outward manifestation of inherent biological deficiency, a deficiency hidden within Jews who did not practice Judaism and who could be detected only through genealogy.

Anti-Semitism provided soil where the Holocaust could grow, but did not cause the Holocaust, any more than soil "causes" any other crop to grow. Nazis used anti-Semitic feelings as fertilizer, nurturing public acceptance of attacks on ordinary persons regardless of whether they had connection with Judaism. What caused the Holocaust was the desire to destroy one's neighbors. If that desire were unique to persons who resided in Germany during the 1930s, then this book would recount a mere historical curiosity. Unfortunately this book's interpretation of the Holocaust argues that its spirit still lives among us, and that we can be filled with so much goodness and compassion that we are oblivious to evil and savagery we visit upon our neighbors. Humans today are no different than villagers who greeted Hitler:

> People . . . wove a carpet of flowers from their gardens. They placed this on the road over which their Führer was to pass. Either word of it reached him somehow or, as one old man in that village is certain, he has very long sight. His car and those that escorted him halted. He got down. Wheels were not allowed to crush the blossoms.
>
> The cars and the escort went around. The Führer walked through the village. He spoke gently to men, women, and children. He took the hands of two little ones who ran to him. Babies went into his strange arms fearlessly.
>
> No one who saw this could correctly call it play-acting. He was moved by the gift of flowers put on his road. He was grateful for love. Goodness shone in his face.
>
> When he had gone, they said: "He is our true German Führer. He would not let a flower, a bird, or a person be crushed if he knew it was to be done. He is enthroned in our hearts. Heaven sent him."[7]

National Socialism is humanity's greatest experience. It is man gloriously in search of his soul.

—Joseph Goebbels[8]

1

IDENTIFICATION

If a group is to be eliminated from society, members of the group must be detected. To detect them, we must have a way to identify characteristics possessed by members and not possessed by the rest of us. And we must use those characteristics to define membership in the targeted group.

Offhand one might think that a Jew can be defined readily with a dictionary, but the task is not straightforward. A confounding factor is the reason a group is targeted. That reason permits the majesty of the law to display all its finery, expanding the definition when needed to sweep up certain individuals, contracting the definition to protect others. Zen masters of the law may take on contortions to disguise the arbitrary nature of their actions. The masters may pretend obedience to a sovereign power that all must obey. But victims understand well enough that such officials merely use law to clothe their naked personal desire.

Precise legal definition of a targeted group is crucial to the destruction process. Until then victims can call upon governmental authorities for protection against vigilante or mob action. Protection might be inadequate or even nonexistent, but at least a victim has reason to cry out, "Help, police!" After the victim becomes a legal target, however, police and courts become mechanisms of destruction rather than protection. Not only the hatred of the public but the power of the state is directed against a victim. Attacks that were extralegal or even illegal become not only legal but necessary. Authorities who ignore the presence of a victim become derelict in their duty to the public. Victims must not only avoid the mob and vigilantes, but avoid law-abiding patriots whose separation from the police is measured by no more than a phone connection. A victim no longer calls for police, for when they come, their guns point in a new direction.

Victims who were formerly enemies of the people now become enemies of the state. This change in status is important. Now bureaucrats take over from the rabble. What was once disorganized becomes scientific, legal, and precise. In addition, more and more officials acquire an interest in the destruction process. Personal careers and departmental budgets become enmeshed in the effort. When ordering an action there is no longer a need to ask why people have been selected as victims; the law authorizes action, and that is justification enough. If I do not issue the directive, my competitor at the next desk will. If my department does not conduct the action, another department will act in order to poach on my budget. The destruction process takes on a momentum independent of any threat that victims pose to society.

This chapter examines the first element of the destruction process, the procedures used to identify who will be victims.

CHARACTERISTICS OF JEWS

This book was written during the 1990s in the United States, a time and place with a consensus that Jews are ordinary human beings. At a stretch one could find characteristics by which Jews differed from non-Jews, but no more than redheads or baseball fans differed from other persons. Characteristics defining all those groups were considered trivial. Tints of anti-Semitism still colored American society, varying in strength from locale to locale. Nonetheless most Americans who learned that an acquaintance was a Jew took the news with equanimity, as if they had learned the acquaintance played chess or shopped at a health food store.

Part of the reason for such equanimity was that, with few exceptions, nothing about a Jew's appearance or behavior differed from anyone else. A handful of Jews could be identified by outward manifestation in clothing or hair style, just as a handful of Roman Catholics could. A handful could be identified by behavior, just as vegetarians could. Those identifying characteristics, however, were actions. Actions can cease. A Jew who gave up those actions could no longer be identified. Moreover, a non-Jew who adopted those actions would be misidentified as a Jew.

If our intention is to eliminate Jews from society, we must use inescapable criteria for defining Jews. If police pound on a door at 3:00 A.M. and roar, "Are you the Jew Schmidt?" we can't have Herr Schmidt send them on their way with the reply, "I'm not a Jew any more." The law must confer on Jews a status that is unaffected by inward belief or outward action. To confer such status the law must go beyond the dictionary definition of Jew. If the goal sought by eliminating Jews is not achieved after that first expansion of definition, the definition will expand again and again as the war on Jews intensifies. The process of definition will encompass persons who the warriors had never intended as victims in the beginning, perhaps even persons who once supported the war.

Having stated the principles involved, let us examine how they guided the process in Nazi Germany. Let us see how Nazis specified characteristics that would distinguish ordinary people from everyone else.

DETECTION OF JEWISH CHARACTERISTICS

One of the first Nazi definitions of Jew came from Alfred Rosenberg in 1920: "A Jew is he whose parents on either side are nationally Jews. Anyone who has a Jewish husband or wife is henceforth a Jew."[1] Although Rosenberg's definition had no legal standing in 1920, after the Nazis achieved control of the German state in 1933 their definitions of Jew were based on the same sort of reasoning as Rosenberg's.

In Rosenberg's first sentence he defined what Jews are not; they are not Germans. More importantly, he establishes an inescapable status. The adverb "nationally" means that, in legal jargon, Jewishness works as a "corruption of blood."[2] Once a Jew, always a Jew. A victim's parent who renounces the Jewish religion remains a Jew. The victim's own religion is irrelevant. One is defined as a Jew not by one's own beliefs or actions, but by those of one's parents. The definition holds one responsible for actions of someone else. Despite later modifications of the definition, that principle of responsibility remained. Perhaps the most notorious illustration was the 1938 Crystal Night fine levied against all Germany's Jews; officially the fine was an atonement because a Jew murdered a Nazi official in France. That element of Crystal Night, an event to be discussed more fully later, shocked much of the world as vicious Nazi creativity. But the fine's origin lay within the legal definition of Jew. The definition itself made such persecution possible.

The second sentence of Rosenberg's definition deepened the pool of victims by defining people as Jewish through a spouse. Those new victims, however, could escape through divorce or death of a spouse. Although that route did work for some persons, it was not offered as a humanitarian gesture. By establishing a class of "voluntary victims" the definition increased pressure on spouses. It also established a class of Germans who could be hounded as traitors to the *Volk*.[3] Jews by birth could not alter their biological destiny (biological in a legal, not a scientific, sense). But Germans who chose to become Jews through marriage were acting with free will. They had no reason to be Jews, so their conduct was despicable.

Rosenberg's marriage clause had an ex post facto element. A German who married a Jew in 1905 had no notice that such conduct transformed the German into a Jew from 1920 forward. People are held accountable for actions they might have avoided if they had known that disapproval would later emerge.

The Rosenberg definition also allowed unsuspecting persons to be transformed into Jews. If a person's classification depended upon the parents' classification, then by extrapolation the parental classification depended on the grandparents, and the grandparents' classification depended on the great-grandparents, and so on. If a person could belong to the Jewish "nationality" regardless of personal religious creed, discovery of previously unknown Jewish ancestors could transform descendants into Jews. An enthusiastic Nazi could become a Jew:

My motherly [reporter] friend unburdened herself desperately: ["]From January 1 [1934] on, press members will have to give evidence of their Aryan descent."

"Why should *you* worry?"

"I have reason, Bella darling. I wrote for my papers, chased all over the place getting them. Finally, I found out that my grandmother was Jewish. Nobody knew anything about it. Now I lose my living."[4]

A U-boat commander recalled, "I signed up for the navy in 1936. Everything went fine until one day I was informed that I'd been discharged. I mean, I looked like any other blond, curly-haired Hitler Youth, and took it for granted that my Aryan *Nachweis* was no problem. But my father had been reactivated as a colonel and had to submit evidence of Aryan heritage. . . . It turned out that although my grandfather's parents had married as Christians, both of them had come from Jewish families. My grandfather was a *Volljude* (100 percent Jewish) by blood. . . . I was completely shocked."[5] Such discoveries were especially awkward if they involved prominent persons. The chairman of the 1936 Nazi Olympic effort had to resign when his Jewish ancestry was learned,[6] and the army officer in charge of constructing the Olympic Village was dismissed from the military due to Jewish lineage.[7] Despite a public pledge of loyalty to Hitler, the number two man in the *Stahlhelm* (a right-wing veterans group allied with the Nazis) lost his position upon discovery of a Jewish forebear.[8] The ambassador to Lithuania was recalled when his Jewish pedigree was revealed,[9] and the same apparently happened to the consul general in Palestine when his wife's Jewish ancestry became known.[10] Not all such revelations were inadvertent. Business and professional rivals would trace one another's family trees in search of ancestry that would remove a competitor from the field.[11]

Rosenberg provided a far surer means of detecting Jews than did the more familiar Nazi racial propaganda about physical characteristics. Many Aryans had physical features ascribed to Jews, and many Jews looked like Aryans. Indeed, the Propaganda Ministry produced a film showing how easily Jews could transform their physical appearance and pass as Aryans.[12] "Blue-eyed Susanne, with the blond braids, who had recently been praised in our 'Racial Theory' class as a perfect example of the build and skull formation of the Nordic type, was abruptly expelled from school after being classified as one-hundred-percent Jewish in accordance with the Nuremberg Laws."[13] By defining who was a Jew through genealogy, rather than religion or personal appearance, Rosenberg succeeded in establishing an inescapable status. One's biological ancestors could not be changed.[14] The need for genealogical documents produced new jobs; licensed genealogical researchers made a living by helping citizens prove their pedigrees.[15] Because many genealogical records were the property of churches, Christian clergy assisted Nazis in identifying who was a Jew.[16] Perhaps an individual clergyman might excuse genealogical assistance by arguing he protected people through documenting their Aryan heritage. But such collaboration also targeted new victims. A mere definition enlisted Christian clergy in the war against Jews. Teachers joined the hunt as well. "Ancestor Treasure Troves," sets of colored cards and boxes, were distributed to school children with directions on tracing their families' genealogy.[17] In 1937 a national competition was held for high-school teachers, in which they sought more effective means of tracing "racial heritage" of local families. "The *Ärzteblatt für Berlin* noted that one teacher, as part of his project for the contest, had managed to uncover a Jew among ancestors of a certain family; the journal reported that descendants of this Jew (baptized in 1685) had been entirely unaware of this aspect of their family background."[18] The importance of definition in the destruction process cannot be overemphasized.[19]

An early legally binding Nazi definition of Jew was supplied in the First Regulation for Administration of the Law for the Restoration of the Professional Civil Service on April 11, 1933: "A person is to be regarded as non-Aryan, who is descended from non-Aryans, especially Jewish parents or grandparents. This holds true even if only one parent or grandparent is of non-Aryan descent. This premise especially obtains if one parent or grandparent was of Jewish faith. . . . If Aryan descent is doubtful, an opinion must be obtained from the expert on racial research commissioned by the Reich Minister of the Interior."[20] In doubtful cases, racial status of great-grandparents would be considered. A September 16 decree allowed civil service workers to be defined as non-Aryan if one great-grandfather was Jewish by descent regardless of the great-grandfather's own religion.[21] In 1934, however, a grandparent was considered Jewish only if both great-grandparents were Jewish.[22]

The civil service definition differs from Rosenberg's concept in several ways. The most obvious is through introduction of the term "Aryan," traditionally used to identify a language group but adopted by Nazis to signify the master race. Their biology may have been crackpot, but here we see again an effort to bestow an inescapable status, this time through genetics. In that era the necessary technology to examine a person's genetic makeup did not exist, so makeup was inferred from gross physical characteristics (color of hair and eyes, shape of nostrils and skull, and the like).[23] Walter Gross, a top Nazi physician and *Honorarprofessor* of Racial Science at the University of Berlin, noted, "Correct racial diagnosis of the individual spouse, as possibilities of observation now stand, almost invariably depends upon the bodily appearance; thus such diagnosis can not or can only incompletely comprehend the quality of psyche and character."[24] The latter point was important. As much as Nazis condemned "Jewish mentality" they were unable to find a reliable biological sign to reveal it. The 1936 edition of an internationally used textbook on genetics and eugenics coauthored by Dr. Fritz Lenz, professor of biology at the University of Berlin, said, "If here, in the first place, the *differences* in the endowment of the Jews and Teutons were stressed, it should not be overlooked, however, that in external mental dispositions they resemble each other, and this is particularly true if 'Teutons' are to designate people of the tall blonde race."[25] Inability to distinguish

Jews by appearance or action is why they were ordered to wear yellow stars. "He [the Jew] was made recognizable by the Jewish star lest, under the mask of an honest man, he carry on inflammatory work inimical to the folk." So said the Army Supreme Command.[26]

Racial science involved artistic license, providing employment for bureaucrats of the Interior Ministry. Their artistic tastes determined subsequent lives—and sometimes deaths—of persons brought before them. "Scientific precision" in definition of Jew actually introduced an arbitrary element to selection of victims. Bureaucrats could shift the boundary that separated victims from the rest of society. And a boundary that shifts does not exist.

By making "Jewish faith" proof of membership in a "non-Aryan" people the April 1933 definition moves into the realm of Lamarckian evolution. Nearly 200 years before the Nazi era, Chevalier de Lamarck argued that physical traits acquired after birth can be passed to offspring. For example, amputation of an arm would eventually cause a person's descendants to be born without an arm. Although absolute disproof of his theory awaited demonstration of DNA's molecular activity in the 1950s, Lamarck's honorable though mistaken work had been thoroughly discredited by the 1930s. And the notion that an intellectual decision (religious faith) affects chromosomes goes far beyond Lamarck's more modest claim.

The April 1933 definition reflected a basic, though unacknowledged, tension in Nazi biological claims. The reliable authority Hans F. K. Gunther reported that Hitler himself believed in Lamarckian evolution,[27] but Nazi scientists spotted the trap laid by such a belief. If one's actions could transform an Aryan into a Jew, perhaps actions could also transform a Jew into an Aryan. If genetic distinction between Jew and Aryan was malleable, no biological basis existed for the Nazi war on Jews. A broad consensus of Nazi racial and genetic scientists held that Lamarckian thought was incorrect, that biological inheritance was governed instead by Mendelian genetics. As understood in that era (an understanding modified decades later as molecular level environmental effects were explored), Mendelian principles demonstrated no environmental effect on genes. A person's race could never change.[28] Statutes based on race were therefore statutes based on science. Hitler's personal belief notwithstanding, his regime held that race was inviolable. The 1937 edition of *Handbook for the Hitler Youth* states, "Environmental influences have never been known to bring about the formation of a new race. That is one more reason for our belief that a Jew remains a Jew, in Germany or in any other country. He can never change his race, even by centuries of residence among another people."[29]

Nonetheless by the 1930s Nazi ideology held that a person's Jewish faith had a biological impact on subsequent generations of offspring. Rosenberg's clever separation of church and race was lost. "Corruption of blood" was transformed from legal principle to ostensible biological fact. "Whoever has Jewish blood in his veins will sooner or later reveal the Jewish part of his character," said *Der Stürmer* in March 1936.[30] Although not all Nazis accepted that newspaper's reports at face value, anti-Semites had long enunciated the principle. Said one *Reichstag* member in 1895, "Every Jew who at this very moment has not as yet transgressed is likely to do so at some future time under given circumstances because his racial characteristics drive him on in that direction."[31] Hitler agreed in 1922, saying it was "beside the point whether the individual Jew is 'decent' or not. In himself he carries those characteristics which Nature has given him, and he cannot ever rid himself of those characteristics. And to us he is harmful."[32] A 1944 SS[33] and police manual illustrates results of the law's April 1933 definition as supported by findings of Nazi scientists: "People who on the basis of their character attitude vow their allegiance to us, thereby prove that they possess Nordic qualities even if externally they do not entirely correspond to the Nordic ideal. The upright vow of allegiance to the Reich by a [non-German] European volunteer, therefore, is not only a political factor but also the expression of a biological attachment."[34] A person's politics revealed that person's biological makeup. By implication a non-Aryan was inherently subversive to the state. And because politics was determined by biology, persuasion was useless against a political opponent. The opponent had to be eliminated from society. A 1944 Wehrmacht instruction book demonstrates this belief: "Who believes in the possibility of improving the parasite (for instance, the louse)? Who believes that there is a way of compromise with a parasite? We have only the choice of being devoured by the parasite or of destroying him. THE JEW MUST BE ANNIHILATED WHEREVER WE MEET HIM!"[35] Such were conclusions permitted by the April 1933 definition of "non-Aryan," which made science yield to political correctness.

A few months after this transformation of science we find a further development in the Homestead Law of September 29 (sometimes called Peasants Farm Law):

(1) Only a person of German or cognate blood may be a peasant.
(2) A person is not considered German or as having cognate blood, if his paternal or maternal ancestors have Jewish or colored blood in their veins.
(3) The first of January, 1800, is the day that decides whether the premises of Section I obtain. In case of doubt whether the premises of Section I obtain, the inheritance court decides on a motion of the [hereditary manor] owner or of the district leader of the peasants.[36]

In contrast to previous definitions, this one limits use of genealogy. Everyone starts with a clean slate on January 1, 1800, and is assumed to be Aryan. Regarding that date a party order declared, "Prior to the emancipation of the Jews the penetration of their blood into German folkdom was virtually impossible."[37] If no ancestor was either non-Aryan or the spouse or offspring of a non-Aryan after January 1, 1800, a person's Aryan status could not be altered by further genealogical exploration. What some ancestor had done in 1799 or earlier was irrelevant. Given the elastic definition of non-Aryan, and eternal corruption of blood, without such a cut-off date the existence of any Aryans became problematical. This new definition blended objective fact and political necessity by retaining the genealogical principle but arbitrarily limiting its application. Even so, Nazi doctrine held that biological Jewish identity could diminish as generations passed, until descendants of Jews could be considered Aryan. For example, normally the great-great-grandchild of baptized Jews was Aryan, as was the great-grandchild of a marriage between Jew and Aryan.[38]

The phrase "blood in their veins" is meant literally. Although researchers of the German Medical Association were never able to devise a blood test that distinguished Aryans from non-Aryans,[39] Nazis nonetheless maintained that a person's ancestry was carried in the blood. "Early this year Dr. Hans Serelman of Niederlungwitz was sent to a concentration camp on the charge of 'race defilement.' . . . The charge against him was based on the fact that to save the life of an Aryan patient the doctor submitted him to a blood transfusion and had given his own non-Aryan blood for the transfusion."[40] In that same year, 1935, a *Sturmabteilung*[41] (SA) man injured in an auto accident was rushed to a nearby Jewish hospital where he received a transfusion of "Jewish blood." An SA tribunal considered whether his possession of Jewish blood required expulsion from the SA. The tribunal ruled that the blood was from a Jew who had fought at the front in World War I, therefore, in keeping with the Hindenburg Exception to the Law for the Restoration of the Professional Civil Service (discussed in our next chapter), civic duty impelled the conclusion that such blood did not contaminate racial purity. The tribunal found, however, that if the Jewish donor had not been covered by the Hindenburg Exception, the SA man's Aryan purity would have been compromised.[42] After the *Anschluss* (the 1938 political joining of Germany and Austria) Viennese hospitals maintained separate blood supplies for Jews and Aryans, so patients would be given blood only from donors of the same race.[43] Many Nazis contended that a blood transfusion could transform an Aryan into a non-Aryan. "Families," according to Hitler, "even if they have only a minute quantity of Jewish blood in their veins, regularly produce, generation by generation, at last one pure Jew."[44]

Administrative regulations[45] accompanying the Reich Citizenship Law[46] (one of the "Nuremberg Decrees" of September 15, 1935) provided definitions that lasted until the end of the Third Reich. The new rules addressed problems caused by the old definitions.

One of the most vexing problems had been the corruption of blood that could transform an Aryan into a Jew upon discovery of a distant Jewish ancestor. The new regulations addressed this problem by starting the genealogical clock on September 15, 1935, by stopping genealogical exploration at the grandparent level, and by establishing degrees of Jewishness—a person was no longer all Jew or not Jew.

Persons who fell somewhere in the middle were described with the term *Mischlinge* (hybrid or crossbreed or mongrel). *Mischlinge* of the first degree were "half Jews," persons not of the Jewish faith and not married to a Jew (as of

September 15, 1935, or later) but who were descended from two Jewish grandparents. *Mischlinge* of the second degree were "quarter Jews," descended from one Jewish grandparent. For genealogical purposes *Mischlinge* grandparents counted as Aryan. Government regulations and penalties stopped at the grandparent level, but assorted Nazi agencies traced pedigree further. The Nazi party refused membership even to *Mischlinge* of the fifth degree, although in law they were generally treated as Aryans. The regime published easily understood charts illustrating *Mischlinge* degrees and their relation to "purebred" Jews and Aryans. A later student of Nazi genetic theories shrewdly noted, "Charts illustrating the various degrees of mixed marriages . . . are exact replicas of the well-known diagrams showing the results of Mendel's experiments. Jewish blood is thus consistently considered as if it were a hereditary characteristic dependent on a single gene."[47] We must remember that such a genealogical scheme has no biological basis and is instead a legal fiction used to sort persons into different categories that determine who will become victims.

Jews suffered far more than *Mischlinge*, but the latter did not escape penalties. Passport restrictions applied against Jews also applied to first-degree *Mischlinge*,[48] and first-degree *Mischlinge* might be included when companies were ordered to dismiss Jewish workers.[49] *Mischlinge* involved in litigation faced judges who had declared their hostility against non-Aryans. Worse yet, Jewish lawyers could represent only Jews, so *Mischlinge* had to use Aryan attorneys who were formally hostile against non-Aryans. Hitler Youth service was a prerequisite for many careers, but *Mischlinge* were barred from the Hitler Youth, thereby closing careers theoretically open to them.[50] *Mischlinge* who lost their jobs could not receive unemployment help from either Nazi or Jewish relief agencies.[51] In that respect *Mischlinge* were worse off than Jews. Nonetheless, although *Mischlinge* had to live under disabilities, most were allowed to live.

Under the genealogical scheme outlined above, corruption of blood still existed but could diminish generation by generation. Chances were small that genealogical research would turn Aryans into *Mischlinge*, let alone into Jews. As happened with the news reporter mentioned above, one would have to discover that, unknown to the family, a grandparent had been a member of the Jewish religious community. (In theory a grandparent's status was determined solely by personal religious faith, not by genealogy of great-grandparents or other ancestors.)[52]

Mischlinge were defined by genealogy. In contrast, Jews were defined not only by genealogy but by marital status and religion. While considering the following rules, remember that "full Jew" is a genealogical classification having nothing to do with personal religious faith. An atheist or a Roman Catholic priest could be a full Jew.[53] This was well understood, as illustrated by a servant's refusal to bring a Christmas Eve dinner in 1934:

"I cannot serve it. There is a Jewess among you."

"Frau von D. is a Catholic—three generations a Catholic. You have served her every Christmas Eve since you entered our service."

"I do not serve her any longer. I am a good German, a *Kerndeutscher*."

"You know well that she is a good German and that her husband was *Kerndeutsch*—he fell fighting for our country."

"I obey the Party. I do not hand food to a woman of Jewish blood ever again."[54]

A 1933 directive ordering companies to fire Jewish employees said, "It is not religion but race that is decisive. Christianized Jews are thus equally affected."[55] Defining Jews by genealogy rather than religious profession greatly expanded the pool of victims. One contemporary observer said the number of German "Jews" more than doubled.[56] That would be in keeping with Nazi rhetoric complaining about "1,000,000 Jews too many in Germany."[57] Another observer said the number tripled, from 600,000 by religious profession to two million by genealogy.[58] A Ministry of Interior official put the number at 1.5 million,[59] a figure also given by a United States Young Men's Christian Association official who examined the situation.[60] Another source put the total at three million,[61] about 5 percent of Germany's population. Still another source said up to four million Germans had at least one Jewish grandparent, disqualifying them from jobs that then became available to Nazis.[62] Another source reported that such persons numbered at least four million.[63] Yet another put the number at four to six million, with the higher number accepted by a *New York Times* editorial writer at the time—10 percent of the population.[64] "I questioned . . . a manufacturer, connoisseur and philosopher, a Christian who was made a Jew by official decree because one of his parents or grandparents was Jewish. . . . He laughs at Hitler's 'distorting of ethnic history.' . . . He laughs at the sheer stupidity of the proscription. But he does not laugh at Hitler."[65]

Under Nuremberg Law regulations anyone descended from four Jewish grandparents was a "full Jew" regardless of the descendant's personal religious faith. That was straight genealogy. Despite the scheme's logic, however, no "three-quarters" Jews existed. A third grandparent bestowed "full Jew" status. An illegitimate child born of a Jew and an Aryan after July 31, 1936, was Jewish regardless of the child's personal religious faith. The illegitimacy regulation was needed, in part, because under Nazi law, marriages could not be contracted between Jews and German Aryans as of September 15, 1935. Churches, synagogues, and foreign governments might consider such couples to be married, but the Third Reich did not. The illegitimacy regulation implied, however, that a child from a marriage contracted between Jew and Aryan before September 15, 1935, might not be Jewish if the child was not a member of the Jewish religious community. In December 1938 Hitler confirmed that interpretation by ruling such offspring to be first-degree *Mischlinge*.[66]

One further factor could determine if a person was a Jew. That factor was nationality; for example, whether the person was a French citizen living in

Germany. A foreign *Mischling* could retain that status in circumstances where a German *Mischling* would become a Jew.[67] Rules on interrelation of nationality with genealogy were no less complex than other regulations we have already examined, but we need not consider details here.

Although all these regulations appeared to give certain persons a right to remain unmolested by Nazi agencies, a distinguished authority has pointed out that "survival in Nazi Germany could not be assured by insisting upon one's rights."[68] In reality, the regulations only guaranteed that certain persons would be targeted as victims, not that the remainder were safe.

Occasionally a targeted person could move aside. Through an official process called Liberation, a full Jew could become a *Mischling* of the first degree, and a first-degree *Mischling* could enter the second degree. Two types of Liberation existed.

"Pseudo Liberation" depended on facts or legal interpretations. For example, in theory the status of great-grandparents was irrelevant, but occasionally theory yielded to situations. A grandparent who belonged to the Jewish religious community could be reclassified as Christian if the grandparent was the child of Christian parents.[69] (That process could go the other direction, however, catastrophically transforming an Aryan into a *Mischling* or a *Mischling* into a Jew by declaring that a Christian grandparent was Jewish because the great-grandparents were Jews.[70])

"Real Liberation" occurred when a person's Nazi zeal was so outstanding as to reveal the person's true Aryan biological makeup that had been unapparent through genealogy. Such an endangered person thereby had motivation to promote the war on Jews with especial vigor. Hitler personally upgraded thousands of persons whose pedigrees would have made them subject to persecutions they advocated.[71]

Through definitions, definers can reveal as much about themselves as about what they define. For example, Liberation based on facts was "pseudo" or false. Liberation based on subjective personal opinion was "real." Such rhetoric holds that belief can overpower facts through a triumph of the will; the objective universe is less important than human desires. For me, your desires are part of the objective universe, and thereby your desires are less important than mine. My will be done. Genealogical rules demonstrate a determination to hold people accountable for actions of others, a philosophy that easily rationalizes punishing innocent persons in lieu of perpetrators who are inaccessible. Such a policy discourages dissent, as dissenters know they endanger others. Through such a policy, authorities also demonstrate they are more concerned about releasing tensions of rage through pursuit of sacrificial victims than about protecting society through pursuit of justice. And although the definition of Jew extrapolates from Lamarckian theory and holds that intellectual activity has physical effects on offspring and their descendants, the definition contradictorily holds that intellectual activity is a manifestation of a person's genetic inheritance. Thought and biology cause each other. Despite confusion in logic, the definition of Jew seeks to establish objective physical criteria for identifying enemies of the state.

In summary, the Nazi definition of Jew portrays the definers as persons filled with rage who believe that opinion is more important than fact, that their opinions are superior to anyone else's, and that their actions express an inescapable biological imperative—to resist their actions is to resist life itself.

In addition to what the definition of Jew reveals about the definers, the *process* of definition reveals something. By establishing bureaucratic rules, persecutors can profess to be as trapped as victims are. Heinrich Himmler provided a classic example when he observed a mobile killing operation in Minsk. In the group of victims he saw a young man with Aryan features—blond hair and blue eyes. Before the gunmen opened fire, Himmler walked over to the man. The following brief exchange occurred.

> "Are you a Jew?"
> "Yes."
> "Are both of your parents Jews?"
> "Yes."
> "Do you have any ancestors who were not Jews?"
> "No."
> "Then I can't help you!"[72]

The second-most powerful man in the Reich felt he lacked the power to whisper, "step aside." He knew the definition of Jew and had to obey the rule. By subservience to cold regulations he and his fellow persecutors wished to evade accountability for their actions. We already see this desire in 1933, long before any Nazi feared trial for crimes against humanity. Although Nazis repeatedly asserted pride in their work, many could reconcile their actions with their consciences only by denying they could choose to avoid action. They understood what was happening, as well as their victims did, and felt ashamed.

PORTRAYAL OF JEWISH CHARACTERISTICS

We have seen how Jews were defined by law, but another type of definition was just as important. That type was through rhetoric. Statements by politicians, bureaucrats, community leaders, and the news media shaped public perception of what Jews were like, and that perception was used to excuse sanctions applied against them. Both law and rhetoric established characteristics by which a Jew could be detected, but those established by rhetoric were far more visceral.

One rhetorical technique involved appeal to a "Communist threat." In the last *Reichstag* elected before the Nazi dictatorship, only two of the one hundred communist members were Jews, and vote totals from Jewish areas showed small support for communist candidates. These facts were even supported by the official Nazi government publication *Wirtschaft und Statistik*.[73]

Anyone who depended on information from government officials or the news media, however, got a very different impression. Hitler had long maintained, "When the Jew makes common cause with bolshevism we must look upon him as an enemy."[74] A British student attending a German university expressed the spirit of the times when he wrote in February 1933, "It is no secret that they [Jews] have financed the Communist activities here."[75] Hitler's "first broadcast speech to the nation after becoming Chancellor," noted one contemporary observer, "was nothing more than a prolonged ranting against 'Jewish Marxism.'"[76] Writing in 1938, the same observer noted, "the noisiest argument against the Jews is their connection with Communism. Hitler never refers to Communism without describing it as 'Jewish Bolshevism', and his most popular claim is that he saved Germany from Communist domination—in other words, from Jewish hegemony."[77] *Mein Kampf* contended that communism was the ultimate expression of Jews' world conspiracy: *"Russian Bolshevism represents the twentieth century attempt of the Jews to gain world-dominion."*[78] "As the Jew battles his way to political power," Hitler declared, "the democratic popular Jew becomes the bloody Jew and tyrant over the people. . . . The most fearful example of this sort is Russia, where he has killed (sometimes with inhuman tortures) or starved to death with truly fanatical savagery close to thirty million persons in order to assure domination over a great people for a crowd of Jewish literati and stock-exchange bandits."[79] "The International Jew," Hitler concluded in *Mein Kampf*, "completely dominates Russia."[80] United States ambassador William Dodd met with Hitler in 1933 shortly after Hitler assumed power: "He spoke of having saved Germany from the Communists and said 59 per cent of the officials of Russia were Jews."[81] Rudolf Hess spoke of "Bolshevism, personified in the Jew" and declared, "Jewry . . . through Marxism and since the war through bolshevism, has been directed against Germany."[82] In 1936 Hans Frank promised that the regime would eliminate the "Jewish pack of bolshevistic preachers."[83] That same year Goebbels declared, "Bolshevism . . . is a pathological, criminal nonsense, demonstrably thought up by the Jews and now, under Jewish leadership, it aims at the destruction of civilized European nations and the creation of an international Jewish world domination."[84] In 1937 Goebbels described Judaism as responsible for communist revolution.[85] One scholar has noted, "Jews and Bolsheviks were virtually synonymous to Hitler" and that the epithet "Jewish Bolshevik" was familiar to Germans of the era.[86] In March 1933 *Der Angriff* characterized victims of raids on an artists' colony section of Berlin as "Jewish literati and drawing-room Bolshevists."[87] That same month Munich's city government announced it would no longer do business with Jewish or Marxist firms.[88] A few months later Speyer's authorities said any company wishing municipal contracts had to certify it was neither Jewish nor "run on 'Marxist' lines."[89] The October 5, 1935, issue of *Der Stürmer* contained an article "The Face of the Jew," featuring a likeness of a Jew wielding the hammer and sickle.[90] Such stereotypes were not limited to the popular press. An article in *Archiv für Psychiatrie und Nervenkrankheiten* declared, "Degenerate art is really morbid because it is an attempted imitation of psychotic and primitive originals by abnormal, more or less degenerated persons, particularly communistic Jews."[91] Writing in the scientific journal *Zentralblatt für Psychotherapie*, G. Eggert praised Friedrich Nietzsche as "the bitterest enemy of . . . communism, and Judaism, the inner unity of which he was the first to perceive and unmask."[92] A July 1933 report from the U.S. Embassy in Berlin noted, "A few days ago, the [Jewish] Advisory Bureau for Physicians was raided by the police because the local Nazi Medical Organization charged that its members were Marxists."[93] In 1934 Martha Dodd, daughter of the United States ambassador to Germany, found Nazi rhetoric equating Jews and communists to be so pervasive that she facetiously expressed surprise that her Jewish acquaintances in Berlin "weren't branded with the hammer and sickle."[94] School children received such indoctrination in racial theory classes; one child recorded in her class notes that "all Jews are communists."[95] In 1936 the traveling exhibit "Bolshevism, World Enemy No. 1" featured picture of Soviet leaders, each captioned "Jew."[96] By 1935 Hitler Youth had to master quizzes such as "Q. Which was the first attempt to create a Jewish World Empire? A. The Russian Revolution, 1917."[97] A visitor to the 1937 Anti-Bolshevist Exhibition reported, "Much of the propaganda material represents an attack on the Jews."[98] In September 1941 General Field Marshal Wilhelm Keitel declared, "The fight against bolshevism demands in the first place also reckless and energetic action against the Jews, the main carriers of bolshevism."[99] A few weeks later General Field Marshal Walter von Reichenau spoke of "the essential aim of the campaign against the Jewish Bolshevist system."[100] News media reports reflected guidelines from Alfred Rosenberg's Ministry for the Occupied Eastern Territories: "In articles on the enemy powers the fraternization between the Jewish-plutocratic and the Jewish-Bolshevist world must be emphasized."[101] Robert Ley's Main Education Office "produced reams of material on 'The Jews in Bolshevism' . . . and 'The Soviet state as the center of Jewish power.'"[102] In 1943 Goebbels described "Jews in the dark corners of the Kremlin as the real bearers of Bolshevism."[103] The Propaganda Ministry issued "Topics of the Time" to guide news media. The October 28, 1944, issue on "Who Rules in the United States" said to stress that "the Roosevelt group is the old Wilson group re-enforced by new Jews and profiteers, to a large extent already strongly marked by bolshevism."[104] A secret internal memorandum from Dr. Eberhard Taubert of the Propaganda Ministry stated, "Our defense action against communism had to be directed against Jewry too, because they are allied."[105] By using such language among themselves, Nazi officials revealed their own acceptance of fantasies they promoted about Jews and communists. A concentration camp survivor reported the same sincere acceptance in conversations by camp guards.[106] Another survivor reported similar attitudes even from non-Jewish *inmates*: "There was a great deal of ugliness against the Jewish ladies. The people really came to believe that the Jews were the root of all evil in Germany. Most of the woman prisoners in the camp actually thought it was because of the Jews that Germany lost the [first world] war. They said this openly to the Jewish women."[107] Nazis' belief in their rhetoric about Jews and communism was demonstrated in actions as well. In November 1941 the German army in front of Moscow desperately needed logistical support, but fifty transport trains were diverted to ship Jews to killing centers.[108] To an outsider such diversion might seem like military folly, but Nazis viewed it as a blow against communism in the unified battle at home and abroad. The date of Dr. Taubert's memo, February 7, 1934, is also important, for we see that the Jew-communist connection dated from the earliest days of the Nazi regime. It was not invented under pressure of later military events on the Eastern front, but was a basic element of the war on Jews from its beginning. The purpose of anticommunist movies such as 1933's *Hitler Youth Quex* and *Hans Westmar* should be considered in an anti-Jewish context as well. During location filming of the latter, Jews in a Berlin neighborhood were forced to be extras shouting communist slogans and giving communist salutes.[109] More than one contemporary account said, "The whole tendency of the film is to identify the Jews with the Communists."[110] The 1939 movie *In Struggle Against the World Enemy: German Volunteers in Spain* showed Jews starting communism in Spain.[111]

After the war Hermann Goering mused, "*Now* I realize that we could have handled the Jews entirely differently. . . . I bet there were plenty who were just as fanatically nationalistic Germans as anybody, and they could have helped the cause.—It was this business of calling Jews Communists and enemies of the State.—God Almighty!"[112] Goering was probably correct about potential Jewish support for Nazism; being victimized by one group does not mean that victims are tolerant of other groups.[113] A friend of mine visited a world-renowned Holocaust refugee and was taken aback by this person's racist comments about inhabitants of the victim's adopted country. Long after the war a former Hitler Youth officer wondered, "Would there have been Jewish Nazis if Hitler had designated only gypsies, for instance, as racially tainted? Very likely, for there were tens of thousands of conservative, nationalistic Jews who longed for a strong leader as much as other Germans."[114] In 1933 Germany's Union of Nationalist Jews was known for its militaristic superpatriot orientation.[115] In August 1933 a British resident in Germany noted a "movement among the older Jews in Frankfurt, to finance a government which would rid the country of the thousands of inferior class Jews who had come into the country from Poland."[116] A distinguished Jew in Berlin told the Britisher, "There is a class of respectable Jews who have been here so long that they too have the love of patriots for Germany. . . . We do not want to see a flood of dishonest, low-class Polish Jews coming into Germany any more than the Christians do."[117] As the Nazis took power one observer noted, "Jews of the possessing classes are inclined to regard their sufferings under Hitler as the lesser of two evils," better than communists seizing power, a fear permeating German society at the time.[118] We have encountered Nazis who discovered they were *Mischlinge*. There is no reason to believe genealogy made support of Nazism any less likely among full Jews than among *Mischlinge*. Genealogy per se does not limit embrace of Nazism. If Jews had not been targeted for destruction, their support of Nazism might have matched levels found among other groups not targeted for destruction. Indeed the *Paulus-Bund* was an organized *Mischlinge* group that sought to serve the Nazi state. The group, formed in July 1933, went through several name changes, and lasted until August 1939. Members included both *Mischlinge* and "racial" Jews, who stoutly declared allegiance to the Nazi regime. The organization showed no sympathy for Jewish sufferings under the Nazis and even joined in rhetoric labeling Jewish thought as Bolshevism.[119] Membership of this almost forgotten organization included the unthinkable: pro-Nazi German Jews (defined as Nazis defined them but who rejected that definition).

Nazi rhetoric not only portrayed Jews as political subversives but also as subversive to public and private morals. "Bolshevism is criminality," Reich Minister Hans Frank declared.[120] In December 1937 U.S. Ambassador Dodd wrote in his diary, "My wife and I went to the old Reichstag building on our way home from Schacht's house. There we saw the so-called anti-Communist pictures about which we had heard. . . . The pictures showed murders, rapes, thefts. . . . Not a crime one could think of but Jews and Communists were performing it. There were two or three thousand visitors present."[121] Four years earlier a visitor to the country related a comment from "probably the most prominent anti-Semite in Germany" who "told me, blandly, that 'we would have no crime if we had no Jews.'"[122] In December 1934 Nazi party district leader (*Gauleiter*) and newspaper editor Julius Streicher told the Congress of National Socialist Lawyers, "One drop of Jewish blood is enough to arouse criminal instincts in a man."[123] Three months later he declared, "Were I to call Christ a Jew, I should be calling him a criminal."[124] At Berlin police headquarters in July 1935, police general Kurt Daluege gave a presentation on "The Jew in Criminal Statistics" and told the news media, "A considerable, if not the main part, of all crooked deals are still invariably perpetrated by Jews."[125] News media hailed Count Wolf Heinrich Graf von Helldorf, installed as Berlin police president that same month, as "our savior from Jewish crime."[126] The intimate connection between Jews and crime, Nazis said, was obvious because the "entire thieves' lingo is of Hebrew origin."[127] New identification cards issued to Jews in summer 1938 included two fingerprints, "usually found only in criminal files."[128] Gerhardt Wagner, the top physician in Nazi medical hierarchy, told the public that Jews tended to be more criminal than non-Jews, citing as examples thievery, purse snatching, and drug dealing.[129] In a mass raid on two cafés in the fashionable Kurfürstendamm district, police rounded up 339 customers, of whom 317 were Jews. Authorities said the raid was directed against "criminal elements, especially drug traffickers and foreign exchange smugglers."[130] When the regime announced its intention of confiscating all private fortunes that had been built illegally, observers assumed wealthy Jews were targeted.[131] An observer noted the Nazi contention that "any money in Jewish hands must have been criminally acquired" and was therefore subject to forfeiture.[132] The manifesto for the April 1, 1933, boycott of Jewish businesses (an event discussed in the next chapter) talked of "Communist and Marxist criminals and their Jewish intellectual instigators."[133] *The Awakening of the Nation*, a history textbook used in Bavarian schools in the mid-1930s, taught that after the world war, "Many Jews and many foreigners collected together: hooligans, criminals and bandits. One had the impression that all the prisons had been opened and that all the prisoners had been let loose."[134] In the 1937 pamphlet "The Jewish Question and School Instruction" Municipal School Inspector Fritz Fink declared "Jewry is Criminality. . . . In deceit, usury, murder, etc. Jews see no crime but consider them as acts pleasing to their God when they are directed against non-Jews."[135] In 1935 a sign at the entrance of Berlin's Darmstadt Herrengarten displayed a rhyme: "This park for criminals like you / Was not intended, cheeky Jew."[136] The previous year Ambassador Dodd noted a conversation where "Countess Helldorf talked again about the vicious Jews who never work and who never live in a country where the population cannot be exploited by them. The Count himself joined his wife in this."[137] Another diplomat reported a 1938 conversation with Foreign Minister Joachim von Ribbentrop in which the Nazi declared that "Jews in Germany without exception were pickpockets, murderers, and thieves."[138] Such sentiments were not mere public bombast but were genuinely believed by the Nazi hierarchy. In a secret meeting with Goering in 1938, SS lieutenant general and commander of the criminal police, Reinhard Heydrich expressed dismay at any prospect of establishing Jewish ghettos, let alone exclusively Jewish towns: They "would remain the permanent hideout for criminals. . . . These towns would be such a heaven for criminals of all sorts that they would be a terrific danger."[139] Years later after ghettos were established outside Germany, a *Kripo* criminal inspector noted the Lodz ghetto contained "about 250,000 Jews, all of whom have more or less criminal tendencies."[140] Even before the Nazi era, a *Reichstag* member proclaimed, "If we did away with the Jews, we could also do away with half the laws now on our books."[141] Referring to Jews, *Das Schwarze Korps* (official magazine of the SS) declared,

> They all sink into criminality, obeying their inherent, blood-conditioned bent. . . .
> The German people do not have the slightest desire to tolerate within their realm hundreds of thousands of criminals who not only seek to live by crime but who thirst for vengeance!
> Still less do we desire to see these hundreds of thousands of pauperized Jews become a breeding place of bolshevism and a receptacle for the criminal subhuman fringe which crumbles off the edge of our own people by natural selection.
> Were we to tolerate such a thing the result might be a conspiracy of the underworld that might be possible in America, but certainly not in Germany.
> At such a stage of development we would be faced with the harsh necessity of rooting out the Jewish underworld in the same manner in which our state, founded on law, extirpates criminals: with fire and sword. The result would be the actual and final end of Jewry in Germany, its absolute annihilation.[142]

Nazi medical authority Gerhardt Wagner declared that Jews were notorious for sexual immorality, particularly in pornography ("exceptionally Jewish") and prostitution.[143] "The relation of Jewry to prostitution and even more to white slavery itself could be studied in Vienna as in probably no other Western European city, with the possible exception of southern French seaport towns," said Hitler. "When I first recognized the Jew as the manager, icily calm and shamelessly businesslike, of this outrageous trade in vice of the offscourings of the metropolis, it sent a chill down my spine."[144] Sexual conduct was a major theme in news media coverage of Jews. "He took this child of poor parents, only 23 years old . . . into his house as a typist. She had to comply with the desires of the old Jew. What frightful things the Jew did to her the neighbors can tell . . . they even saw him through his open window with the girl, in a state which absolutely defies description. . . . When are we going to get a law that finally frees non-Jewish women from the danger of defilement by an alien race?"[145] A children's story book published in 1938, *The Poison Mushroom*, contained the following tale:

Inge sits in the reception room of the Jew doctor. She has to wait a long time. She looks through the journals which are on the table. But she is most [sic] too nervous to read even a few sentences. Again and again she remembers the talk with her mother. And again and again her mind reflects on the warnings of her leader of the BDM [*Bund Deutscher Mädel* or "League of German Girls"]: "A German must not consult a Jew doctor! And particularly not a German girl! Many a girl that went to a Jew doctor to be cured, found disease and disgrace!"

When Inge had entered the waiting room, she experienced an extraordinary incident. From the doctor's consulting room she could hear the sound of crying. She heard the voice of a young girl: "Doctor, doctor leave me alone!"

Then she heard the scornful laughing of a man. And then all of a sudden it became absolutely silent. Inge had listened breathlessly.

"What may be the meaning of all this?" she asked herself and her heart was pounding. And again she thought of the warning of her leader in the BDM.

Inge was already waiting for an hour. Again she takes the journals in an endeavor to read. Then the door opens. Inge looks up. The Jew appears. She screams. In terror she drops the paper. Frightened she jumps up. Her eyes stare into the face of the Jewish doctor. And this face is the face of the devil. In the middle of this devil's face is a huge crooked nose. Behind the spectacles two criminal eyes. And the thick lips are grinning. A grinning that expresses: "Now I got you at last, you little German girl!"

And then the Jew approaches her. His fleshy fingers stretch out after her. But now Inge has her wits. Before the Jew can grab hold of her, she hits the fat face of the Jew doctor with her hand. Then one jump to the door. Breathlessly Inge runs down the stairs. Breathlessly she escapes the Jew house.[146]

Julius Streicher was *Gauleiter* of Franconia and constantly publicized tales of Jewish sexuality. An eyewitness left this account of a speech Streicher gave in Hamburg during August 1935:

"In a town in Westphalia lived the daughter of a professor, a well-bred, decent German girl. She had set her mind on marrying a Jewish pig. No remonstrations were of the slightest avail. After the Jew had been baptised, some parson was found who performed the ceremony. . . .

"Well, then, everything was hotsy-totsy and merrily they did . . ." (Here Streicher grinned and paused. A couple sitting next to us looked at one another, rather shocked. But the Hitler Youth were all ears and the Storm Troopers grinning.) "Then, nine months went by. . . . When the professor's daughter wanted to see her newly born, what, fellow Germans, do you think was lying in the cradle? A LITTLE MONKEY!" (When he said this the vast hall was dead silent. One or two persons rose and left the hall. Streicher then shouted: "Shall I go on? All those for, raise their hands!" Everyone remaining raised their hands, and from the centre there was some clapping. Streicher went on.) . . .

"The little Yid's mother got a divorce from her Jew husband. . . . When she came back home she met a German childhood friend, now an S.S. man. In time the two got married. Evidently cohabiting with a Jew had ruined her character, for she kept quiet about her marriage to the Jewish pig. Well—nine months went by once more. When the S.S. man came to look at his son in the cradle, he was horrified, for what do you think he saw lying there? What? Another LITTLE MONKEY, another little Jew boy. . . .

"During intercourse between this girl and the Jew pig, Jewish blood had flowed into her body with his seed. During the time the seed takes to develop, the blood of the growing child beat in the same circulation as that of its mother. Nine long months the Jewish blood of the child thus ran through its mother's veins, until her blood was totally infected. And this blood predominates in its mother's blood, even if she has another child, made by an Aryan father. This means that Jewish brats will come for at least ten generations, polluting the blood of their children and their children's children."[147]

The process was explained more clinically by *Der Stürmer* in its 1935 New Year's issue:

The male sperm in cohabitation is partially or completely absorbed by the female and thus enters her bloodstream. One single cohabitation of a Jew with an Aryan woman is sufficient to poison her blood forever. Together with the alien albumen she has absorbed the alien soul. Never again will she be able to bear purely Aryan children. . . . Now we know why the Jew uses every artifice of seduction in order to ravish German girls at as early an age as possible, why the Jewish doctor rapes his patients while they are under anaesthetic. He wants the German girl and the German woman to absorb the alien sperm of a Jew. . . . He has been aware of the secrets of the race question for centuries and therefore plans systematically the annihilation of the nations which are superior to him.[148]

These extended quotations offer a flavor of the information that government officials and news media gave the public about Jewish immorality. Persons who view Jews as ordinary people may regard such information as absurd, but it was taken seriously by citizens of the Reich, and its acceptance in Germany was as wide as its distribution. "Marxism . . . and sexual immorality—were but phases of a Jewish plot against the Fatherland. . . . Its primary weapons have been prostitution and syphilis . . . and Bolsehvism."[149] When an 8:00 P.M. curfew was established for Jews after war broke out in 1939, German news media explained, "Jews have not infrequently taken advantage of the blackout to molest Aryan women."[150]

The modern reader has been spared coarse details considered suitable for children's education on this issue. *Der Stürmer* was widely used in the classroom, with students assigned to memorize passages and to compose essays about the subject matter.[151] "When my daddy brought home the new issue to-day," one thirteen-year-old girl said, "I grabbed it right away as I always do."[152] A visitor to a Hitler Youth camp remembered when the boys "were dismissed and crowded to the *Stürmer*-stall to get the last issue of Streicher's paper. Young boys gazed at the cartoons in rapt admiration; and, when I asked the Black Guard officer with me whether he did not see anything funny in the grotesqueries of *Der Stürmer*, he replied: 'It is not funny. They must be taught the truth about the Jews. It is part of their spiritual upbringing.'. . . I looked back at the growing groups round the newspapers and then at a cartoon in my hand showing a Jew disembowelling a beautiful young German girl."[153] Speaking of *Der Stürmer*, in 1938 an observer declared, "On young people in Germany it had probably more effect than any other agency in persuading them to think of Jews and of the children of a Jewish parent as unclean and untouchable."[154] Older schoolchildren sometimes debated whether fantastic news media stories about Jews could possibly be true. Years later one recalled, "A lot of boys found it hard to believe that there wasn't something to it. 'All those papers can't be lying, can they? It's on the radio too, every day.'"[155] Although expressing reservation about the explicit nature of some stories, in 1935 the mayor of a university town declared, "The public has also welcomed the fact that the *Stuermer* is now to be seen in the display boxes, since every Folk-Comrade wants to be kept up to the minute on the Jewish Question."[156] *Der Stürmer*'s contents were endorsed by Reich Youth leader Baldur von Schirach,[157] by Heinrich Himmler,[158] and by Hitler himself.[159] *Der Stürmer* was *the* definitive source of information about the Jewish threat.

The anti-Jewish education program in schools was integrated into the general curriculum.[160] Teachers encouraged pupils to apply lessons in real life. In October 1935 one little girl told a family gathering that her teacher read to us out of a book about Jews . . . that they are evil . . . they look like devils . . . they should all be killed. He said we should spit at them whenever we see them. . . . On our way home . . . Ursel and I saw an old woman. She looked very poor, and we thought she might be Jewish. Ursel said we should spit at her. So she ran up to her and spat on her coat . . . I didn't spit, Aunt Bella. I thought it was disgusting. Ursel yelled at her: "Old Jew witch!" She says that tomorrow she will tell the teacher I wouldn't spit, too.[161]

When her teacher asked her the next day "Do you admit that all Jews are damnable and vile?" the girl stood her ground and said no. That night the Gestapo arrested her father.[162] Authorities encouraged teachers to probe into students' home life,[163] and encouraged children to think something was wrong if their parents failed to support the war on Jews. A man later recalled his reactions in 1938 as a ten-year-old child during Crystal Night:

It was still dark outside when I woke and heard a strange man's voice coming out of the kitchen. . . .

It was Levi, the Jewish livestock dealer. . . . A Jew, a Jew—it kept running through my head. I was not at all happy that he was sitting in our kitchen. . . .

I had already been a member of the *Jungvolk* [a branch of Hitler Youth] for ten months. In our small village on the French border, the leader of the *Jungvolk* group was our teacher. He had already talked to us about the Jews. . . . We boys had the task of convincing our parents not to do business with Jews. And here was this Jew sitting in our kitchen. . . .

I was in despair. Although my father opposed my teacher and refused to buy me a brown shirt, I respected my teacher. . . . And here was my father, a friend of Jews. I just couldn't figure it out.

When it got dark, my father took Levi across the border. When he came back my mother asked him, 'Are you sure nobody saw you?' 'You can rest assured,' my father told her, and at that moment I saw a smile light up my mother's face. And for the first time in my life I wished I wasn't my parents' son.[164]

Those who made war on Jews portrayed them as disease carriers. The 1938 children's story book quoted above (*The Poison Mushroom*) noted, "Many a girl that went to a Jew doctor to be cured, found disease and disgrace!" A 1936 children's picture book by Elvira Bauer included a page about a Jewish butcher: "He sells half refuse instead of meat. A piece of meat lies on the floor, the cat claws another. This doesn't worry the Jewish butcher since the meat increases in weight. Besides, one mustn't forget, he won't have to eat it himself."[165] A member of a Nazi household recalled,

Aunt Anna came for a visit. Everyone sat around the living room table and drank coffee while she told a story. . . . Tante Anna said that one of the Jewesses living across the road from her always took some work with her when she went to the outhouse. She even would take a bowl of dough with her. She kneaded the dough while she sat on the toilet. They could hear her slap the dough around while she did her thing in the outhouse! "*Pfui Teufel!*" they all said. They couldn't go on eating their cake and they asked Tante Anna to stop.

After Tante Anna's story, I could never look at dough without seeing a dark Jewess kneading and slapping a pale mass of dough into submission. Pale dough reminded me of unwashed hands. Jews had pale, unwashed hands. Jews were connected with toilets, urination, and defecation.[166]

A woman recalled Nazi Berlin: "In 1933, when I was seventeen, my father took my sister Grete and me to the eastern part of the city to see real Jews, in the Granary District. It horrified us that such people existed. The police were just conducting a raid—the types they rounded up! Lice-ridden, dressed in rags."[167] A September 1938 issue of *Der Stürmer* declared: "Jews are pests and disseminators of diseases."[168] Hans Frank, a Hitler cabinet member and Governor-General of Poland described Jews as "carriers of diseases and germs."[169] When Jewish railroad passengers were prohibited in Nazi-occupied Poland, a newspaper headline declared, "Germ-carriers Banned from Railways."[170] At the notorious Wannsee Conference (which approved plans for mass killings of Jews across Europe), one official of Frank's government noted "the Jew as carrier of epidemics spelled a great danger."[171] Earlier the top medical official of Frank's government suggested that Warsaw's Jews be put in a ghetto to prevent them from spreading spotted fever through the general population.[172] A renowned German psychologist described Jews as "latent carriers of tuberculosis,"[173] and Nazi physicians attempted to demonstrate that certain diseases were more common among Jews.[174] Nazi rhetoric went further yet and characterized Jews as causing not only physical but societal disease: "In whatever country they settle and spread themselves out, they produce the same effects as are produced in the human body by germs. And in the same way as the human body defends itself against the intruding germs and tries to expel them, the non-Jewish peoples defend themselves against the intrusion and the spreading of the Jews."[175] A U-boat officer wrote in his diary that Jews "sought to poison our nation like a plague spot."[176] An SS brigadier general declared, "We must burn out this bubonic plague." [177] In Vichy France a poster proclaimed, "Against Jewish leprosy, for French purity."[178] The March 1941 issue of the academic journal *Zeitschrift für Geopolitic* discussed population movements in Europe with an article noting "about 400,000 Jews left the Reich borders and will not see Germany any more. Thank God, we have eliminated those foreign bodies."[179] A soldier's letter in a February 1942 *Der Stürmer* declared, "When the sword of the Führer has exterminated this pest, he will also have freed Europe and the whole world of this central seat of diseases."[180] Hitler himself used disease rhetoric when referring to Jews.[181] As with rhetoric linking Jews to communists, rhetoric linking Jews to disease was promoted by motion pictures. The 1940 documentary *The Eternal Jew* emphasized Jews as disease carriers.[182] Other films dealing with this theme ranged from *The Inheritance* in 1935 and *Hereditary Defective* in 1936 (documentaries about hereditary disease) to *The Victim of the Past: The Sin Against Blood and Race* in 1937. The latter, a broadly distributed film, "not only contrasted 'healthy German citizens' (girls doing gymnastics, etc.) with regressed occupants of back wards, but spoke of Jewish mental patients and of the 'frightening transgression' of the law of natural selection, which must be reinstated 'by humane methods.'"[183] A student of rhetoric about Jews as disease carriers and biological pests noted, "These verbal images and biological concepts weakened and effaced the moral scruples, if such still existed, and enfeebled also any potential resistance among the millions who . . . knew . . . what was happening."[184]

The Jewish evil was summarized by a leaflet reprinted in the September 25, 1935, *Basler Nationalzeitung*:

> Fellow German,
> do you know:
>
> that the Jew
> ravishes . . . . your child
> defiles . . . . your wife
> defiles . . . . your sister
> defiles . . . . your sweetheart
> murders . . . . your parents
> steals . . . . your goods
> insults . . . . your honor
> ridicules . . . your customs
> ruins . . . . your church
> corrupts . . . . your culture
> contaminates . . your race
>
> that the Jew
> slanders . . . . you
> cheats . . . . you
> robs . . . . you
> regards . . . . you as cattle
>
> that Jewish
> doctors murder you slowly
> lawyers never try to get you your rights
> provision shops sell you rotten foodstuffs
> butchers' shops are filthier than pigsties
>
> that the Jew
> has to act as above said in accordance
> with the laws of his Talmud, for to do
> so is a "deed good in the sight of
> God."[185]

The Ministry for Foreign Affairs officially summarized the situation facing Germany in 1938: "The advance made by Jewish influence and the destructive Jewish spirit in politics, economy and culture paralyzed the power and will of the German people. . . . The healing of this sickness among the people was therefore certainly one of the most important requirements."[186] Arthur Seyss-Inquart, Reich Commissioner of the Netherlands, noted that Germany had once before paid a heavy price for ignoring the peril posed by Jews: "It was really they, who stuck the knife in the back of the German army which broke the resistance of the Germans, and in the year 1918, they who wanted to dissolve and decompose all national tradition and also moral and religious beliefs of the German people. The Jews for us are not Dutchman. *They are those enemies, with whom we can neither come to an armistice nor to peace.*"[187]

Given the hazardous effect that Jews were thought to have on individuals and on society, and given that such hazard was believed to be an inherent biological characteristic of Jews and could not be eliminated from them, the only solution was to eliminate the disease carriers from society. Hermann Goering explained in 1934, "Whatever has happened so far has been a defensive measure in the interest of our people; it was a reaction against the ruin which this race has brought upon us."[188] In August 1935 *Das Schwarze Korps* declared, "The Jewish problem will only be solved when these parasites in our body politic have been deprived of every opportunity of profiting from the lives of Germans and of continuing their disintegrating activity in the sphere of culture."[189] About the same time Hitler proclaimed that Jews should be "removed from all professions, ghettoised, restricted to a particular territory, where they can wander about, in accordance with their character, while the German people looks on, as one looks at animals in the wild."[190] In January 1939 the Ministry for Foreign Affairs officially declared, "The final goal of German Jewish Policy is the emigration of all the Jews living in Reich territory."[191] As we shall see, to encourage such emigration Jews were pushed to the margins of society, denied opportunity for gainful employment and even for purchase of food. The resulting squalor was then cited as confirmation of Jews' beastiality:

> "Der Stürmer" sent its photographer to various ghettos in the East. A member of the "Stürmer" staff is well acquainted with the Jews; nothing can surprise him easily. But what our contributor saw in these ghettos was a unique experience even for him. He wrote:
> "What my eyes and my Leica camera saw here convinced me that the Jews are not human beings but children of the devil and the spawn of crime . . . It is hard to see how it was possible that this scum of humanity was for centuries looked upon as God's chosen people by the non-Jews . . . This Satanic race really has no right to exist."[192]

German motion pictures promoted attacks on Jews, vividly dramatizing stereotypes promoted in other communications media. The 1933 film *Hans Westmar* included sequences showing Jews conducting themselves boorishly in a dance hall and enjoying a bountiful meal in front of malnourished Aryans.[193] In 1940 Propaganda Minister Joseph Goebbels personally supervised the climax of *Jew Süss* in which the Jewish villain Süss Oppenheimer is executed after raping a German maiden, and the city's Jews are driven out. A town resident declares, "May the citizens of other states never forget this lesson."[194] The effect on audiences was powerful. The Nazi Party's intelligence and security agency *Sicherheitsdienst* (the SD) reported demonstrations against Jews by persons who saw the film.[195] Movie-goers leaving a showing in Berlin shouted, "Drive the Jews from the Kurfürstendamm! Kick the last Jews out of Germany!"[196] Just after watching the movie a group of Hitler Youth in Austria murdered a Jewish man they encountered on the street outside the theater.[197] Joseph Wulf recalled that the film was routinely shown in areas where anti-Jewish actions were scheduled, to arouse the populace against local Jews.[198] Box office receipts demonstrated its popularity with the general public, and special exhibitions of the film were presented to troops, police, and SS men. *The Eternal Jew*, an early 1940s documentary described as "perhaps the most hideous three-quarters-of-an-hour in film history,"[199] featured scenes of Jewish "depravity" under forced ghetto life and a horrifying sequence of animals being tortured in a spurious "kosher" slaughtering ritual. Years later a film critic who found the message repulsive nonetheless called the movie one of the most powerful propaganda films ever made.[200] Anti-Semitic scenes appeared even in lighter entertainment items ranging from 1934's *I For You, You For Me* to 1942's *Rembrandt*.[201] For example, in *Der Weg ins Freie*, a romance set during the 1848 revolution, Metternich seeks to promote the Rothschild fortune.[202] A drama about horse racing, *Riding for Germany . . .*, portrayed bookmakers as stereotypical Jews. *Robert and Bertram* and *Linen from Ireland* were comedies including Jewish subhumans to ridicule. Jews served as contrasts to heros in *Above All in the World* (war drama), *Carl Peters* (drama about German colonial Africa), *Homecoming*, and *Venus on Trial*.[203] In the 1940 feature film *Bismarck* a Jew tries to kill the Second Reich's founder, and a Jew blinds the founder of the Transvaal state in 1941's *Ohm Kruger*.[204] Films included casual anti-Jewish scenes having nothing to do with plot: In 1941's *Return* a Jewish merchant throws invective at an Aryan woman who will not buy from him.[205] Anti-semitism was not limited to Nazi productions. The Swedish film *Petterson and Bendel* was well received in Germany during 1935 and dealt with conflict that a Jewish businessman brought to a peasant.[206] Movies may have provided audiences with escape from much of daily life, but not from anti-Jewish agitation. Hatred of Jews pervaded the Reich.

One of the most alarming characteristics that Nazis found among Jews was a desire to ruin Aryan society. Perceived damage from Jews was not merely collateral to their nature but a deliberate attack. We have already sampled examples cited by Nazis, and these attacks were epitomized by alleged ritual murders of Aryans by Jews. In addition to citing many alleged individual instances, *Der Stürmer* long argued that Jews started World War I in order to exterminate the Aryan people. In 1936 a careful critic of this proposition said in astonishment, "A people of 60 millions is seriously told that the Jews intended its literal extermination: 'The most frightful ritual murder that the world has ever seen was to be perpetrated; the Aryanry of the world, the flower of mankind, was to be rooted out. This was the will of pan-Jewry, and these were the commands of the Jewish Kahal.'"[207] The critic observed, "It is perhaps difficult to imagine any purpose for this constant pressing of fantastic ritual murder charges against the Jews, unless to inspire for them such hatred as will result in direct violence against them on the part of the population."[208] Speaking of Nazis killed in street battles, *Der Angriff* (*The Attack*) shouted in March 1933, "Who have our dead comrades on their consciences? Who is responsible for all these murders of innocent political fighters? The Jews!"[209] A year before Germany hosted the 1936 Olympics, *Dietwart*, official journal of the Reich Sports Leadership, asked, "Wouldn't one kill wild beasts, if they were man-eating, even if they happened to look like men? And are the Jews any different from man eaters?"[210] In 1936 Streicher declared, "Jews always attained their ends through wholesale murder."[211] Stories of ritual murder by Jews were widely believed by the German populace. Years later a man related a childhood memory from 1941:

> One day, while I pretended I was playing in a corner while the adults spoke to each other in low voices, I heard them say that the German army in Czechoslovakia had captured a nest of Jews who had kidnapped and killed little Christian boys and girls and used their blood in baking matzos. They said they had found the small carcasses in a kosher butcher shop hanging from hooks like pigs and cows. *I* was a little Christian boy.
>
> . . . My mind assembled from various elements what my ears had extracted from the adults' conversations—lurid scenes of terror over and over again. I was always on the verge of being captured by dark hairy Jews who wanted to hang me from a hook.[212]

In May 1943 M. Froehling stated a good citizen's indignation in *Der Stürmer*: "A people which, like the Jews, has included murder in its rites and which has for thousands of years indulged in ritual murder, is a community of murderers. It no longer has a right to exist."[213] Ernst Hiemer concurred the next month: "A people who are mass murderers *in accordance with their law*, who are murderers of children and old people *in accordance with their law*, have no longer a right to exist."[214]

The "necessity" to kill all Jews becomes easier to accept if one believes they are not human. We have already seen rhetoric describing Jews as disease-carrying organisms and foreign bodies. Hans Frank, president of the German Academy of Law, wrote in his diary, "I could not eliminate all lice and Jews in only a year's time."[215] Walter Buch, supreme judge of the Nazi party court, declared in the October 21, 1938, issue of *Deutsche Justiz*: "The Jew is not a human being. He is a phenomenon of putrefaction."[216] The previous month *Der Stürmer* reminded readers that a Jew "is not 'also a human being,' but a germ. A parasite, an enemy, an evil-doer, a disseminator of diseases who must be destroyed in the interest of mankind."[217] Hitler often used such metaphors.[218] In *Mein Kampf* he described Jews as "a ferment of decomposition"[219] and warned that any Jew "remains a typical parasite, spreading like a harmful bacillus wherever a suitable medium invites it. And the effect of his existence is also like that of parasites: wherever he occurs, the host nation dies off sooner or later."[220] In a January 1937 speech he declared, "We endeavour, as well as we can, to make the German people immune against this infection. A part of our measures is the avoidance of any close relationship with the carriers of this poisonous bacillus."[221] During a February 1942 conversation Hitler commented, "The discovery of the Jewish virus is one of the greatest revolutions that have taken place in the world. The battle we are engaged in is of the same sort as the battle waged, during the last century, by Pasteur and Koch."[222] The secret memorandum of an April 1943 conversation showed Hitler saying

> Where the Jews were left to themselves, as for instance in Poland, the most terrible misery and decay prevailed. They are just pure parasites. In Poland this state of affairs had been fundamentally cleared up. If the Jews there did not want to work, they were shot. If they could not work, they had to succumb. They had to be treated like tuberculosis bacillae, with which a healthy body may become infected. This was not cruel, if one remembered that even innocent creatures of nature, such as hares and deer, have to be killed, so that no harm is caused by them. Why should the beasts who wanted to bring us Bolshevism be spared more?[223]

Such metaphors push the nonhuman description so far that we may fail to understand that some Nazi officials regarded Jews as literally nonhuman. In the mid-1930s Martha Dodd, daughter of the U.S. ambassador to Germany, noticed "the Nazi attitude, which I once heard expressed by a supposedly intelligent assistant of von Ribbentrop, to consider Negroes as animals, and utterly unequal to enter the [Olympic] Games. This young man elaborated his thesis, saying that, of course, if the Germans had had the bad sportsmanship to enter deer or another species of fleet-footed animal, they could have taken the honors from America in the track events. He added that it was an unfair advantage we took when we let non-humans, like Owens and other Negro athletes, compete with fine human Germanic products. . . . I reflected that this attitude of theirs, slightly modified, applied to anyone not a member of Aryan Nazidom."[224] Hitler declared that marriages between Aryans and Jews produced "monstrous beings, half man, half monkey."[225] On another occasion he declared, "When I confront the Aryan with the Jew and call the one a human being, I must call the other by a different name. The two are as widely separated as man from beast."[226] Hitler warned that if Jews achieved victory in their struggle for world domination, "then this planet will once more, as millions of years ago, move through the ether devoid of human beings."[227] If a planet filled with Jews would be devoid of human beings, then Jews are nonhuman.[228] A German Jew recalled a conversation from September 1938: "I heard a child asking his mother: 'what kind of human beings are these, Mother?' And the mother answered: 'These are no human beings, these are Jews."[229] A Nazi manual said the Jew "who to all appearance is a biologically homogeneous natural creation with hands, feet, and some sort of brain, with eyes and a mouth, is all the same a totally different, a terrifying creature; he is endowed with human features—though merely a sketch version of the true human being—, mentally, spiritually he stands lower than an animal."[230] In the Nazi slogan "*Deutschland erwache, Juda verrecke!*" the verb *verrecken* ("perish like a beast") reveals that Jews are not human, as this verb refers to destroying animals rather than people.[231] A student of such rhetoric found that "to the general mass of the people the Jew no longer appeared as a human being but as some lower animal, like worms and insects, terrible and incomprehensible in their destructive effect."[232]

To appreciate the impact of anti-Jewish rhetoric, we must remember that it came not only from politicians and reporters but from highly regarded scholars and scientists. The University of Heidelberg's rector declared, "If every branch of science is focussed on the racial totality of life, the ramified and independent sciences are thereby connected in one great sense and meaning, and by a common idea."[233] In 1937 Dr. Eduard Hermann, "dean of German linguists," and a professor at the University of Göttingen declared, "Today, national socialism knocks at the door of every scholarly discipline and asks: what have you to offer me?"[234] The response was overwhelming. Animal behaviorists found "the Nordic chick is better-behaved and more efficient in feeding than the Mediterranean chick. . . . The poultry-yard confutes the liberal-bolshevik claim that race differences are really cultural differences, because race difference among chicks cannot be accounted for by culture."[235] Other scholars found "the direction of private life can be misinterpreted individualistically,"[236] therefore Nazi intrusion in private life promoted mental health. Said one German scholar, "The viewpoint and purpose of German psychology have always been totalitarian—to get at the center of human existence."[237] With the cooperation of German academia, six or more full-scale institutes devoted themselves to the Jewish problem.[238] That total does not include dozens of institutes devoted to racial hygiene.[239] One of the most careful students of Nazi medical practices later noted, "Science (especially biomedical science) under the Nazis cannot simply be seen in terms of a fundamentally 'passive' or 'apolitical' scientific community responding to purely external political forces; on the contrary, there is strong evidence that scientists actively designed and administered central aspects of National Socialist racial policy."[240] Enthusiastic support from world renowned German scholars and scientists lent plausibility and respectability to the Nazi agenda, setting perimeters for debate about steps to deal with the Jewish problem, perimeters obscuring that the "Jewish problem" itself was imaginary.

The Kaiser Wilhelm Institute for Anthropology, Heredity, and Eugenics thrived under Nazi largess. (In 1935 funding for racial hygiene research exceeded the combined funding of the Kaiser Wilhelm Institutes for Physics and Chemistry.)[241] Hundreds of scholarly reports from the Anthropology Institute were published in the 1930s. The Institute's experts routinely advised on disputes about whether someone was Aryan, or suffering from genetically transmitted disease. Such expert opinions were not only valuable to Reich agencies that paid for them, but important also to persons whose lives depended on them.

Racial hygiene grant proposals to the German Research Council had to pass stringent peer review. Among those with sufficient scientific merit to justify funding was a study of twins proposed by Otmar von Verschuer: "My assistant Dr. [Josef] Mengele (M.D., Ph.D.) has joined me in this branch of research. He is presently employed as Haupsturmführer and camp physician in the concentration camp at Auschwitz. Anthropological investigations on the most diverse racial groups of this concentration camp are being carried out."[242] Such studies were sought by German academia before World War II. Dr. Sigmund Rascher, who gained notoriety for his vivisection experiments at Dachau, requested access to inmates in May 1939.[243]

German scholars were well aware of what their work promoted. Academics reported to the Institute for German Eastern Work about mass murders in the Ukraine: "Winniza: 40,000 Jews have been liquidated in the area."[244] An architect involved with the institute was not only an expert on the Rococo but helped design Auschwitz extermination camp facilities.[245] Years later an authority on the institute's affairs dryly noted, "German academic staff worked there because they had careers to make," careers that suffered little postwar harm from service at the institute.[246]

The Reich Institute for the History of the New Germany was created in 1935 and operated with generous government funding. The next year its director, historian Walter Frank, noted that the Institute was establishing one of the world's finest libraries on the Jewish problem; by 1940 the collection contained 20,000 volumes.[247] In 1936 the Institute set up a Research Department for the Jewish Question. Nobel Prize physicist Philipp Lenard sent greetings on the Department's opening.[248] That year the University of Munich hosted a Department conference, attended by rectors from various universities and representatives from all Reich ministries. There Dr. Karl Alexander von Müller, Professor of History at the University of Munich and president of the Bavarian Academy of Sciences, publicly praised the department as "a unique scientific laboratory for this [Jewish] question."[249] At a 1938 conference, again hosted by the University of Munich, Director Frank called the Institute "the center of anti-Semitism in German science."[250] After Julius Streicher's address to the academic gathering, Frank lauded Streicher's presentation of "science experienced in practice."[251] Later that year the Institute held a general history conference where Frank said, "Just as the outrage of World Judaism was followed by the political and economic counterblow of the Reich [Crystal Night and measures inspired by it], so in scholarship there will be a reply in that we continue to strengthen the anti-Jewish wing of our research work."[252] In 1941 a student of German historiography found current themes no different from those existing long before 1933, merely "intensification of tendencies which already were pronounced before the advent of the Nazi regime."[253]

A 1936 academic conference on "Jewry in Jurisprudence" featured papers by scholars from prestigious universities. The introductory address was given by Carl Schmitt, Professor of Constitutional and International Law, University of Berlin. (Schmitt was famed for his theory that no compromise is possible with a foe, that one side in a dispute must be destroyed.[254] This became an important principle of Nazi criminal law.) Schmitt told the conference: "We must free the German spirit from all Jewish falsifications, falsifications of the concept 'spirit' which made possible for Jewish emigrants to call 'unspiritual' the marvelous struggle of Gauleiter Streicher."[255] In 1939 Streicher sponsored a lecture series by a Dr. Deeg at the University of Berlin on "Jews in German Legal History."[256]

Nazi theorist Alfred Rosenberg set up the Institute for Research into the Jewish Question, headquartered in Frankfurt. The city provided RM 160,000 to build the Institute's collection of reference books. Confiscations from Jewish libraries also helped build the collection, which eventually totaled over 500,000 volumes. A publicity release by the Institute described its collection as having "a degree of completeness as regards the literature on the Jewish question as never before in Europe or elsewhere. In the New Order of Europe Organization *the* library for the Jewish question not only for Europe but for the world will arise in Frankfurt am Main."[257] Dr. Wilhelm Grau described the Institute as "a mental power-house."[258] Attenders at a March 1941 Institute conference heard Alfred Rosenberg say, "For Europe the Jewish question will be solved only when the last Jew will have left the European continent."[259] That summer he became Minister for the Occupied Eastern Territories, where Nazis conducted wholesale murder of Jews. In 1943 Dr. Alfred Baeumler, Professor of Philosophy at the University of Berlin, declared, "In days to come one will adore in Rosenberg one of the greatest German educators against halfness. . . . He early recognized that the deeper and more significant the contrasts that wrestle with each other, the more valueless a compromise."[260]

In 1943 Dr. Hans Praesent declared that "German universities, too, have recognized their duty to contribute building stones for the study of Jewry."[261] He noted thirty-two dissertations on the Jewish problem produced between 1939 and 1942. In 1944 he said, "German universities more and more recognized the new way the problem has been posed and contributed to its solution through university studies suitable for the purpose. They are chiefly conducted by young historians, but also by jurists, economists, Germanists, students in journalism, as well as by medical and race students."[262] The latter discipline was of particular importance. In the mid-1940s Dr. Karl Metzger, Professor of Racial Policy, Dresden School of Technology, called racial science "a recognized international science."[263] A contemporary skeptic questioned, however, "whether contrary scientific conclusions would be admitted as valid objections to a dogma, the truth of which is held to be attested by inner conviction."[264] In this regard the University of Heidelberg's rector frankly declared, "The extent to which the science of race has already caught up to the actuality and significance of race, is not a decisive question."[265] A shrewd critic in that era noted, "Anthropology and ethnology become the political sciences *par excellence*."[266] The political nature alone of racial science makes talent for prophecy unnecessary in seeing the ominous portent of Dr. Metzger's declaration that "races originate as a result of natural or artificial breeding selections. For this purpose the breeder makes use of the means of rigid selection, of isolation, and inconsiderate extinction of all descendants who do not fit into the breeding goal."[267]

In association with distinguished colleagues, world famous psychologist Erik Jaensch, professor at the University of Marburg and president of the German Association of Psychology, claimed scientific proof that certain humans had tissue and plasma impelling them to corrupt any society in which they existed.[268] Jaensch labeled such persons as the antitype and warned, "Jewry is the main representative of the Antitype and embodies him in a large compact mass (which is of course the cause of the danger)."[269] He called for whatever steps were needed to protect humanity from the threat. In 1942 an opponent of Jaensch's scholarship saw its dark implications and admonished, "Jaensch and his followers have created . . . a weapon of murderous possibilities."[270]

Hitler appreciated the credibility given to his agenda by German scholars. In 1939 he told the *Reichstag*, "The time of propagandistic defenselessness of the non-Jewish peoples is over. National Socialist Germany and Fascist Italy possess those institutions which can, if necessary, enlighten the world about the essence of a question of which many peoples are aware instinctively although it is unclear to them scientifically."[271] In 1941 Hitler cried, "The international Jew! . . . We have been following his footsteps for so many years and probably for the first time we have in this Reich elucidated in a methodical, scholarly way this human problem and phenomenon."[272]

As Hitler rose to power, Dr. Philipp Lenard, winner of the 1905 Nobel Prize for physics, and Dr. Johannes Stark, winner of the 1919 Nobel Prize for physics, declared, "In Hitler and his comrades we discern the same spirit which we always looked for, strove toward, developed out of ourselves in our work that it might be deep going and successful; the spirit of clarity without residue, of honesty toward the outer world, and simultaneously of inner unity. . . . We admire and adore it likewise in Hitler."[273] Just before Hitler became chancellor Dr. Lenard repeated his praise, "What is it that attracts me so to Hitler, who himself is no scientist? It is the respect for truth which I always have observed in him, his wish to embrace the truth and bring it to power."[274] Professor Jaensch reflected on Hitler's rise thusly: "The fighter with the fist had to follow his own path, and the fighter with the brain had to tread also his own—both well conscious that they belong inseparably together, that they strive toward the same goal but by different means."[275] Dr. Max Clara, Professor of Anatomy at the University of Leipzig, said in the 1941–1942 central German university catalog, of which he was the editor: "Today we can proudly state that scholarship contributed its share to the success of the Führer's great plans."[276] Such contributions could be handsomely rewarded; in 1937 the regime passed out RM 100,000 prizes to assorted professors.[277]

In a March 1941 academic conference at the Frankfurt Institute for Research into the Jewish Question, Norway's Nazi leader Vidkun Quisling noted, "The Jewish question cannot be solved simply by exterminating or sterilizing the Jews."[278] At first glance such a notion may seem startling. But disappearance of all Jews would not mean an end to the war on Jews, because vigilance must be maintained against Jewish characteristics emerging in other populations. Alfred Rosenberg's colleague August Schirmer gave the same academic conference an example: "The last part of this European task is still before us. England, whose plutocratic élite is so keen about giving itself the air of stemming from the ten lost tribes of Israel, faces her annihilation. She has identified herself with Jewry, she went the road of Jewry—she shall go down to the bitter end."[279] As Dr. Wolfgang Meyer-Christian explained three years later in a well-received memo to Propaganda Ministry, "The public at large considers the Jewish question settled." This was an illusion, however, caused by elimination of Jews from German life. "Only the domestic German side of the Jewish problem has been settled by the Reich's policy toward the Jews. In its entirety the problem not only continues to exist, but since 1933 it has acquired a most tremendous acuteness and poignancy, and must therefore be brought to view more than ever and with greater force than ever."[280] The disappearance of Germany's Jews was not evidence that the war on Jews had been won; it was proof that the war must be prosecuted with more vigor than ever. Now resources could be directed against Jews who threatened Germany from outside its borders. "Not only is Germany not safe in the face of the Jews as long as one Jew lives in Europe, but also the Jewish question is hardly solved in Europe so long as Jews live in the rest of the world," warned *Der Stürmer* in 1942.[281] Said Hitler in 1943, "The alliance of the arch-capitalist states of the West, or even more so of America, with the mendacious mock-socialist regime of bolshevism [USSR] is conceivable only because leadership in both of the cases lies in the hands of international Jewry, even if the personalities visible from without seem to contradict this thesis."[282]

In summary, the rhetoric of those who fought the war on Jews portrayed victims as subversive to the nation's political and social order, as engaged in free-wheeling sexual conduct, as carriers of disease, and as subhumans who degraded neighborhoods and entire cities. (Even before the Nazi era a *Reichstag* member declared, "The Jews have achieved what no foreign enemy was ever able to achieve: They have driven the people from the city to the suburbs. And that's how things are wherever Jews have settled in numbers.")[283] Moreover, these subhuman creatures killed individual citizens and promoted destruction of values that citizens had always cherished. In self-defense, society had to eliminate these creatures. At first, victims were excluded from full participation n German society. When results were judged inadequate, victims were forced to leave the German country. Despite all these efforts the Reich's Jewish population continued to grow because the Reich's borders expanded through diplomatic agreement and military conquest, and the danger posed by the Jewish population grew along with its numbers. By necessity these germs and parasites then had to be killed. Everything else had been tried. And even as a final solution was being achieved in Axis Europe, those who made war on Jews faced the frightening prospect of Jews roaming free elsewhere in the world and taking over society after society, endangering the Reich. Even as smoke from the Reich's last Jew went up the last chimney, Nazis knew their mission to save civilization had just begun.

With our historical knowledge of what the Nazis did, a striking aspect in their rhetoric is the similarity between their fantasies about Jewish characteristics and the reality of Nazi characteristics. (We refer to active Nazis who promoted the party program, not Germans who were *pro forma* members paying dues and attending meetings in order to avoid harassment.)[284] If we substitute the word "Nazi" for "Jew" in the 1935 *Basler Nationalzeitung* leaflet quoted above, the description becomes accurate. When Nazis describe Jews as warmongers and mass murderers "in accordance with their law," the match becomes eerie. We begin to understand why the war on Jews could never end. Nazis were projecting what they loathed about themselves on to their victims. Nazis could not survive without victims.

Prosecutors at the Nuremberg Military Tribunal argued that anti-Jewish rhetoric established an atmosphere that permitted violence.[285] Already by 1934 an observer could describe the atmosphere:

> Feeling rushed into the vacuum created by the isolation of the Jew from normal society. It created a kind of ecstasy of vindictive and cowardly hate. One who has been in Germany under older conditions simply finds incredible the things which are said not by victory-crazed politicians but by porters, children, house-wives, peasants. The gamut of abuse runs all the way from ribald songs to personal insults. Schoolboys shout ditties in which Jews are made to roll in veritable verbal ordure; women voice sentiments akin to those which distinguished the murderous parisiennes of 1789.[286]

Julius Streicher, who did not always speak in bombast, once reflected, "It is primarily necessary that the public conscience be aroused to realize that there is a Jewish problem, so that laws that sooner or later must be enacted may take root in the public conscience. Only when every one understands . . . will the ground be prepared for further serious work."[287] "Words *can* kill," Heinrich Boell warns, "and it is solely a question of conscience whether one allows language to slip into fields of thought where it will become murderous."[288] One student who pondered the relation of rhetoric to violence found that the work of "doctors and biologists who helped to implant the Nazi ideology . . . raises the question of their criminal responsibility. . . . The perverted system of morals which emerged in the Third Reich was at least as criminal as the deeds of those who were perhaps only the packhorses in the enterprise."[289] One of the packhorses, on trial for participation in a mobile killing squad, declared, "When for years, for decades, the doctrine is preached that the Slav race is an inferior race and Jews not even human, then such an outcome is inevitable."[290] Nuremberg tribunal prosecutors, too, saw the power hidden in rhetoric of hate, saw that hyperbole can become reality. "It would be a strange law, indeed, which would say that if a man killed the Pole or one Jew, his prior threats to and assaults upon that Pole or Jew were relevant evidence of the motive with which he acted, but would deny the same proof, when the same man, or in this case men, killed millions."[291] In speaking of Julius Streicher, prosecutors said:

> In the early days he was preaching persecution. As persecution took place he preached extermination and annihilation and, as millions of Jews were exterminated and annihilated, in the Ghettos of the East, he cried out for more and more.
>
> The crime of Streicher is that he made these crimes possible, which they would never have been had it not been for him and for those like him. Without Streicher and his propaganda, the Kaltenbrunners, the Himmlers, the General Stroops would have had nobody to do their orders.
>
> In its extent Streicher's crime is probably greater and more far-reaching than that of any of the other defendants. The mischief which they caused ceased with their capture. The effects of this man's crime, of the poison that he has put into the minds of millions of young boys and girls goes on.[292]

Philologist and Nazi victim Victor Klemperer has noted, "Nazism . . . crept into the flesh and blood of the masses by means of single words, turns of phrase and stock expressions which, imposed upon the people a million times over in continuous reiteration, were mechanically and unconsciously absorbed by them." Klemperer concluded, "Words can act like tiny doses of arsenic: they are swallowed without being noticed, they appear to have no effect, but after a while the poison has done its work."[293] Speaking of the Reich's general "anti-Jewish education" effort, a Nuremberg prosecutor declared, "It will take generations of mental and moral sanitation to stamp out this Nazi plague. Thus the crime lives after the criminals."[294] In the 1990s someone spent two years touring areas of eastern Europe that had been occupied by the Nazis and reported, "Even today the notion of ritual murder [of Christians by Jews] is still rooted in people's minds, at least in rural areas. I didn't meet anyone who said they didn't believe in its existence. I met people who said they didn't know. One man even told me that when his sister worked as an apprentice for the Jews he trembled every day for fear she would not return."[295] In 1992 a public opinion survey found that over one-fourth of Germany's citizens believed that under Hitler "Jews were at least partly at fault for the way they were treated."[296]

How they were treated is our next topic of discussion.

2

OSTRACISM

A person having the status of Jew was forbidden to do things permitted to other persons. Such conduct was criminal for Jews; they were forbidden to engage in activities inherent to normal life, from driving a car to holding a job. Such a policy allowed Jews to roam through a community but excluded them from community life. They were the living dead.

This chapter surveys the process by which Nazi law turned autonomous human beings into zombies.

MOB VERSUS BUREAUCRAT

After the Nazis ascended to power anti-Jewish actions fell into two general categories. One was vigilante justice. The other was use of state power. The difference in approach was immaterial for victims, but perpetrators found state power to be so efficient that vigilante action virtually disappeared. The triumph of state power in this competition is important for our discussion because that triumph created a series of defendants in Nuremberg Military Tribunal proceedings—prosecutors and judges who were found guilty of obeying unjust law.

The phrase "Nazi legal system" may sound like an oxymoron, but the regime did have laws and law enforcement officers. There was a Ministry of Justice and a court system filled with attorneys. "Some of the more turbulent Brownshirt leaders coined a scoffing word combining *Legality* and *Adolf* [*Adolphe Légalité*], and even Joseph Goebbels said that he [Hitler] had a 'legality complex.'"[1] Hitler's attitude leaked downward. Heinrich Himmler once sighed to a colleague about the regime's early days: "Everywhere I was knocking up against people in SS uniforms, in themselves dear, nice, decent people, who saw their task as that of supplying all my orders with a kind of legal respectability and pointing out to me at what points my measures contradicted existing enactments and were therefore not binding in law."[2] Someone who views Nazi jurisprudence from the perspective of American legal tradition may see only arbitrary action and wanton brutality. But law officers found guilty at Nuremberg did serve ideals higher than themselves; their ideals simply corroded traditional legal guarantees, and in Germany loss of those guarantees eventually corrupted all law enforcement.

Corruption was expedited by lack of a legal tradition. Prior to the founding of modern Germany in 1870, justice was meted out by rulers of German kingdoms. Only with the formation of the Second Reich in 1870 did lawyers emerge as a profession. The percentage of lawyers affiliated with government was much higher in Germany than in the United States, coloring the profession's attitude toward government power. That attitude was reflected in a courtroom etiquette where prosecutors addressed the court while physically located on a level shared with the judge, but defense attorneys operated below in a pit with the accused person (whose guilt was assumed in fact if not in law—the acquittal rate in 1932 was 15.05 percent).[3] Moreover, judges were civil service workers, appointed not because of eminence but because they were bureaucrats on a particular career track. Someone familiar with the German legal profession noted that as Hitler rose to power "the bar was overcrowded, divided, frequently anti-Semitic, conservative, wishing they were in uniform." He concluded, "If in 1933 we had been looking for a source of probable opposition to Hitler, the last place we would have looked to would have been the bench and the bar."[4]

When Hitler became chancellor of Germany the country had a written constitution which served as the republic's fundamental law. In law and in fact the constitution protected personal liberties associated with democracy. Principles of German jurisprudence resembled those of America's. The constitution could be changed by formal amendment, but another method was accepted by custom. That method was for Germany's parliament, the *Reichstag*, to pass a law by the two-thirds majority required for a constitutional amendment. A law passed by such a majority superseded any constitutional provisions inconsistent with the law. Such a law could make narrow exceptions for a particular situation, or make exceptions so broad as to delete a constitutional provision for all situations. Also, in an emergency the Reich president was authorized to suspend parts of the constitution.

Soon after Hitler took office in 1933 an arson fire burned the *Reichstag* building. This shocking act heightened public fears that had already elevated Hitler to power as a strong man to deal with a national crisis. An hour after the fire began Hitler announced that it had been set by communists, a synonym for Jews in Nazi parlance. He had no evidence to support his view but "was convinced of it," according to Hermann Goering. "The Fuehrer wanted it this way."[5] This was nothing new. For years Nazi agitators had been warning of communist danger "until in 1932 it culminated in the creation of an anti-Communist psychosis in Germany. . . . Of necessity, this agitation had to exaggerate the gravity of the Communist threat. The Nazi propagandists succeeded in creating a pseudo-situation, in which a Communist revolution was imminent. They could not afford to take any note of the facts."[6] After the *Reichstag* fire, at Hitler's instigation the Reich president issued an emergency decree for defense against communism on February 28.[7] The decree suspended various sections of the constitution "until further notice." The same sort of presidential decree had been issued more than once under the Weimar Republic (the regime preceding the Nazis), and no public alarm was apparent about the latest measure. Suspended sections of the constitution included numbers 114 ("freedom of the person is inviolable"), 115 ("every German's home is his sanctuary and inviolable"), and 118 (forbidding limits on free speech by employers).[8] The emergency decree explicitly stated that

> restrictions on personal liberty, on the right of free expression of opinion, including freedom of the press, on the right of assembly and the right of association, and violations of the privacy of postal telegraphic, and telephonic communications, and warrants for house-searches, orders for confiscations as well as restrictions on property, are also permissible beyond the legal limits otherwise prescribed.

In addition the decree said, "Whoever provokes or incites to an act contrary to public welfare is to be punished with a penitentiary sentence [or], under mitigating circumstances, with imprisonment of not less than three months." Gestapo head Rudolf Diels (Himmler did not head the Gestapo until 1934)[9] noted that the Nazis, who controlled Germany's police, now had legal power to do anything, and victims had no appeal.[10] Administrative rules told police that the decree not only removed constitutional limits on their power but also removed "all other Reich and state limitations in this matter." The regulations said "additional permissible actions will be directed primarily against the communists, but also against all those working with the communists or even indirectly supporting or promoting their criminal aims." Regulations told police to act against "democratic parties or organizations, when such measures serve for the defense against such communist tendencies in their broadest meaning."[11] The Nationalist *Börsen-Zeitung* explained that the decree included "all those who, without themselves being Communists, cooperate with Communism, or are sufficiently suspect of sympathizing with Bolshevism."[12] Goering explained that anyone seeking to create discontent with government policy was a Marxist.[13]

On March 24, the *Reichstag* passed the Law to Remove the Distress of People and State, also called the Enabling Act.[14] This allowed the Reich Cabinet, selected by Hitler, to make laws having the same validity as any passed by the *Reichstag*. Moreover, these cabinet decrees could disregard the constitution. As with presidential decrees suspending the constitution, enabling acts were familiar in German legal tradition. Various cabinets that ruled during Weimar's last tumultuous years all ruled by decree through virtue of enabling acts. Indeed Hitler had accepted the chancellorship with the understanding that the *Reichstag* would pass an enabling act for his cabinet.[15] The *Reichstag* majority passing this law was large enough to have passed the act as a constitutional amendment instead of a law, therefore (as noted above) the act was constitutional. The majority was large enough because the Roman Catholic Center Party joined with the Nazis in this vote, producing a yea total of 444. Although police and security forces (acting under the emergency decree to fight communism) arrested enough Communist and Social Democrat *Reichstag* members to minimize the opposition vote, that step did not affect the outcome. Even if all those deputies had been present Hitler would have needed only 431 votes to get the necessary two-thirds majority. Support from the Roman Catholic Center Party, not arrest of opponents, was the key to Nazi victory.[16]

In practical effect the *Reichstag* repealed the constitution on March 24, and made Hitler's cabinet decrees supreme law of the land. These cabinet actions were formalities; one cabinet member could not recall a single instance in which he and his colleagues refused to issue any decree Hitler wanted.[17] The cabinet was so irrelevant that it stopped meeting in 1937, and by custom Hitler acquired power to issue decrees on his own authority.[18] A contemporary observer of Hitler noted, "The spitting machine-guns used by the police against him in 1923 converted him for ever to a fervent belief in legal methods. . . . The interesting conjecture thus arises—would Hitler have achieved power if the Weimar constitution had not contained clauses that permitted a revolution by abusing the spirit of the law while adhering to its outward form? If it had been a matter of barricades and a bloody *putcsh*, would Hitler have met the test? Or would he have stood by, as he always stood, limp and helpless, on the platform, in the fighting days of his movement, watching the mêlée below him?"[19]

Another key measure in 1933 was the "Law on Securing the Unity of Party and State."[20] Article I proclaimed, "The National Socialistic German Labor Party is the bearer of the concept of the German State and is inseparable from the state." This did not mean that party and state were identical. Rather, the party inspired state actions; the state looked to the party for guidance. In August 1933 a German scholar told Rudolf Hess about an American's interest in this development, and Hess replied, "It is no longer the question of a 'party' in the sense of the 'custom' practiced since Washington's time, that we are striving for, but this party is a section of the State itself."[21] Courts now built their rulings on party resolutions and programs and on speeches and writings from Hitler and party officials.[22] For example in early 1934 a high court upheld an employer's dismissal of a Jewish movie director without notice, citing as legal authority speeches by Hitler and Goebbels.[23] In 1935 this procedure formally entered the criminal code: "The Reich Supreme Court as the highest German tribunal must consider it its duty to effect an interpretation of the law which takes into account the change of ideology and of legal concepts which the new state has brought about." The court need not "show consideration for the jurisdiction of the past brought about by other ideologies and other legal concepts."[24]

Upon the death of President Paul von Hindenburg in August 1934, the Succession Act[25] eliminated the last technical obstacle to legal personal rule by Hitler. This new cabinet decree combined the offices of president and chancellor, making Hitler head of government and head of state, with all powers of both offices to rule by decree. In theory this cabinet action overstepped one of the handful of powers that the *Reichstag* had still reserved for itself, but in mid-August a vote of the people made Hitler president by a 90 percent majority. In effect the election ratified the intent of the cabinet decree. Hitler was now supreme dictator ostensibly by popular demand ("ostensibly" because election officials were not fastidious about secret ballots,[26] and consequences that befell opponents of the regime were already notorious).

The Third Reich had no formal constitution. Someone anchored in the American legal tradition might describe Nazi jurisprudence as no more than a civilized veneer allowing police, prosecutors, and judges to gratify personal desires in the name of justice. That element certainly pervaded Nazi jurisprudence. Those personal desires, however, emerged from ideals and principles to which most officials were steadfastly loyal. An American might view their actions as arbitrary because victims could find no protection in statutes, regulations, or precedents. Officials did not rely on such sources for their authority, however, but instead relied on two principles (which were used to interpret statutes, regulations, and precedents): civic duty and the educational nature of law (sometimes called "law by analogy").

The first principle was civic duty. One had a civic duty to uphold the law, and the law's purpose was to protect the state.[27] As a Nazi commentator aptly said in 1934, "The *Gestapo* protect the community rather than the individuals."[28] Civic duty was a positive obligation. A citizen who stood aloof from civic life was not neutral, but dangerous. For example the purpose of elections was not for citizens to make choices but for citizens to affirm their support of government measures. When half the patients voting from Düsseldorf's Marien Hospital cast "no" votes in a 1934 election where the regime wanted "yes" votes, the local medical society leader directed member physicians to boycott the hospital to force its closing.[29] Failure to vote was evidence of opposition to the state. (Jews thereby felt compelled to cast ballots in favor of regime, and for that reason many welcomed the eventual disfranchisement ending that grotesquery.)[30] In 1936 a Court of Honor disbarred an attorney who cast no vote: "Through his failure to participate in the election, not only did he give evidence of his own lack of loyalty to other members of the community, but also this conduct of the defendant was such as to raise doubts about the solidarity of the German legal profession and its commitment to the Führer and the state."[31] Workers could be fired for failure to vote.[32] Rough justice was also administered: "Nazis Set Fire to Ruttenburg Bishop's Home, Incensed at His Refusal to Vote In Plebiscite."[33] Failure to vote subjected citizens to pillorying,[34] as did voting without enthusiasm.[35] Citizens had many other civic duties. A court ruled that a public employee's failure to make "voluntary" charitable contributions to the government's Winter Relief Fund, on top of contributions already made by the employee to private charities, was a failure of civic duty that comprised a misdemeanor: "For him liberty is the right to neglect all his duties except where they are explicitly required by law. He has abstained from participation in community enterprises merely because he wanted to show that as a 'free' man he could not be coerced."[36] Another court ruling upheld firing a worker for not contributing enough to Winter Relief even though he contributed. He got his job back when he agreed to donate about 5 percent of his monthly pay.[37] A 1935 criminal case involved members of a Roman Catholic youth group who continued to meet in spite of a government ban on church youth groups. A state supreme court declared that civic duty, not actual effects of citizens' actions, justified criminalization of innocuous private activity: "Such a public display of personal opinion or belief can all too easily become an encouragement to Communists, Communist sympathizers, or persons currently of unsettled political allegiance, who would then develop and spread the opinion that the National Socialist state did not have the people behind it."[38] In other words, the point was not that danger existed in harmless personal activity, but that such activity sent the wrong message to the German people. Another high court decision of 1935 demonstrated civic duty in jurisprudence. Jehovah's Witnesses sought relief from Nazi persecution by appealing to Article 137 of the old pre-Nazi constitution. "Granted the validity of Art. 137," the court ruled, "its correct application does not prevent the suppression of a religious association if the activities of that association are incompatible with public order."[39] The state had determined that Jehovah's Witnesses should be suppressed, and civic duty required courts to protect the state's determination even if such protection disregarded exact wording found in any laws. In 1934 Nazi legal theorist Carl Schmitt declared, "Today everyone will recognize that the maxim 'No crime without punishment' takes priority over the maxim 'No punishment without law' as the higher and stronger legal truth."[40] The challenge was putting the new maxim into practice; in 1934 Goering complained about defendants still having so many legal rights that convictions could be impeded.[41] One listener recalled Goebbels telling a group of judges some years later, "While making his decisions the judge had to proceed less from the law than from the basic idea that the offender was to be eliminated from the community."[42] Disregard for statutory language brings us to the second guiding principle of Nazi jurisprudence.

The second principle was the educational nature of law. In 1933 Interior Ministry official Dr. Achim Gercke declared, "The laws are mainly educational and give direction. This aspect of the laws should not be underestimated. . . . Decrees give the general direction."[43] In 1936 the Commission for National Socialist Economic Policy declared, "He who sticks to the letter of the law or refuses to go beyond it, because the orders are not given to do so, confirms the fact that he is willing to do only the minimum of what the community asks of him."[44] Specifics in a law were examples to guide officials in their actions, to help them see the spirit of the societal goal illustrated by the law so they could use their initiative to accomplish the goal. A law's language was not intended to limit that task. For example, the Law for the Restoration of the Professional Civil Service[45] spoke only of dismissing Jewish government employees. In the spirit of that law, however, University of Freiburg rector Martin Heidegger halted fellowship payments to Jewish students.[46] Even though no law prohibited marriages between Aryans and Jews, in summer 1935 a Wetzlar court upheld officials who refused to permit such marriages. A contemporary account noted the court "opposed the principle that because a thing is not prohibited [by a law's language] it is therefore permitted."[47] Those examples are from civil law; in 1935 the educational principle was entered explicitly into criminal code:

Article 2
Whoever commits an act which the law declares as punishable or which deserves punishment according to the fundamental idea of a penal law or the sound sentiment of the people, shall be punished. If no specific penal law can be directly applied to the act, it shall be punished according to the law whose underlying principle can be most readily applied to the act.[48]

Article 170a
If an act deserves punishment according to the sound sentiment of the people, but is not declared punishable in the law, the prosecution will examine whether the underlying principle of a penal law can be applied to the act and whether justice can be helped to triumph by the analogous application of this penal law.[49]

Article 267a
If the trial shows that the defendant committed an act which deserves punishment according to the sound sentiment of the people, but is not declared punishable by the law, then the court will examine whether the underlying principle of a penal law applies to the act and whether justice can be helped to triumph by the proper application of that penal law.[50]

In 1937 Minister of Justice Franz Gürtner explained.

A law which originates from the rule: Nulla poena sine lege[51] regards only such action as illegal which violates an existing clause of a punitive law. . . . National Socialism substitutes for the conception of formal wrong the idea of factual wrong: it considers every attack against the welfare of the people's community, every violation of the requirements of the life of a nation as wrong. . . . As a result, the law gives up all claim to be an exclusive source for the determination of right and wrong. . . . The legislator is aware of the fact that he cannot give exhaustive regulations for all the situations in life; therefore he entrusts the judge with filling the remaining gaps. . . . [The judge] interprets the existing regulations not literally but according to their spirit and basic thoughts.[52]

Judges did limit themselves when exercising that right. They imposed punishments harsher than those prescribed for a criminal act because prescribed punishments merely indicated how serious the act was compared to others, but judges did not disregard express provisions of a statute defining a criminal act. For example, judges did not use a law against seduction of females under age sixteen to punish someone for seducing a female aged over sixteen; the age specification was considered an explicit limitation defining the offense and not mere educational guidance. Judges could extrapolate but could not invent an offense having no basis whatsoever in written law.[53] Any inconvenience caused by such limitation could be eased, however. Justice Minister Otto Thierack declared, "Every judge is at liberty to call on me in case he thinks that a law compels him to render a judgment not compatible with real life. In such an emergency it will be my task to provide him with the law he needs."[54]

In effect the educational nature of law merges law with morality. People who do not act as they should must be punished, regardless of what the law says. Acts, if intended to help the state, become permissible even if formally proscribed. And so courts become the moral guardian of society. During World War II a student of the Nazi legal system dryly observed that in Germany the "attempt of the legislator and of the judiciary to use the criminal law to raise the moral standards of the community, appears, when measured by the results achieved, as . . . premature."[55]

With civic duty and the educational nature of law as guiding principles, officials could do almost anything they believed would promote the public good. That did not mean they could do anything else. A judge would face deep trouble by ordering sexual favors from a law-abiding citizen. A Gestapo man who helped himself to confiscated property could expect severe punishment. On the topic of confiscated Jewish property Himmler noted, "This wealth should, as a matter of course, be handed over to the Reich without reserve. We have taken none of it for ourselves. Individual men who have lapsed will be punished in accordance with an order I issued at the beginning, which gave this warning: Whoever takes so much as a mark of it, is a dead man. A number of SS men—there are not very many of them—have fallen short, and they will die, without mercy."[56] Goering concurred about misappropriated goods, "I shall not hesitate to act ruthlessly in any case where such a trick is played. If the individual involved is prominent, I shall see the Fuehrer within two hours and report him."[57] Such statements were not idle. Vienna *Gauleiter* Josef Bürckel sent to Dachau a dozen Nazi officials who demonstrated corruption in confiscations of Jewish property.[58] Others, "fearful for their safety, have asked to be relieved of their tasks."[59] Even high Nazi figures trembled when accused of corruption involving Jewish property. Julius Streicher once exclaimed to an associate, "The police have found out about the Mars shares. We will simply say that the shares were not bought for me but for the Fraenkische Tageszeitung!!"[60] Streicher was dismissed from office because of such venality. Officials could exceed any written law, but their actions had to be consistent with civic duty. That limit was real but would be unapparent to anyone who thinks the purpose of law is to protect individual citizens. Nazis believed law was intended to protect the state.

Such a legal philosophy guarantees harshness. A judge would violate civic duty by imposing a penalty less severe than called for by the law. Any doubts in a case must be settled in favor of the state. Mere accusations (including the act of arrest) become sufficient to impose grave penalties, because if a defendant's story differs from a police officer's, the state's safety requires the police version to be accepted. Formal trials are needed less and less. A police officer who fails to act upon gossip could allow a social malcontent to injure the state. Failing to act upon anonymous accusations would prove that the police officer lacks sufficient sense of civic duty, a lack meriting punishment. The SS extended police power to all citizens in Jewish matters; in 1935 *Das Schwarze Korps* (the official SS journal) said anyone could legally arrest a Jew for any violation. If the Jew resisted, the private citizen could use force. If later investigation showed the citizen was mistaken, no punishment would occur.[61] That policy was a license for vigilante violence. Streicher, for example, gave *Der Stürmer* vendors standing orders to arrest Jewish members of Aryan-Jewish couples.[62]

The penal code itself called for harshness whenever doubt arose. For example, before Hitler took office Article 2 of the code said, "For no act may punishment be imposed unless such punishment is prescribed by statute before the act is committed. In the event of any change in the statute between the time of commission of an act and the time of rendering a decision, the most lenient statute shall apply."[63] In 1935 this article was amended to say, "A law issued for a limited time only is to be applied to those criminal acts which were committed during its validity, even after its validity has expired."[64] In other words, the harsher statute shall apply. That general principle was also expressed in specific statutes. A 1933 decree allowed capital punishment for assorted acts committed between January 31 and February 28 even though the acts had been legal then.[65] Highway robbery only became a death-penalty offense in 1938, but Nazis extended the penalty's coverage to offenses perpetrated any time after 1935.[66] Amendments to the criminal code introduced the same spirit into appeals:

Article 358
Even if the judgment has been contested only by the defendant or his legal representative or by the prosecution in his favor, it can be changed against the interests of the defendant.[67]

Article 373
Even if resumption of the proceedings has been applied for only by the defendant or his legal representative or by the prosecution in his favor, the sentence can be changed against the interest of the defendant.[68]

Nazis said these amendments introduced more fairness into the judicial system by "removal of one-sided limitations of the courts deciding on legal appeals."[69] The effect was to encourage harshness. Nuremberg Military Tribunal prosecutors noted that *Judges' Letters*, a confidential publication distributed to judges by the Ministry of Justice, was "filled with exhortations to the utmost ruthlessness in the imposition of sentences."[70] In 1935 Hans Frank, president of the Germany Academy of Law, told the International Congress on Penal Law and Prison Problems, "We have from the beginning emphasized that the National Socialist State knows no humanitarian scruples so far as the criminal is concerned. National Socialism stands in the position of a state of war against criminal elements. I can give you the assurance, gentlemen, that the National Socialist jurist is a fanatical exponent of the principle of reprisal, yes, of intimidation."[71] Under a decree of September 1939[72] prosecutors could appeal acquittals. A contemporary critic noted the power to reopen a case meant "it is the prosecutor who actually determines the final judgment."[73] Even so, concern about judicial leniency lingered. A judge recalled that *Der Stürmer* and *Das Schwarze Korps* "took delight in distorting reports of trials and in naming those judges who had imposed [insufficiently harsh] sentences which the party considered intolerable."[74] In April 1942 Hitler had the *Reichstag* authorize him to remove any judge from office.[75] That authorization was superfluous because the 1933 Law for the Restoration of the Professional Civil Service already allowed dismissal of judges for any reason.[76] Still, the regime worried that remaining judges were too soft. In September 1942 the Reich Minister of Justice authorized "special treatment at the hands of the police in cases where judicial sentences are not severe enough."[77] Such was already the custom. In 1936 an Aryan woman related how her Jewish husband refused to loan money to a man. The disappointed man then denounced the woman for slandering Nazi officials. The judge found her innocent, but the Gestapo sent her to a concentration camp.[78] In 1937 Heydrich ordered that race polluters be put into protective custody after serving the prison term imposed by a court.[79] The next year a former Social Democrat managed to avoid conviction for disseminating unlawful political literature. Lawyer and client exchanged hearty mutual congratulations outside the courthouse, and went their separate ways. "Up the street Peter [the lawyer] had turned to wave a final goodbye. He was just in time to see his client being marched away between two uniformed guards and bundled into a green van parked beside the roadway. . . . Peter's client had simply vanished without trace."[80] Unlike "arrest" which was a prelude to trial, "protective custody" was administrative incarceration to protect the state and lasted until authorities thought the person no longer threatened the state.

In November 1942 the Ministry of Justice confidentially directed that "courts will forego the carrying out of regular criminal procedures" against Jews. Jews "henceforth shall be turned over to the police" for retribution.[81] The following April the Ministry authorized police to place Jews under administrative imprisonment whenever judicial imprisonment sentences ended.[82] Three months later the Ministry publicly codified its earlier confidential directive: "Criminal actions committed by Jews shall be punished by the police."[83]

Nazi jurisprudence did not actually engage in arbitrary action. "Arbitrary" implies freedom of action. Nazi jurisprudence encouraged only harshness. Mercy was discouraged. Hans Frank said Germany "makes no concessions to criminals; it does not negotiate with them, it stamps them out."[84] (Keep in mind that a "criminal" under the Nazi dictatorship could be an ordinary person who engaged in behavior common to a democratic society.) A system that pushes in only one direction is not arbitrary.

That observation returns us to the conflict of mob versus bureaucrat. Nazi law codified mob violence. As discussed in chapter one, a system was devised to identify victims. Now we see a system by which those victims can be persecuted at will. The High Administrative Court of Saxony said in 1935, "'Law' as the common law, i.e. as the orderly way in which the people lives as a community, is recognized as taking precedence over the statutes themselves."[85] Said senior SS and Security Services leader Werner Best, "This means that the orderly or regular way in which the people fulfills the 'police' task through its 'voices'— organizations and individuals—is 'police' law, which takes precedence over statutory law."[86] Once victims are apprehended, their fate is determined only by their captors' sense of civic duty, not by any guarantees of due process or civil liberties. By codifying mob violence, state actions merge with vigilante actions.

The character of violence changes, however. More and more often drunken SA (storm trooper) thugs were replaced by cool university graduates of the SS. The latter were more efficient and thorough, having both a grasp of the big picture and small detail, and they crowded Old Fighters out of anti-Jewish actions. Instead of a brawl that smashed a Jewish shopkeeper's business and which ran the proprietor into the next town, the proprietor disappeared into "protective custody," and the government sold the shop's assets. Victims were still brutalized, but public decorum was preserved. The mob was now comprised of government officials who worked their will upon victims. Mob violence moved from streets to the courts. The mob became more civilized in speech, but still brutalized ordinary people. Nazi legal officials replaced vigilantes with a system that efficiently accomplished what vigilantes wanted. All in the name of civic duty.

Although Nazis best articulated civic duty and the educational nature of law, they were not alien to German legal tradition.[87] Said one scholar familiar with pre-Nazi jurisprudence, "The jurist must put himself outside of the body of the existing rules. He must closely observe the facts of life, economics and other social phenomena. He must know the political tendencies of the community." The scholar added, "A right, a legal relation cannot exist outside a given body of law by which it is created."[88] Such thinking helped many German lawyers and judges adapt to the Nazi legal system. "The German judge," said another authority, "is unaffected by intellectual doubts as to the intrinsic justice of the legal rule he has to apply, provided it is enacted by the authority of the state, and he does not question whether the authority is legitimate or not."[89] The absolute rejection of natural law in such thinking was tempered in a special way by Nazi legal theorists. Helmut Nicolai said in 1934, "*According to German legal thinking law does not arise from the statute but is there before the statute*. An outrage is still an outrage although out of some ground or other it has not been designated as such by legislation."[90] Nazis argued that natural law grants rights to prosecutors and the state but not to victims.

Before we examine operation of Nazi anti-Jewish laws, we should note one more general Nazi legal principle. That principle was the extension of German criminal law to foreign countries. In 1940 the following language was added to the Reich criminal code: "German criminal law will be applied to the following acts committed by a foreigner abroad, independently of the laws of the place of commitment: . . . unauthorized sale of narcotics."[91] Prosecutors at the Nuremberg Military Tribunal described that extension as criminal, and it formed part of the indictment against Ministry of Justice defendants.[92] Once the extension principle was established, coverage of one criminal statute after another was extended to other countries.[93] The *Frankfurter Zeitung* exulted, "Only a powerful great power can enforce this principle in practice."[94] In 1939 and 1940 Nazi law enforcement agents were active in the United States.[95] In 1935 Reich Minister of the Interior Wilhelm Frick noted that Nazi law officers had abducted persons in Holland, Switzerland, and Czechoslovakia to stand trial in Germany.[96] In addition to activity acknowledged by Frick, Nazi kidnap squads operated in England, France, and Denmark.[97] We speak here of unlawful kidnappings, not lawful extraditions. Such activity was well known at the time. In 1935 the United States ambassador to Germany wrote in his diary, "On my right sat the wife of the Swiss Minister who, on Monday last, made a formal protest against the Nazi kidnapping of a Jew, named Jacob, who has been writing able anti-Nazi articles for the Swiss and French press the last two years. Jacob was a German citizen before 1933. He is now in jail, to be tried for treason."[98]

Having considered the basis of Nazi law, we can now consider its operation in real life.

BOYCOTT AS AN ELEMENT OF OSTRACISM

For ease of understanding, the ostracism portion of the destruction process is here subdivided into various topics. In practice all subdivisions can occur simultaneously, as can other aspects of the destruction process. For example, Nazis began to arrest and kill Jews soon after Hitler became chancellor, before ostracism had been completed. Nonetheless mass annihilation did not occur until preceding stages of the destruction process had been fulfilled. There is a natural progression from one stage to another, although incidents classified as parts of various stages can occur at any time in the destruction process.

Having established a means to identify victims, ostracism of those victims begins with boycott. By "boycott" we mean social pressure to avoid dealing with victims. Because of civic duty and intermingling of the Nazi party with the state, we can rarely say that a boycott action was strictly voluntary with no element of compulsion. We can, however, make a general distinction between acts committed by citizens on their own behalf, and acts committed by government agents on order of the state. When speaking of "boycott" we mean actions of ordinary citizens.

Frequent Nazi admonitions to ostracize Jews, along with publicity and punishments given to boycott violators, can be misinterpreted as meaning the regime had difficulty in gaining the population's cooperation. In fact, great popular support existed for anti-Jewish measures. Ubiquitous admonitions should be interpreted in the context of, say, numerous Partnership for a Drug-Free

America announcements in the United States during the 1980s and 1990s. Repeated exhortations to avoid drug use did not mean that most Americans supported drug users; on the contrary, most Americans supported the war on drug users with enthusiasm.

One factor promoting widespread support for the war on Jews was ostracism, excluding Jews from normal society. Rhetoric described in the previous chapter became more credible because it met no refutation from real life examples of Jews living ordinary productive lives; stereotypes went unchallenged.[99] In 1936 the Aryan wife of a Jew declared, "It is impossible to imagine what it is like to live among 60,000,000 people all pledged to be your enemies."[100] True enough, but perhaps conditions documented in the following pages can aid our comprehension.

Hans Quecke noted in volume five of his 1941 study *Building of the Third Reich*, "A task of special political significance and economic importance arose as an absolute necessity out of the National Socialist conception of state and economy, namely, *the eradication of Jewish influence from the economy.*"[101] From the start, Nazi officials were forthright about that goal. In 1934 one onlooker reported, "Impartial observers have been informed by leading Nazi officials that they are determined to close all economic opportunities completely to the Jews and to render them wholly helpless and destitute."[102]

In pursuance of a Jew-free economy, Nazis announced a nationwide boycott of Jewish businesses to begin on April 1, 1933. In part the measure was intended to mollify anti-Semites who were demanding action now that the Nazis controlled the government. Local actions were already proceeding with rude vigor; Frankfurt storm troopers had jailed thirty-five Jewish businessmen; Annaberg Nazis had imprisoned every Jewish merchant in town; Worms Nazis filled some Jewish stores with tear gas and vandalized others; thugs with swastika armbands descended on a Jewish-owned hotel in Magdeburg and wrecked its dining room; Nazis from Kassel invaded the Tietz department stores, where they "threatened and photographed every customer"; ominous crowds forced Jewish stores to close elsewhere; where vigilantes failed, police occasionally shut down defiant shops that had remained open.[103] Senior party officials wanted the April 1 boycott to be peaceful in order to demonstrate the party's control over members. "We expect iron discipline," Goebbels said. "This must be for the whole world a wonderful show of unity and manly training. To those abroad who believe that we could not manage it, we want to show that we have the people in our hand."[104] The action was cancelled after one day due to the number of citizens who made a show of patronizing Jewish businesses in protest of the boycott. Cancellation, however, was hardly a victory for tolerance. Said one German aristocrat, "I am glad that the Nazis were obliged to give the 'stop' signal the first night. However, I hope it has taught the Jews a lesson. They should all leave Germany and bide their time outside."[105] Although the one-day effort demonstrated a difference of opinion among the citizenry, it also demonstrated that actions against Jews were socially acceptable.

Having established the social acceptability of boycotting Jews, further actions depended on the interest level of individuals and groups across Germany. A United States diplomat noted a public declaration by Goering that "police in Germany were not supported by the Government for the purpose of protecting Jewish stores."[106] In 1935 *Das Schwarze Korps* and the Ministry of Justice publication *Die Deutsche Justiz* called for prosecution of Jews who protested boycott signs labeling their shops as Jewish.[107] Later the regime ordered permanent marking of Jewish shops.[108] "It does not do for innumerable citizens to daily buy from Jews and to fill the pockets of our enemies with their money," said *Der Stürmer*. "He who buys from Jews takes goods and wages from his citizens."[109]

In cities more and more Aryan businesses became unwilling to deal with Jews. Hotels demurred when Jews sought to register as guests, and restaurants declined to serve.[110] "Large signs hang in cafe and shop windows—'Only traitors talk or deal with Jews'; 'Jews visit this place at the risk of their lives'; 'Israel, there is no room for you here.'"[111] While dining at Berlin's elegant Café Josty a woman noticed a couple waiting for their meal at the next table. "A page boy had just placed a teacup with a slip of paper in it before the young man. The young couple read the slip of paper and blushed. They seemed about to rise from their seats. At our table, the first champagne was opened with a loud pop. 'May I take the liberty?' I said to them in French, and removed the slip of paper from their table and translated it to my party. 'We do not serve Jews,' read the notice."[112] Ostracism by businesses could be not only deeply personal but coldly institutional. Commercial directories deleted Jewish listings,[113] and Jewish businesses found themselves unable to place ads in telephone directories, in newspapers, on radio, or in the German State Railway system.[114] Refusal of advertising to Jewish firms became routine and crippling.[115] Jewish firms were even cut off from bulk rates when mailing advertisements unless addressees were Jewish.[116] Circulation restrictions on Jewish newspapers, such as forbidding them to be sold on the street or in railroad stations after October 1935,[117] limited the impact of what little advertising remained available to Jewish businesses.

In small towns the campaign against Jewish business was promoted by rhetoric poisoning the commercial atmosphere. *Der Stürmer* boasted with pride, "In thousands of towns and villages signs and posters say: 'Jews are not wanted here!'"[118] A contemporary chronicler found the boast accurate. "The sign 'No Jews Allowed' is proudly flaunted by the municipalities of Oberrosbach, Unterrossbach, Limbach, Norderney, Gross Groebach, Marburg, Herolsberg, Bubenfurth, Mittelfranken, Boedelsee, Glasbeck, Westphalia Giessen, Ansbach, Neidenberg, Nordseebad."[119] Some signs were lit up at night like billboards.[120] Proud villages displayed a white flag to proclaim they were Jew-free.[121] In Germany the Osann-am-Mosel town council resolved: "No Jew or Jewess is permitted to move into Osann. No Jew can rent or buy a house or land in Osann. No craftsman, merchant or any other citizen can get work or orders in the town if he has had anything to do with a Jew. Purchases from Jews mean treason against the people and the nation."[122] Other towns passed similar resolutions.[123] In 1934 a swastika banner flew in celebration from the former house of the last Jew to leave the Hersbruck district of thirty-six villages.[124] A traveler in Germany that year left this description:

> On and on we went. My heart sang. I was happy—happy to have Marie, happy to be traveling through a German Christmas-card landscape to Christmas in a German home. A bunny scuttled across a field. We saw a little boy with red cap and red mittens. Smoke rose from house chimneys. . . .
>
> The road dipped, leading into a valley threaded with villages—villages as charmingly built as the others we had passed, but strangely quiet. Dusk was gathering. Each had its *Christbaum*; yet not one was lit. At the entrance and exit of every village, and sometimes before houses, stood a sign against Jews. . . .
>
> "*Juden dürfen hier nicht bleiben*" (Jews may not stay here)—"*Wer die Juden unterstüzt fördert den Kommunismus*" (Who helps the Jews helps Communism)—"*Juden unerwünscht*" (Jews not wanted)—"*Wer da naht mit platten Füssen, mit Haaren kraus und Nasen krumm, der soll nicht unser Land geniessen, der muss hinaus, der muss hinaus*" (This flat-footed stranger, with kinky hair and hooked nose, he shall not our land enjoy, he must leave, he must leave)—"*Deutschland! erwache aus deinem bösen Traum, gib fremden Juden in deinem Reich nich Raum!*" (Germany! awake from thy bad dream, give stranger Jews in thy Reich no room)—"*Juda, entweihe aus unsrem deutschen Haus!*" (Jews, vacate our German house)—these were among the things we read. The writings before house doors were on white sheets stretched between two posts thrust into the ground and plainly lettered in black. They all had to do with women either married or engaged to men of Jewish blood. They were personal allusions to each girl or woman, and of a sexual vileness I would not have believed had I not seen them.[125]

The rhetoric campaign helped devastate rural Jewish business. "Since the spring of 1933," wrote one contemporary observer, "Jewish businessmen and shopkeepers in the small country towns have been ruined and forced to give up their businesses and leave their homes."[126] Another observer reported in 1934, "Frightful anxiety is rocking the edifice of small-town Jewry."[127]

Because Jewish businesses were integrated with the rest of the German economy, decline of Jewish mercantile prosperity could affect Aryan firms. In the summer of 1935 Jewish retail shoe shops began to cancel standing orders with Aryan shoe manufacturers because Aryan customers refused to buy the products. Nazis could hardly admit that anti-Jewish actions were harming Aryan workers. Instead the party in Pirmasens, a town where the economy depended on footwear manufacturing, labeled the cancellations as a Jewish plot: "The Jew is again trying to brandish his whip at us. He wants to browbeat National Socialist Pirmasens. But we say that we mean war to the knife on anyone who threatens our workshops. From now on we will not set foot in another Jewish shop, not enter another Jewish doctor's waiting-room. No more dealings with Jews!"[128] The

Homestead Law's anti-Jewish element had another type of unexpected effect. That law converted small peasant holdings into hereditary landed estates that could not be sold, and excluded any Jew from this new petty nobility. Because the land was immune from creditors, however, agribusiness suppliers demanded cash transactions from farmers. The law's anti-Jewish element had the ironic effect of causing some farmers to claim Jewish ancestry in order to maintain credit lines and stay in business.[129]

Throughout Germany all sorts of organizations asked Jewish members to depart: veterans groups, student groups, skat clubs, rabbit breeder societies.[130] Aryan business partners had the right to expel Jewish partners.[131] All prominent Jewish members of Berlin's Chamber of Commerce were forced out by April 1933. *Völkischer Beobachter* reported "the most important Chamber of Commerce in Germany has thus become 'Jew-free.'"[132] Jews were excluded from golf courses; even the Wannsee country club, whose members were sophisticated and wealthy, expelled Jewish members.[133] Prohibitions extended to charitable activity. The Central Organization for German Deaf ended monthly benefits paid to Jewish members,[134] and the Ministry of Posts and Telegraphs cancelled discounts formerly applied to monthly phone bills of blind Jewish war veterans.[135] Charities refused to take donations from Jews. Said one Rhineland official, "I should like to point out to all departments the impropriety of accepting contributions from Jews while, at the same time, opposing the Jewish Race on the basis of folkish considerations."[136] Nazis denied that Jews could benefit the community in any way, even as providers of charity.

Enforcement of the boycott could be brutal. When a Jewish typist complained in 1933 that Nazi coworkers made the office atmosphere intolerable, they denounced her for sowing atrocity propaganda; she was sentenced to eight months' incarceration.[137] If shops were vandalized, Jewish owners were given about two hours to repair damage. Otherwise they would be accused of promoting blight. A young Jew talked with an owner cleaning up a ruined store. "They got my phone number and made me come all the way here. My wife said don't go, but they said they'd fine me a thousand marks and put me in jail if I didn't clean up immediately. So I came and cleaned up. People stood around and watched me. I was bending down to pick up some big glass pieces and somebody kicked me from behind and I fell right into the pile of glass."[138] A Berlin resident went to a store of Jewish friends. "Their shop was in ruins. . . . Three S. A. men, roaring with obscene laughter, forced the trembling old man to pick up the broken glass with hands that were covered with blood."[139] The SS was no gentler in discouraging blight, beating a store owner who pleaded that he lacked the physical strength to remove debris scattered from his shop.[140]

Enforcement of the boycott went beyond Jewish victims, to Aryans who broke the boycott and even to relatives of those Aryans. An insurance clerk had to leave her job because of harassment from fellow employees who objected to her Christian father working for Jews.[141] A regional party directive issued in 1933 stated, "No German will speak to a Jew if it is not absolutely necessary."[142]

Aryans tending town garden plots became fearful of speaking to Jews tending an adjoining plot, fearing job loss and ostracism of family members.[143] In 1933 a Jewish husband and Roman Catholic wife unsuccessfully sought advice from a priest: "He was scared of getting mixed up with us."[144] A friendly game of cards between Jew and Aryan was declared race defilement.[145] In the mid-1930s an Aryan was threatened with job loss if he continued visiting the house of an old friend whose grandmother had been Jewish. When asked how he planned to respond to the threat he replied, "I can't live if I lose my job."[146] Said one contemporary observer, "No one living in a village or little town could venture to set foot in a Jew's business premises or his house without being reviled."[147] A 1933 party directive not only ordered members to cease associating with Jews, but to cease associating with Aryans who dealt with Jews.[148] Such visits were chancy even in cosmopolitan Berlin. A Berlin Nazi visited someone known to sympathize with Jews. The Nazi emerged from the residence after dark and discovered that his automobile had been vandalized. The sympathizer wrote, "I thought of course that it had been injured in the process of attempted theft. He was confident that it was a warning to him from the Secret Police that his visits . . . were unwelcome."[149] Juergen Ohlsen, who portrayed the lead role in the acclaimed 1933 movie *Hitler Youth Quex*, was ostracized two years later for playing tennis with a Jewish friend.[150] When the Nazi head of a traveling circus appeared in court with a Jewish lawyer, the court not only refused to let the lawyer plead but removed the Nazi from his job and forbade him to hold an executive position in any other company.[151] In July 1933 Tilsit's city council withdrew municipal business from an attorney who made compassionate remarks about a Jewish attorney's plight.[152] Aryans lost their leases to communal meadows from Mainz-Bischofsheim if they were discovered doing business with Jews.[153] Two Aryan doctors were disciplined for involvement with a foreign Jew's house purchase.[154] A government official in Brunswick was disciplined for letting a Jewish salesman store a sample case in the official's attic.[155] A paper mill executive found himself in protective custody in 1934 for hiring the son of a Jewish refugee.[156] The previous year public welfare recipients, ranging from the destitute to ordinary newlyweds, were ordered to avoid spending their aid in Jewish shops.[157] By July 1935 recipients who patronized a Jewish shop lost their public assistance: "He who still nowadays satisfies his needs by purchase of goods of any kind whatsoever from the Jews imperils the generosity of those foremost in helping him to combat hunger and cold. I therefore feel obliged to exclude from assistance by the National Socialist Welfare organisation every needy person so depraved as to shut himself out from the community in this way."[158] An incident in autumn 1938 illustrated the boycott's scope. A Bonn Jew clearing debris from her smashed shop accepted help in the task from the wife of a renowned professor at the university. "He suffered such harassment that he emigrated to England with his family as soon as circumstances permitted. The intervening months were a period of quarantine during which a total of three people—out of the Professor's entire social and professional circle—called on him under cover of darkness. He received one other communication from the outside world: a letter from a group of colleagues expressing regret that he had forfeited an honourable exit from the university through his wife's lack of instinct."[159]

The Jewish boycott gave Aryans an opportunity to settle private grievances against fellow Aryans. Nazi officials were overwhelmed by spiteful "patriotic" reports.[160] "Most turn out to be malicious suspicions or backbiting," declared one police officer.[161] Goering expressed disgust at the extent of denunciations for minor infractions of the Jewish boycott.[162] Even Hitler complained, "I cannot bring myself to believe that this despicable practice is always dictated by the desire to bring guilty persons before the bar of justice. Too often selfishness and petty personal spite are the motives."[163] He added in disgust, "We are living at present in a sea of denunciations and human meanness."[164] Justice Minister Thierack admonished citizens that the Reich did not expect them to pass on every suspicion to police.[165] By May 1933 the situation was so bad that a decree forbade denouncing people for private revenge.[166] Five years later the practice of denouncing government workers in order to get their jobs remained so prevalent that a new directive said no one could get a specific vacant public office if that person had informed on that specific officeholder.[167] Nonetheless many citizens continued to use the war on Jews to make war on fellow Aryans. In October 1938 a Würzburg waitress denounced her employer for saying he would be glad to have Jewish customers. Investigation found that he had said no such thing, and that the waitress was taking revenge for being unable to switch jobs without paying the employer a penalty.[168] A tenant behind on rent reported the landlady for having Jewish friends, a report that the Gestapo found to be groundless harassment.[169] Indeed one scholar examining court cases found that almost all boycott violation charges laid against Aryans, even if upheld, were based on grudges rather than concern about the war on Jews. Another scholar found that almost 40 percent of denunciations in Gestapo files were positively due to personal grudges. Still another student of Gestapo files declared, "Paid informers or agents are conspicuous by their absence. . . . Perhaps there was enough volunteered information to make the use of agents superfluous."[170]

Aryans accused of boycott violation were pilloried. "The 'German Labour Front' office in Cologne has posted on the wall, in the form of a 'Wanted' or 'Arrest' notice, photographs of women entering or leaving Jewish shops, with the words: 'Fie! These traitors bought from Jews. *Who knows them?*'"[171] Photos were also taken for display in theaters and publication in newspapers.[172] In 1933 an Aryan shop window in Corbach-Waldeck was reserved for display of offending names.[173] Names could be listed in newspapers and posted in town halls as well.[174] One observer in the 1930s reported "'Shame Boards' installed by Party agencies adorn the streets, branding 'traitors' by inclusion of their names under the heading 'Fellow-citizens who maintain friendly relations with Jews or buy in Jewish stores.'"[175] In Langenzenn and Behringersdorf citizens were told they faced being paraded through town with signs around their necks if they dared to violate the boycott.[176] Aschaffenburg housewives faced close questioning for patronizing Jews,[177] and the National Socialist Retailers and Handicraft Organization sent threatening letters to Aryan housewives who bought from Jewish merchants.[178] A 1933 directive from the Coblenz-Trier Nazi party district organization told local committees how to get the names: "Secure female clerks from Jewish stores, who can then very easily name those who purchase in Jewish shops. This demands some caution and has to be done with the greatest secrecy." The party tried to guarantee equivalent employment to any female clerks who got fired for this spying.[179] Party leaders elsewhere took a more direct approach, simply having police and brownshirt thugs convince a merchant to reveal the names of customers.[180] Still another method was effective; bank clerks would watch checks clearing through the bank and notify the party if an Aryan had written a check to a Jewish firm.[181]

Der Stürmer featured letters to the editor by which readers with a grievance against anyone could pillory that person. (In October 1935 one citizen privately noted that *Stürmer* gossip "always" came from "the shadiest elements in our town.")[182] The newspaper was displayed in "*Stürmer* boxes" (glass-covered exhibit cases) throughout Germany, where passers-by could read letters such as these:

> In Bruttig, in the lovely Moselkrampen, there is a boarding school for children. . . . The National-Socialist communal counsellor has . . . put a ban on Jewish children being cared for at the school. There was great sorrow over this among those who bow down to the Jews. To overcome this "bad state of affairs", the wife of the richest peasant in Bruttig, Mrs. Nik. Loenarz, decided to look after the Jewish children. She now goes out for walks with Jewish children in bright daylight. No wonder the Loenarz family buys meat from the Jew. *"Tell me with whom you consort and I will tell you who you are."*[183]

> The wife of the farmer from Menzel, from Gross-Schiresdorf, near Goldberg, buys her shoes from a Jew, though her husband, as a farmer Stahlhelm-member, belongs to the SAR. Dear "Stuermer", we National Socialists of Silesa will work hard to make every compatriot realize the Jewish question. But the nation should also know who are the people who sabotage our defensive struggle.[184]

"We children in Roth do our bit too," wrote one nine-year-old girl. "Some of our class often stand in front of Baer's shop and when people want to go in, we shout: 'You ought to be ashamed, shopping at a Jew's; fie upon you!' Then the women blush crimson and go away. Well *Stürmer*, you like that, don't you?"[185] Max Bukert, a teacher at Overbeckstrasse School in Cologne-Ehrenfeld, wrote,

> I give lectures on the Jewish question to all my senior forms. . . . How deeply rooted the lesson is already is emphasized by the following little experience which I had with a nine-year-old boy in my class.
>   One day he came to school and said: "Please, Sir, yesterday I was out with mother. Just as we passed the stores (evidently Jewish owned) she remembered

she wanted some reels of cotton. She tried to give me the money to slip into the stores to buy them. Whereupon I told my mother: 'You don't get me going in there, go yourself! But, let me tell you, if you do I'll tell teacher tomorrow. Then he'll send for you and it may not be so pleasant for you.'"[186]

Male photographers from *Der Stürmer* snapped women as they patronized a Jewish-owned business or chatted on the street with a Jew. Sample captions: "This young woman shopped at a Jew's shop; her husband is employed at the State Theatre," "In the face of (name follows) is mirrored the shamelessness and lack of self-respect which have resulted in her from contact with a Jew. In the face of the Jew (name follows) gleams satanic joy."[187] When a storm troop leader pilloried a fellow storm trooper's wife for race defilement, she denied sexual involvement with her Jewish friend and sought an injunction against her accuser. Instead the Breslau court upheld the charge: "Even if she was not intimate with the Jew Spanier, her behaviour with him, particularly having regard to present day ideas, was inexcusable and certainly constituted race-defilement."[188] Breslau was known for toughness on this topic. Breslau SA men would march around town, stop at homes of Aryan women "defiling the race" via relations with Jewish men, and there shout denouncements while scrawling the women's names in the street.[189] The *Schlesische Tageszeitung* published such names in a feature called "On the Pillory."[190] In 1933 the newspaper *Hakenkreuzbanner* pilloried one Aryan female daily for race defilement, printing her name and address: "All girls and women so named have been ruined socially, morally and economically. . . . Mannheim women and girls live in terror lest some one denounce them for, however false the denunciation may be, they have no redress. Complaints against the Nazi powers are laughed out of court."[191] A simple handshake with a Jew of the opposite sex was enough to bring charges of race defilement.[192] Villification by *Der Stürmer* was taken seriously. When a woman sought a city job in Aschaffendburg, a police background check found "She appears in regard to morals to be pretty decadent, because before the National Socialist uprising she entertained relations with Jews about which at the time even the *Stürmer* reported."[193] A Frankfurt-on-the-Oder Law Court refused an injunction requested by a woman who *Der Stürmer* had pilloried for using familiar form of address to a Jew: "It must be a matter of course and duty of honour for every German citizen to sacrifice even personal friendship, and its ties of loyalty, to the loyalty and duty which he owes to the Fatherland. It is the task of everyone to do what he can to help to reduce Jewish influence in public life. To that end the social ostracism and isolation of individual Jews is essential."[194]

Appeals to courts may have been fruitless but they were understandable, given the serious consequences that could result from being pilloried. Shopping at a Jewish store or using services from a Jewish physician or attorney was a firing offense for any municipal employee of Frankenberg.[195] By 1938 private employers were allowed to fire workers without compensation for the same reason.[196] And such job loss might well be followed by SS action and by public ordeal, such as being marched through town.[197] Government employees were fired if their *relatives* patronized a Jewish-owned department store.[198] A man recalled a scene between his parents: "My father found a shopping bag from Alsberg's and scolded my mother for shopping in a Jewish store when she was the wife of a Party member and a district court presiding judge. . . . Mother said she would do her shopping wherever she pleased. . . . My father begged her to consider the harm it would do to him if she were seen entering or leaving a Jewish store."[199] In 1935 police in Paderborn had to break up a mob menacing the town hall after the spouse of a senior town official was discovered buying from a Jewish department store.[200] Government employees were even fired if *their* employees patronized a Jewish-owned business. Bonn University's rector and the law school's dean lost their appointments when their maids obtained meat from a Jewish butcher.[201] In November 1935 Nazis expelled Berlin's mayor Heinrich Sahm from the party, action which ultimately cost him his mayoralty, because he twice patronized Jewish businesses.[202] And offenders risked more than their jobs.

> *Order for the Initiation of Criminal Proceedings*
> I initiate an inquiry against notary Dr. Kurt Prelle of Naumburg. . . .
> It has become doubtful whether notary Dr. Prelle can still be relied upon to lend his active support to the National Socialist State at all times. . . .
> He was accused of having made a purchase from the Jew Max Cohn in Naumburg (Saale) on 24 December 1935. On 18 February 1936 . . . he submitted a questionable justification in which he explained that not he himself but his wife without his knowledge had bought picture postcards from the Jew Cohn for a total of 10 Reichspfennig. . . .
>
> Berlin, 6 December 1938
> The Reich Minister of Justice[203]

The Nazi state followed a zero-tolerance policy for commerce with Jews, and three years after the original ten pfennig offense Dr. Prelle was about to pay a heavy price.

Government endorsement of private intimidation, combined with courts that refused redress to victims, encouraged a climate of violence. In March 1933 an American diplomat in Berlin noted, "Prior to the elections on March 5 the admirable police force of Germany was able to restrain the uniformed National-Socialists from excesses against the Jews" but afterward beatings and other attacks became common.[204] "One day here in Heilbronn," said an eyewitness in the mid-1930s, "squads of Nazi troops, each about a hundred strong, marched through the town. In the main streets they shouted their slogans: 'Perish Judah,' 'Out with the Jews,' etc."[205] Brass bands accompanied such parades in Berlin.[206] During a 1935 campaign against Jewish ice cream parlors in Berlin menacing "squads of young anti-Semites marched up and down shouting and displaying placards."[207] One sign proclaimed, "Jews violate children."[208] Customers were chased and abused; one "ice cream and confectionary shop was completely wrecked, the proprietor was badly beaten and his girl assistant was knocked unconscious."[209] Police responded by ordering shopkeepers to close.[210] In Vienna soon after the *Anschluss* Aryans who patronized Jewish businesses were marched around town through booing crowds, wearing signs inscribed "I am an Aryan pig. I bought from a Jewish shop."[211] A similar atmosphere prevailed in Berlin: "Two of the largest Jewish-owned establishments in the Kurfuerstendamm were the objects today of crowds that blocked the entrances. Prospective buyers were compelled to elbow their way through the hostile crowds and when they emerged they were loudly booed."[212] From *Hessische Volkswacht* of Kassel in 1933: "A Jew, Walther Lieberg, maintained relations with a Christian girl. The girl's mother did nothing to terminate these relations, but suffered them. The Christian girl took the ground that the new government could not interfere with her private life. To enlighten these people and bring home to them the heinousness of their conduct, a detachment of Hitler guards paraded the Jew, his sweetheart and her mother through the streets of Kassel."[213] A large crowd in Kassel watched as the man "with a semi-shaven head was marched through the streets between two women, who were wearing hats, but whose heads seemed to observers also to have been shaven. The man, a Jewish manufacturer in the middle thirties, wore a placard with the words, 'I, a Jew, have defiled German girls.' The women were alleged to be his mistress and her mother."[214] In summer 1933 a Jew and a non-Jew identified as lovers were displayed around Nuremberg in an open car, wearing signs proclaiming, "I have dishonoured a German woman" and "I have surrendered myself to a Jew."[215] Later that summer, while in Nuremberg the son and daughter of U.S. Ambassador William E. Dodd saw storm troopers grab a petite and fragile teenage girl found in company with a Jewish man, shave her head, parade her through streets and into cabarets while shouting ridicule at her and forcing her to wear a sign, "I have offered myself to a Jew." A lusty crowd of 2,000 accompanied the SA men and their pillory victim. The young woman was hospitalized for mental collapse.[216] That was in 1933.

By August 1935 feelings surrounding the boycott of Jews were so intense that a simple pillory notice in *Der Stürmer* could have mortal consequences:

> *Meerane*. The Jewish business apprentice, Willi Wertheim, living at 57, Crotlenlaiderstrasse, Meerane, maintains a race-defiling association with the German embroideress, Charlotte Ahnert. The girl's parents live at 26, Crotenlaiderstrasse [*sic*]. They agree with the choice of their daughter. The behaviour of the Jew and his degenerate girl friend has long caused public indignation.[217]

Nazis thereupon took the man to a concentration camp and tortured him to death. They also arrested the Aryan woman. Her relatives eventually found her in a hospital. One wrote, "She was bandaged all over and could hardly make herself understood. She had been beaten mercilessly in the camp and then had been made to sign a statement that she had been 'well treated.'"[218]

REVOCATION OF LEGAL RIGHTS AS AN ELEMENT OF OSTRACISM

Boycott measures depended on public cooperation. Admittedly the boycott involved an element of governmental coercion. Government officers might instigate, look the other way, or give full official cooperation in boycott actions. Nonetheless, although tremendous and sometimes violent pressures may have been applied to force obedience to the boycott, actions we have examined thus far have their origins in private shunning.

As the 1930s progressed, however, in addition to private shunning the state began to strip Jews of legal rights. This stripping was based solely on a person's status as Jew, not on any act committed by the person. The revocation process had two elements. The first element involved governmental orders. The second element is less familiar to Americans, and was comprised of fascist industrial codes. The Nazi party promoted fascism. Fascism may well have been the most innovative development in capitalism since *laissez faire* challenged mercantilism. Fascism organizes an economy by industry, ostensibly rising above arguments between labor and management (by eliminating workers' rights) while promoting national prosperity through streamlining industrial practices (by trust and cartel arrangements giving large corporations control of an industry). For example, the most influential members of the baking industry (typically persons running large companies) draw up a code by which the industry operates. Everyone in the baking industry—whether worker, manager, or owner—must obey the industry code. The code can specify conditions that suppliers and workers must meet—for example, no Jews allowed. Upon state approval of the code, the industry or profession becomes self-governing, much like guilds used to be. Membership is compulsory in order to engage in the industry or profession. A bakery that offends German honor by using Jewish suppliers or employees, or an Aryan employee who persists in "confusing selfish interests with the common interest"[219] would be declared in violation of the industry code. The employee can be fired by the bakery, or the bakery can be closed down by the code administrator, and government will take any action needed to enforce the administrator's decision. That action can include fines or imprisonment. The code is written and policed by private individuals with no accountability to the public, but their decisions are enforced by the state.

With this brief sketch of the fascist system we can appreciate the power of decisions we shall encounter from various Reich industrial or professional associations. Those decisions might come from a private group, but have far greater consequences than pronouncements from American industrial or professional organizations.

Revocation of legal rights followed a typical sequence. First agitation arose about a situation. Next private action occurred, ranging from peaceful shunning to vigilante violence. Finally the state supported the aggressors and turned against their victims.[220] For example *Der Stürmer* and other agitators pounded the theme of sexual exploitation of Aryan female servants by male Jewish employers. In

July 1935 the Nazi party newsletter called for a law forbidding Jews from employing Aryan domestics.[221] Two months later such a law was passed. Another example: Agitators claimed that Jews ruined towns, and such claims were followed by posting of "keep out" signs at town outskirts, forbidding entry to Jews. Those private actions set the climate for the national state's first bans on travel by Jews in 1938 (localities had enacted restrictions earlier; for example, in March 1933 Breslau forbade Jewish residents to leave Germany; in April Koenigsberg officials invalidated Jews' passports;[222] and passport restrictions then spread through Bavaria and later through northern Germany).[223] Still another example: In cities more and more stores refused to sell to Jews, and hotels refused to register Jewish guests. Those private actions set the climate for state bans: On August 6, 1935, authorities in Bad Tölz evicted 350 Jewish guests from a resort in the Bavarian Alps foothills.[224] Although the agitation-vigilantism-law sequence is not documented throughout the general account that follows, we may safely assume that anti-Jewish measures often climaxed such a sequence. The sequence informally allowed authorities to go beyond the law's limits. For example, under the Hindenburg Exception (discussed below) certain Jewish lawyers were exempt from restrictions on their practices, but Aryans who used those attorneys were pilloried.[225] To avoid that consequence Aryans avoided using Jewish lawyers, and that boycott thereby accomplished what the law could not yet do—limit the livelihood of those Jewish lawyers. Revocations of legal rights also dovetailed with other Nazi policies. For example, starting in 1935, when Jews tried to acquire real estate, officials refused to register the deed.[226] Because that refusal included inheritances, Jewish legatees had to sell their property claim to Aryans, thereby promoting the Aryanization program described in the next chapter. The ban also prevented Jews from buying houses, promoting the concentration program described in chapter four.

Measures against Jewish drivers were underway by 1935, not in response to poor driving behavior, but simply to send a message that Jews were not tolerated in Germany. In 1935 Jews could no longer park their cars on streets or squares in Horrweiler, and the next year Rommersheim enacted the same restriction.[227] Apparently in 1936, someone who emerged from six months in a concentration camp was denied a driver's license, and in January 1937 the Prussian Supreme Administrative Court upheld the denial: "There is no longer such a thing as an unpolitical phase of life," the court said. "The community has a right to be protected from its enemies in every sphere of life."[228] Eighteen months later a Berlin resident wrote, "Friends informed me that non-Aryan drivers were dragged from their cars. They were taken to police stations and released after a day or two."[229] After two more months passed the same person reported, "A decree has been issued directing non-Aryan automobiles to change their license plates. The new numbers are 'Jewish numbers.' From 355,000 upward."[230] That way police could easily target drivers for harassment. At the same time *Der Stürmer* was agitating to revoke Jews' drivers licenses.[231] Finally in December 1938 Himmler issued the following decree: "For general security and police reasons and for the protection of the public I herewith prohibit all Jews of German nationality living in Germany from driving mechanized vehicles of all kinds and herewith repeal their drivers' licenses, effective immediately."[232] In addition to general harassment value, the timing of Himmler's decree suggests a more ominous purpose: thwarting advice from Jewish leaders who urged compatriots to acquire cars and trucks so they could flee pogroms.[233]

Loss of driver's licenses was more than an inconvenience. Loss of licenses could mean loss of jobs. Car pools with an Aryan driver were impossible, and public transportation was forbidden to Jews. In 1933 Coburg banned Jews from the town's streetcars.[234] Magdeburg followed suit, with streetcar signs saying "Jews are not desired here."[235] In December 1938 Göttingen's city council barred Jews from buses.[236] A Jew wrote,

> I want to get on the tram, I am only permitted to use the footplate, and only when I go to the factory, and only when the factory is more than six kilometres from my home, and only when the footplate is strictly separate from the interior of the carriage; I want to get on, it is late, and if I don't arrive punctually for work, the foreman can report me to the Gestapo. Someone drags me off: "Go on foot, it's a lot healthier!" . . . A car brakes as it goes along the empty street, a strange head leans out: "Are you still alive, you damn pig? They should run you over, across your belly!"[237]

Such incidents led Reinhard Heydrich, head of the Reich Main Security Office, to note "complaints on disturbances through the use of public transportation (street cars, subway, buses, in Berlin also the S-railway) by Jews increase constantly."[238] He thereupon tightened the criteria a Jew must meet to get a police pass authorizing use of public transit.

Gestapo revocation of other types of licenses illustrated police power to disregard civil decisions of courts, in addition to disregard of criminal decisions by courts. In June 1938 the Gestapo's legal counsel Werner Best said, "If the administrative courts repeatedly grant peddler's license to Jews . . . , the *Gestapo*, in executing its commission to protect the people and the state from the danger resident in such elements, will confiscate those licenses."[239]

Simple pleasures such as swimming at a beach were denied to Jews. Soon after the Nazis took power in 1933, Jews were banned at public bathing beaches in growing numbers of towns.[240] An American recalled "Jews were forbidden to bathe in Wannsee, a popular lake near Berlin. I was shocked and disgusted and could scarcely believe that it was a government edict—as it was. For two years my favorite lake was Gross Glienicke, a beautiful, serene and quiet spot among hills and trees near Berlin. In 1935 I saw the inhuman black notice posted on the edge of the bathing beach: *Jews Not Admitted*. I never went there again."[241] In July 1935, another observer noted, "Placards inscribed 'Jews to be impaled' were carried along the [Wannsee] beach, then the Jewish visitors were struck and driven away from the beach."[242] Nazis in Hesse argued that Niederrad had insufficient beach space, so excluding Jews would relieve crowding.[243] That action was a typical Nazi response to shortage of a commodity: Nazis eliminated Jewish consumer demand instead of expanding the commodity's supply. Beginning in 1933 many municipalities banned Jews from public swimming baths for "maintenance of cleanliness and public morality."[244] In July 1935 the SS authorized arrest of any Jew who "behaves himself in a noisy or obtrusive manner in German baths,"[245] perhaps diminishing relaxation obtained by Jews at baths where they were still permitted. The Westerland sea resort told Jews to stay away in 1934;[246] the next year the Bad Dürckheim health resort prohibited Jews from its gardens;[247] and in 1936 Berlin's Jewish children were forbidden to enter Bad Klingenberg on Lake Rummelsburg at the start of summer vacation from Berlin's public schools.[248] "A mob singing anti-Semitic songs paraded through the streets of the Baltic seashore resort Misdroy last night, carrying placards with the ultimatum: 'Jews, we give you twenty-four hours to get out.'"[249] Misdroy innkeepers cooperated by evicting all Jewish guests.[250] At the Feldafing holiday resort "schoolboys have been marching through the streets singing anti-Jewish songs of an offensive description." Officials there resolved to erect banners across all roads to Feldafing, saying "Jews are undesirable."[251] In 1937 general restrictions were placed on use of health resorts by Jews. Mineral water halls and baths could be used by Jews only at certain times, and Jews were banned outright from gardens, sports areas, and guest houses of resorts.[252] General rules could be adapted to local needs; at Baden-Baden Jews could go to concerts and to gambling halls, but not the hall of drinking waters, the inhalatorium, or public baths.[253] In 1938 Jews were even forbidden to sun bathe.[254]

The "Aryan Paragraph" of the 1933 Reich civil service law, discussed more fully later in this chapter, eliminated Jews from government jobs. In keeping with civic duty and the educational nature of law, various private organizations applied the Aryan Paragraph to their memberships. Athletic associations are a good example.[255] In April 1933 the German Swimming Association adopted the paragraph and required affiliated clubs to expel Jews. The Union of Professional Boxers ousted its Jewish members in April. Also that month the German Lawn Tennis Association banned Jews from the organization's committees and as players at international meets such as the Davis Cup. In May the German Gymnastic Union and the German Rowing Association adopted the paragraph. In June the German Skiing Union did so, in July the All-German Chess Association, in October the Red-White Lawn Tennis Club (extended to spouses of Jews in November). Finally in December 1933 the regime ordered Jews out of all sports clubs, from cycling associations to ping pong groups. Internationally known Jewish athletes could no longer compete, an outcome praised by a Nazi book *The Spirit of Sport in the Third Reich*, which said Jewish leadership in athletics was "worse than cholera, tuberculosis, syphilis."[256] In Nuremberg, Jews could not even be spectators at the city stadium.[257]

Jews were prohibited from other recreation as well. "No admittance to Jews" signs appeared on Nuremberg's amusement spots in 1934.[258] The next year Weimar's top movie theater announced that Jews would not be admitted, and any who deceived the ticket window would be ejected upon discovery.[259] Coburg had the same movie ban.[260] In 1935 Jews could not buy tickets for a boat excursion on the Rhine.[261] Having lost their fishing licenses in 1933, in 1937 they could no longer have hunting permits either.[262] "You can't even take a quiet walk in the park without running into a yellow sign on a bench announcing that 'Jews are forbidden' to sit there."[263] By June 1938 police were banning Jews from certain parks altogether.[264] The Prussian State Library began restricting access by Jewish readers in 1933;[265] Magdeburg's libraries and museums were closed to Jews; and Rothemann city officials banned Jews from the public library, not because Jews were unruly or in any way offensive but to eliminate "contact with German citizens."[266]

Nor were the children forgotten. Puppet shows portrayed heroes bashing Jewish enemies.[267] Juvenile literature at school and at home promoted the war on Jews, as did toys. News item: "An enterprising firm of toy manufacturers has produced a game called 'Out with the Jews,' which is played on a board on which little non-Aryan figures move at the throw of the dice, as each player attempts to get his Jews from Germany to Palestine."[268] Elvira Bauer's book *The Poison Mushroom,* mentioned in the previous chapter, told children about Jewish harm to blessings showered upon Aryans by God. The book's pictures of Jewish children portray them as mean and repulsive, and one illustration shows Jewish elementary students being attacked by schoolmates.[269]

Insidious as juvenile books and games might have been, modifications in the educational system probably had a greater effect on children. Since the world war, physical plants of the German educational system had been lagging behind demand, resulting in overcrowding. Instead of calling for a massive construction program, a Nazi manifesto issued in connection with the April 1, 1933, commercial boycott demanded that the percentage of Jews enrolled in secondary schools and universities be limited to their percentage in the general population.[270] On April 25 the Law Against Overcrowding of German Schools and Higher Institutions mandated such an enrollment limitation in high schools and universities.[271] The University of Leipzig immediately imposed a ten-semester moratorium on admitting Jewish students; Bavarian universities banned Jews from medical studies; and by year's end no teacher's college in the Reich would accept Jewish students.[272] Jews who continued as students in various schools did so with the same restrictions imposed on foreigners.[273] In addition many could not use school libraries or student meal rooms.[274] In May 1933 at the University of Frankfurt uniformed Nazi students confiscated student identification cards from Jewish fellow students and ordered them to leave the university grounds forever.[275] In December 1933 the Minister of Education limited university enrollments to students who were "physically and spiritually mature and of strict nationalistic reliability"—in other words, no Jews need apply.[276] Final exams were cancelled for Jewish pharmacology students in December 1934, leaving them unable to complete their courses.[277] (Travel to the exam site was impaired anyway; by 1934 student discounts on streetcar and railway tickets were denied to Jews.)[278] All Jewish students in Prussia were forbidden to take final exams that year.[279] Laws passed from 1933 to 1935 forbade Jews to take examinations required for entry into professions of business, pharmacy, dentistry, general medical practice, and veterinary medicine.[280] From 1935 forward Jewish students found themselves largely excluded from universities, although enrollment was still legal.[281] As of April 1937 universities ceased awarding doctorate degrees to Jews. Even if they had finished their dissertations they found their degrees withheld.[282] As of June 1938 Jews were formally banned from Germany's university classes.[283] In November Jews were prohibited from technical schools as well.[284] Also that month Jews were ordered to pay back all student loans within two weeks regardless of the contracted repayment schedule. Anyone who failed to meet that new repayment deadline was subject to "police action."[285]

Jewish school children in elementary grades faced assorted cruelties every day. A Jewish boy who returned to school after an illness discovered a change in the opening of the school day. He was astonished when the teacher shouted, "Heil Hitler!" and the class responded likewise. "I was still standing there with my mouth wide open. The teacher smiled and said quite kindly: 'The Jewish boys are excused from giving the Hitler salute.'"[286] One Jewish girl felt "awkward and embarrassed" each morning when she had to remain seated and quiet while Aryan pupils began the day by standing with the patriotic shout, "Heil Hitler!"[287] "School turned into hell," a Jewish boy recalled.[288] One adult observer of Nazi education found that students "enjoy having enemies whom they can flog and attack. Jews . . . are free targets."[289] Another adult in 1934 spoke of a Berlin street scene, of "a Jewish schoolboy about 8 years old being beaten in the street by his 'German' comrades. 'He is a Jew!' they shouted. A crowd gathered but did not interfere."[290] Still another report said Jewish schoolchildren were "despised by their school-fellows" and by teachers. One Jewish boy who wanted to play in sports "was forced to stand before the class and repeat aloud, 'I don't want to play.'"[291] In 1935 the Bavarian Education Authority decreed: "Non-Aryan pupils, whether boys or girls, must not be taken on school outings. During the break period of their own class they must attend lessons in some other class selected by the headmaster."[292] A thirteen-year-old Jewish schoolgirl took these notes in her racial theory class:

1. The Jewish race is much inferior to the Negro race.
2. All Jews have crooked legs, fat bellies, curly hair, and an untrustworthy look.
3. Jews are responsible for the World War.
4. They are to blame for the armistice of 1918 and they made the Peace of Versailles.
5. They were the cause of the inflation.
6. They brought on downfall of the Roman Empire.
7. Marx is a great criminal.
8. All Jews are communists.
9. They are the rulers of Russia.[293]

A thirteen-year-old boy wrote in 1933:

> I was the only Jew in my class. Until Easter I was a Protestant, then they found out that my father was a Jew and so I became one. After that everything was different. No one would be friends with me. No one would answer me. In school no one would sit next to me. They all used to want to before, as I was the best in the class and they all wanted to crib. Now I had to sit all alone on the back bench. At first I was frightfully unhappy—more so as the masters who always used to like me could not stand the sight of me any more. When they came into the classroom everyone had to jump up and with right hand outstretched, shout "Heil, Hitler!" I did too—or I didn't. I don't know. If I did, then the whole class would shout, "The Jew is profaning our greeting!" And if I didn't, the master shouted, "You wait, you Marxist bastard!" Then I was ordered to shout "Heil, Hitler!" alone three times. The whole class laughed. I was so afraid. . . .
>
> Once I did not know the answer—I used always to know before—so he asked me if the only thing I could do was "Fires and murders like my father." Once when I could not answer, the history master said I should be slaughtered like father. I tried to pull myself together, but tears used to sometimes come and then they used to say I was a dirty coward like the rest of the Marxists. . . .
>
> In drawing I had to do nothing but swastikas. Once I got detention because I drew a crooked one. Then the master wrote in his book, "For ridiculing the German symbol."[294]

An adult reported that same year:

> In the kindergarten games, when every child represents some animal, the Jewish ones are made pigs. After having been made a pig for several days in succession, a little Jewish girl of six refused to go to the school any more. Boys and girls who used to play with the Jews now turn their backs to them. The teachers show frozen faces to the Jewish children; they will lose their posts if they do not. Many Jewish children come home with swastikas cut in their clothes. Their books are smeared with the sign. Little Jewish girls at a school near Hindenburg had their school aprons cut into swastika shape.[295]

A school girl remembered the day after Crystal Night:

> About half an hour after school started the principal, a very mild-mannered, soft-spoken, kind man came to class. He pointed at me and said, "Get out, you dirty Jew." I heard his words, but I couldn't believe what I had heard. I asked him to repeat what he had said. He came over to me, grabbed me by my elbow and pushed me out the door. "Get out, you dirty Jew!" I stood in the hall trying to understand what I had done to make him so angry, afraid that my parents would be angry, too, if I went home from school so early. Kids came out wearing their coats. Some of them pushed me and called me a dirty Jew as they passed. I didn't know what to do.[296]

Someone who observed a German elementary school said:

> During morning break the children were filing past the door of the school
> canteen where they were given a cup of milk and a piece of bread. The little
> girls were standing in a row awaiting their turn. But whenever a Jewish girl's
> turn came the matron would shout: 'Get away you Jewess. Next, please!' This
> scene was re-enacted every day. The little Jewish children were not spared the
> mortification of being made to stand in the queue. They were not saved the
> humiliation of stretching out their hands for the cup. . . . Christian children had
> daily to bear witness to such things that they might be taught how to treat a
> hungry Jewish child.[297]

Terminology such as "Christian children" is misleading, as Nazis were ordinarily
concerned more with genealogy than with religious profession. We have already
seen an account from a Protestant boy who was classified as Jew, as were all
Mischlinge before September 1935. The situation of such students was as difficult
as that faced by any other Jew.[298] A later scholar found "their reaction took the
form of abnormal behaviour, severe illness, even thoughts of suicide."[299] A report
from 1933 states, "Jewish children come home from school depressed and deeply
hurt. . . . A seven-year-old lad began at a school in Berlin last Easter. Here he
received his first impression of the boycott of Jewish children. His face streaming
with tears, he came home and cried, 'Mother, I don't want to be a Jew.'"[300]

In addition to attacking people, young and old, the war on Jews attacked
"Jewish culture." In 1933 a Reich Chamber of Music was organized to control
musical composition and performance in accordance with Aryan principles.[301]
Members were forbidden to instruct Jews in music.[302] By 1936 non-Aryan
composers (living and dead), conductors, soloists, and other musicians were
banned from performance in Germany.[303] Such prohibitions were monitored; a
conductor lost his job for permitting performance of a piece composed by a
Jew.[304] In 1934 musicologist Walter Abendroth described contemporary music as
"a bacillus which had produced laziness, implanted into the cultural body by
hostile agents. . . . This musical bolshevism has had its golden age."[305] Writing
in *Musik und Rasse* musicologist Richard Eichenauer said, "Insofar as atonalists
. . . are Jewish, they obey a law of their race, in consequence of which they must
attempt to destroy generically alien harmony."[306] Ludwig Altmann described jazz
as a "barbarian invasion supported by Jews."[307] *Zeitschrift für Musik* declared,
"An end is to be made of a music that Juda-izes, be-niggers and is without
soul."[308] Similar actions were taken against non-Aryan dance steps; the SA
publication *S. A. Mann* described the Lambeth Walk as "Jewish mischief and
animalistic hopping."[309] *Das Schwarze Korps* announced that any Aryan was
authorized to arrest anyone "who performs arrogant contortions of his limbs in
a public dance hall."[310] The Reich Chamber of Music and Chamber of Theaters
announced "new and foreign dances . . . must henceforth be performed before
judges and certified to be unobjectionable before they can be popularized."[311]

Elimination of Jewish influence from musical sound may seem extreme but was matched, if not exceeded, by other actions to purify Aryan culture. Color could become Aryan. In 1936 a Jewish cattle dealer was sentenced to six weeks of incarceration for wearing brown trousers. The victim protested that all cattle dealers customarily wore brown pants at work, but the court said that a Jew who wore brown trousers could be mistaken for an SA man.[312] The oral identification alphabet provided another example of extreme Aryan purity. That alphabet was used by radio and telephone operators to assure correct understanding when reading sequences of letters aloud (A-Adam, B-Baker, C-Charlie, etc.). A newspaper announced Nazi plans to delete Jewish names from the German oral identification alphabet: D-David, I-Isidor, N-Nathan, R-Rebecca, S-Samuel, Z-Zacharius[313]—even telephone operators joined the war on Jews.

Curtailment of civic rights was another element of the war. A decree of March 1936 said Jews could no longer vote in *Reichstag* elections.[314] The Reich Citizenship Law[315] was eventually interpreted as forbidding all Jews from exercising any suffrage.[316] Effects of that ban were broader than Americans might think. As we have seen, failure to vote was evidence that someone was an enemy of the people. One Aryan government official urged his Jewish wife to vote in an election, lest inquiry reveal her genealogical background and endanger his job. She was caught. The court rejected her defense that she was a baptized Christian, and fined her RM 2,000 for casting an illegal vote. Charges against her husband were dropped.[317] This example illustrates how assorted Nazi policies dovetailed: They targeted victims by genealogy rather than religion, ostracized people for not voting, threatened the livelihood of someone who associated with a Jew, encouraged break-up of marriages between Jews and Aryans. Such dovetailing is one reason why the war on Jews was so effective.

In addition to outright limitations on legal rights, Jews were forced to take on obligations that further limited them. One of the most important obligations dealt with their names. Because nothing about a Jew's appearance or actions necessarily differed from an Aryan's, in everyday life a Jew could easily pass as an Aryan and evade anti-Jewish sanctions.[318] In 1935 Jewish artists and performers were forbidden to use pseudonyms lest the professional names deceive anyone into treating the Jews as Aryans.[319] Three years later officials published a list of 316 Jewish names, allowing the assumption that anyone with such a name was Jewish.[320] This assumption, however, could create problems for Aryans with such names, while allowing Jews with non-Jewish names to escape identification. Aryan parents therefore were forbidden to give Jewish-sounding names to their children.[321] Jewish parents were forbidden to give Aryan-sounding names to their children.[322] A decree of August 1938 required male Jews to take on the additional given name Israel, and females Sara, by the first of the year.[323] The day after the decree's application to *Mischlinge* was announced, one *Mischling* said, "I was bathed in sweat last night. It was plain, common fear."[324] The additional name had to be given in any business transaction involving the Jew's name, from writing a check to arranging a parcel delivery. In 1938 Oskar

Rosenthal delivered a report of suspicious activity to a policeman, while standing "with his hands at his side, and said, as Nazi protocol required, '*Ich bin der Jude*, Oskar Israel Rosen[thal].'"[325] Deliberate failure to give the "Jewish name" was punishable by six months in prison, accidental failure by one month. The name requirement tightened ostracism, not only by reducing a Jew's opportunities to evade sanctions but by damaging any alibi that sympathetic merchants could offer if their dealings with the Jew became known. Merchants had new motivation to refuse service. Eventually the "Jewish name" had to be used in nonbusiness contexts as well, such as telephone directories.[326]

Identifying a Jew by name proved insufficient. Racial identity cards had long been carried by people in Germany but were not readily visible.[327] Public transit schedules would snarl if streetcar conductors asked each rider's name and confirmed the answer with the rider's identity papers. Normal city life could not continue if police stopped and checked every pedestrian in districts forbidden to Jews. The point of anti-Jewish regulations was to make life easier for Aryans, not harder. In September 1941 the Interior Minister ordered Jews in Germany to wear a yellow star insignia whenever they appeared in public.[328] Goebbels explained, "Whoever wears a Jewish star is thus marked an enemy of the people."[329] Wrote one wearer of the star, "A conventional, good-natured-looking man came towards me, carefully leading a small boy by the hand. He stopped before me. 'Look at that, Horst! He is responsible for everything!'"[330] Another wearer recalled passing a crowd: "They began yelling, 'There goes a Jew girl! This is all their fault!' The headlines they had read that morning in the newspapers began to have an effect. The people picked up stones and gravel and threw them at me, a 15-year-old girl."[331] A girl in Eastern Galicia cried, "Mother, I am afraid to walk in the street. Look, there is nobody in the street. People don't like to show up with the badge."[332] The yellow badge was the final solution to the problem of instantly identifying Jews who walked among their fellow human beings.

A similar purpose was served by an October 1938 decree invalidating passports held by Jews. The documents could be restored only if authorities stamped them with a red "J" to signify the holder as Jewish.[333] This identification marked the holder for special harassment when trying to leave the country. As one Jew neared the border, Nazi officials told her she either had to leave the train or admit she was illegally trying to smuggle her jewels out of Germany. They told her to sign a confession and turn over the jewels if she wanted to proceed. "I signed. I had to get out of this country. This was a country to get out of if you had to do it naked. . . . The statement, together with my jewels, had gone into the pockets of my tormenters."[334] The "J" passport stigma, incidentally, was suggested to the Nazi regime by Swiss officials who wanted an easy way to identify Jews so visas could be denied to any wishing to flee to Switzerland.[335] New distinctive domestic identification cards were issued for Jews to use in Germany as well.[336]

One of the three very important Nuremberg decrees of September 1935 prohibited Jews from displaying the German flag, a practice already prohibited by administrative action,[337] and now punishable by fine and one-year imprisonment.[338] Offhand this may seem a petty nod to jingoism, but it also helped identify Jews. Any household without a German flag on appropriate occasions would stand out, and its members would become targets.[339] One civil servant was fired after no swastika flag was noticed flying from his apartment;[340] an engineer found himself under protective custody for the same conduct.[341] Even before the September decree Frankfurt police declared that display of swastika flags by Jews during a town celebration was "not desired." An observer speculated that the few buildings without flags were connected with Jews: "The flag incident . . . [was] designed to make Jews unpopular among patriotic Germans."[342] The situation was a dilemma: Any Jew who failed to fly a flag would be punished for not showing support of the regime, but any Jew would be punished for flying the flag. Later the flag prohibition was extended to spouses of Jews and *Mischlinge*,[343] expanding persecution to households with an Aryan member. Similar thinking guided the November 1937 law denying Jews permission to use the "German greeting" (an outstretched right arm accompanied by the words "Heil Hitler").[344] The German greeting was as common as "hello" or "goodby," and "Heil Hitler!" was the standard closing in business correspondence. Anyone who failed to use it stood apart from the community and was shunned. Disciplinary proceedings censured an attorney who neglected to give the German greeting in court,[345] and such failure was a firing offense for government employees.[346]

We shall later examine other specifics of the 1935 Nuremberg decrees, but we should note here the energizing effect they had on anti-Jewish action. Labor exchanges around the country received copies of the Nuremberg decrees and were ordered to follow their spirit. Exchanges used them to turn away unemployed Jews seeking to register for jobs.[347] Citing the decrees as inspirational, the Gas and Electrical Supply Corporation of Mayence decided to halt service to residences and businesses of Jewish customers. The action was duplicated by the Electricity and Gas Co-operative of Wiesbaden.[348]

Just as private boycott actions against Jews led to laws that required such actions, so did private sanctions against boycott violators lead to laws that punished violators. In 1933 civil servants could be fired if seen in friendly conversation with a Jew or patronizing a Jewish store.[349] Nurses at the Düsseldorf Pediatrics Clinic gave a medal of appreciation to a Jewish physician who was expelled from the staff in 1935. They were each punished with a RM 10 fine.[350] Nazis who worked at Wertheim's department store in Berlin were disciplined for giving a birthday bouquet to a Jewish clerk.[351] In September 1935 the Municipal Council of Oppenheim on the Rhine announced, "Townspeople who have any business or personal dealings with Jews shall receive no rebate of taxes."[352] Schotten's city council declared, "Those fellow-citizens who have business dealings or maintain friendly relations with Jews, will no longer receive municipal contracts or any kind of relief."[353] The same sorts of resolutions passed elsewhere; in 1935 the Merkenfritz town council proclaimed, "Whoever, as a German and a fellow-citizen of Merkenfritz, does any business with Jews, shelters one or flirts with one, is a traitor to the German people and its Fuehrer, and in this municipality can obtain no business and receive no municipal contracts."[354] Coburg's city employees were ordered to avoid contact not only with Jews but with Aryan spouses and *Mischlinge* children.[355]

The May 1935 Military Service Law excluded Jews from membership in the regular armed forces. That did not mean such persons were exempt from wartime military duty, merely that they were fit only for auxiliary status. The law's function was to affirm second-class citizenship for Jews, not to relieve them from any duties.[356] A side angle was revenue. Men of military age but who did not serve (i.e., Jews) had to pay a penalty tax until age forty-five.[357]

In July 1933 many naturalized Jews lost their German citizenship.[358] Those Jews could not be citizens. The September 1935 Nuremberg decree on citizenship[359] was implemented by a series of administrative rules. The first was issued in November.[360] It stripped all Jews of their citizenship, disfranchised them, and disqualified them from holding any public office except that of public school teacher in Jewish schools (the rule promised that such teachers would be dealt with later). Although Jews could no longer be citizens, they remained German nationals. Six years later, however, Jews could even lose German nationality (a loss that forfeited their property to the government).[361] Just as it was important to define who was a Jew, it was also important to define what a Jew was not. A Jew was not a citizen, not a fellow member of the community whose word could be trusted. In a 1939 senior judicial conference courts were advised that testimony of Jews should be evaluated with "extreme caution" and "no verdict should be passed . . . when a sentence would exclusively be based on the testimony of a Jew."[362] Noted one incredulous observer, "At times, judges, in their opinions, have gone to great lengths to bring in a non-aryan connection. In one case, a defendant was found to lack appreciation of the national socialist world outlook because he had a sister who was married to a non-aryan!"[363]

At this point in our narrative we reach the arbitrary dividing point of Crystal Night (called the Isaac Affair by Nazis), November 9–10 1938. Crystal Night is often described as the start of the Holocaust. This carefully orchestrated night of rampage against Jewish businesses, homes, synagogues, and people was so dramatic that it made headlines around the world. In reality, however, the night and its aftermath simply continued anti-Jewish action that had been underway ever since Nazis took over the German government. The simultaneous nationwide activity of Crystal Night was extraordinary, but the night's outrages were no different from those that had been occurring on a daily basis. Thus far we have described revocations of rights that occurred before Crystal Night. If these revocations are no different in character from those that followed Crystal Night (described below) we may conclude that the Holocaust had been proceeding in a robust fashion for years before outside observers awoke to what was happening.

At a meeting of top Nazis immediately after Crystal Night Goebbels announced,

> I deem it necessary to issue a decree forbidding the Jews to enter German theaters, moving [picture] houses, and circuses. . . . Our theaters are overcrowded, we have hardly any room. . . . Furthermore, there ought to be a decree barring Jews from German beaches and resorts. . . . It'll also have to be considered if it might not become necessary to forbid Jews to enter German forests. In the Grunewald, whole herds of them are running around. . . . Furthermore, Jews should not be allowed to sit around in German parks. I am thinking of the whispering campaign on the part of Jewish women in the public gardens at Fehrbelliner Platz. They go and sit with German mothers and their children and begin to gossip and incite. I see in this a particularly grave danger.[364]

Another participant at the meeting, Reinhard Heydrich, added,

> Cultural activities in holiday resorts may be considered an additional feature, not absolutely necessary for the individual. Many German Volksgenessen [*sic*] are unable to improve their health through a stay at a resort town. I don't see why the Jew should go to these places at all.[365]

As of November 12, Jews could no longer patronize plays, movies, concerts, art shows, or certain restaurants.[366] As of November 29, local government officials were authorized to establish curfews for Jews and to forbid their entry into any specified area at any time.[367] As of December 6, Berlin police banned Jews from

> 1. All theaters, cinemas, cabarets, public concert and lecture halls, museums, amusement places, the exhibition halls at the Messedamm including the exhibition area and radio-tower, the Deutschlandhalle and the Sports-place, the Reichs-sports-field, and all sports-places including the ice-skating rinks.
> 2. All public and private bathing establishments and indoor baths as well as open-air baths.
> 3. The Wilhelmstrasse from the Leipziger Strasse up to Unter den Linden including the Wilhelmplatz.
> 4. The Vossstrasse from the Hermann-Goering-Strasse up to the Wilhelmstrasse.
> 5. The Reich-Honor-Monument including the sidewalk on the north side of Unter den Linden from the university to the Military Historical Museum.[368]

A contemporary report warned that the ban "will soon be extended to include a large number of Berlin streets. In this respect the main streets and thoroughfares of Berlin especially come into consideration, because in these streets in particular Jewry even today more or less dominates the street scene. . . . Furthermore, the Jews can figure on being restricted to purely Jewish inns in the future."[369] Berlin police later ordered Jews to keep out of barber and beauty shops, prohibited purchase of newspapers by Jews, and even made pet ownership illegal for Jews.[370] "I heard later that Heydrich had also been planning a ban on house plants."[371] In November 1938 all hunting licenses were withdrawn from Jews.[372] In December the Bad Nauheim health spa banned Jews.[373] That same month government employment offices formally stopped serving Jews seeking jobs.[374] Also Reich Minister of Education Bernhard Rust forbade access to libraries and laboratories by dismissed Jewish professors and lecturers wishing to conduct private research.[375] On the Day of National Solidarity (December 3) all Jews nationwide had to remain indoors from noon until 8:00 P.M.,[376] and thereafter individual localities could enact similar restrictions whenever desired.[377] As of September 1939 Jews had to stay indoors every day between 9:00 P.M. and 5:00 A.M. during the summer, with the restriction extended one hour in each direction during winter. They were also forbidden to possess radios.[378] Eventually their telephones were confiscated, and they were forbidden to use public telephones.[379] (As early as 1933 Hamburg forbade Jewish merchants from having public telephone booths in their stores.)[380] Gradually Jews were ordered to give up other amenities of western civilization: typewriters, phonographs, cameras, electric irons, space heaters.[381]

In December 1938 Goering reported a series of decisions from Hitler.[382] Hitler ordered German railroads to ban Jews from dining cars and sleeping cars. Moreover they were barred from "hotels and restaurants which are mainly visited by Party members. . . . The ban can further be pronounced for swimming pools, certain public squares, resort towns, etc." In addition to those bans decided by Hitler, in December, police forbade Jews from appearing in certain districts of Berlin. If a Jew was summoned to such an area, police permission was required to obey the summons—thereby establishing an effective way to whipsaw victims.[383]

That same month a Jew received the following correspondence from a health insurance agency: "We feel compelled to point out to you as a Jewish member, that your continued membership is highly undesirable due to your race, because on the one hand we cannot expect our Aryan members to stay on in the same organization with you and thus possibly be forced to support you with their means in case of illness, and on the other hand our employees refuse to deal with the affairs of Jewish members after the events of November 9/10. We thus urge you to declare your withdrawal and in such case are prepared to set aside the time for notice and to effect the immediate cancellation of your membership."[384]

Children received attention. At the post-Crystal Night meeting of top Nazis mentioned above, Goebbels declared, "Jewish children are still allowed in German schools. That's impossible. It is out of the question that any boy should sit beside a Jewish boy in a German gymnasium and receive lessons in German history."[385] Goebbels was correct that efforts to segregate public school students by genealogy[386] had been widely evaded. In theory Jewish students aged six to fourteen years were banned from Aryan public schools in spring 1936,[387] but through loopholes over 35 percent of all Jewish school children still attended non-Jewish schools in 1937.[388] Two days after Goebbels complained, Education Minister Rust decreed, "Jews are not allowed to attend German schools. They may only attend Jewish schools. In so far as it has not occurred already, all Jews currently attending a German school are to be dismissed immediately."[389] In December Rust also formally forbade Jews to attend German universities.[390]

In October 1941 friendship became a crime. Aryans and Jews who maintained friendships became subject to protective custody and concentration camp internment.[391]

JOB DISMISSALS

In addition to discriminations designed to eliminate Jews from social life and to deny them necessities of physical life, an additional series of measures sought to deny Jews the *means to obtain* necessities of life even if Jews could locate them. One of the most effective measures was to deny jobs to Jews, thereby reducing their ability to afford necessities.

When Aryan students used firecrackers, stink bombs, and tear gas to protest lectures by Jewish professors, university administrations expelled the professors rather than the students.[392] "Lecturing is difficult," said one professor in 1934, "for a man cannot give his best to the class when he is continually haunted by the fear that some Nazi student may rise and order him to stop, accusing him of un-German ideas, as a result of which the Rector would say regretfully that, in the interests of peace and order, a resignation would be welcome."[393] Nazi students were known to bodily eject such teachers from the classroom.[394] The U.S. ambassador to Germany confided to his diary, "My friend Professor Wolfgang Windelband called and sadly informed me that he had been ordered to give up his position and go to Halle. He says he will resign rather than obey the arbitrary order. 'If I went to Halle there would be Hitler Jugend demonstrations against me, no students would register for my work, and in a few months I would be dismissed.'"[395] Students were not the only members of the academic community promoting departure of certain teachers and professors. A U.S. diplomat in Berlin once mused about an Aryan who "used to be one of my instructors at Harvard University, and I have seen quite a bit of him during my last four years in Germany. . . . It disgusted me to see with what opportunism Schoenemann has thrown himself into the lap of the National-Socialists. His conduct during the early months of the regime when the Jewish persecutions and other excesses had shocked all decent people, was . . . disgusting."[396] The April 7, 1933, Law for the Restoration of the Professional Civil Service, discussed below, removed most Jews from teaching positions.[397] Jews were even expelled from faculties of private schools in 1933.[398] The next July Jews were disqualified as university teaching assistants, and in December 1934 Jews were forbidden to present work that would qualify them to lecture at universities.[399] In 1935 Education Minister Rust even forbade Aryan university students from using Jewish tutors;[400] a bulletin board warning at the University of Berlin implied that violators would not pass their exams.[401] The next year Jewish tutors were ordered to stop providing their services.[402] Early in 1935 a contemporary account noted that Berlin was free of non-Aryan professors.[403] In addition to opening positions for Aryan academics, such measures saved money. Due to arcane rules of German faculty rank, many dismissed Jewish faculty members lost pension benefits along with their jobs. They also lost pensions if they emigrated. And of course many of the remainder who qualified for pensions never received them, in the spirit of civic duty.[404]

When the Nazis took power, medical practitioners were suffering economic hardship because there were too many doctors for too few paying patients.[405] "In medical school my fellow students were often complaining that opportunities for doctors were getting worse every year, because Germany had so many doctors. But if Hitler came to power he would 'eliminate' our Jewish competition, and then we 'Aryans' could have a profitable practice."[406] Germany had a National Health Service in which patients could choose their own doctors from the program's "panel" of approved practitioners, and fees charged by those private practice physicians were paid by the national health insurance program. Most physicians participated in the national health care plan. Fraternal groups, mutual benefit societies, factory sick funds, fascist guild sick funds, employers, and private insurance companies also had panels that members had to use in order to receive benefits. About 85 percent of a participating physician's or dentist's income depended on panel patients.[407] In March Jewish physicians of Duisburg found they could no longer collect fees for services they had rendered to health service patients.[408] An April 1933 directive extended the Law for the Restoration of the Professional Civil Service to National Health Service panels without regard to the Hindenburg Exception (discussed below, which would otherwise exempt some Jewish physicians from discrimination).[409] In the same month patients using the National Health Service learned that the government would no longer pay for treatment by Jewish physicians,[410] such as cases where an Aryan panel doctor referred the patient to a Jewish specialist. Because National Health Service coverage was being extended to all Aryan workers, greater numbers of citizens had strong economic motivation to boycott Jewish practitioners (whose bills would not be paid by the national health plan). "It is obviously the national duty of insured persons to refrain from being treated by Jewish medical practitioners," said the chairman of Berlin's Municipal Health Insurance Institute.[411] Employers reminded sick workers of that duty if they sought to use the company program. The German General Electric Company wrote to an employee who wanted to keep using a Jewish practitioner, "We expect you to employ an Aryan physician. Otherwise, we cannot guarantee the payment of the benefits."[412] Frankfurt-am-Main prohibited city workers from using Jewish doctors even if they were on a worker's panel.[413] Fascist guilds also implemented such restrictions; the Association of Office Workers' Health Insurance Societies forbade its three million members to use Jewish doctors in panel treatment.[414] The boycott provided yet another economic incentive to patients in March 1934; anyone eligible for a pension due to illness could receive it only if all treatment for the affliction, from the very beginning, came from Aryan physicians.[415] Such tactics helped ruin practices of Jewish physicians protected by the Hindenburg Exception. Patients did not have to interrogate their doctors on genealogy; published lists of panel doctors were coded to reveal that information. In one list a period was found after names of Aryan practitioners, a comma after Jews, and a semicolon appeared after Aryans married to a Jew;[416] in another list an asterisk marked names of Jewish doctors.[417] By March 1933 few Jewish physicians could treat patients in either the National Health Service or any private insurance program, and most of the remainder were excluded that summer.[418] The insurance boycott was a tremendous blow to practices of Jewish doctors, and a boon to Aryan doctors who snatched that business. ("The leading German medical association," said a U.S. diplomat, "has now concluded an agreement with private sick benefit insurance companies whereby the latter agree not to pay bills submitted by Aryans for treatment by Jewish doctors.")[419] As early as April 1933 Munich's mayor forbade Jewish physicians from treating Aryan patients in the National Health Service and directed that only cadavers of Jews could be dissected by Jewish physicians.[420] The same month the Baden Medical Association declared that Jewish physicians could treat only Jewish patients, and that all Jewish physicians would be expelled from any official positions they held.[421] Other medical chambers began expelling Jewish physicians.[422] Said one visitor in 1933, "While I was in Berlin an announcement was published of a forthcoming meeting of the Berlin Medical Association. The announcement carried, in black-faced type, this line: 'Jews will not be admitted.'"[423] Officials around the country kept National Health Service patients from using hospitals that had Jewish administrators.[424] During the summer of 1933 Jewish dentists and dental technicians were excluded as national health insurance care providers.[425] In August Jewish doctors could no longer consult with Aryan doctors, a prohibition driving away patients suffering from any complicated ailment.[426] Prior to then a Jewish physician who consulted on an Aryan colleague's panel case might have a private arrangement with the Aryan to get a percentage of the panel fee. The German medical guild closed that loophole in August, announcing that any Aryan doctor who engaged in such conduct would be fined 150 percent of the panel fee.[427] Earlier most Jewish physicians had been removed from municipal hospitals:[428] A headline in *Der Angriff* proclaimed, "Clean-up in Municipal Hospitals."[429] In Bavaria a Nazi official noted that the Enabling Act would authorize hospitals to "get rid of the gentlemen for good" despite their employment contracts.[430] By autumn 1933 Jewish physicians were banned from private clinics and hospitals, as well as public ones.[431] That action devastated Jewish surgeons' private practices (in addition to previous loss of their panel practices).[432] In November 1933 Aryan doctors, dentists, and dental technicians practicing in cities with populations exceeding 100,000 were removed from National Health Service panels and institutions if their spouses were Jewish.[433] In spring 1934 the ban on Jewish medical care providers in the national system was broadened to include Aryan providers whose spouses were Jewish.[434] Before the end of 1933 most private health care organizations fulfilled their civic duty by firing non-Aryan physicians.[435] In the spirit of civic duty, medical schools began requiring doctor candidates to meet eligibility qualifications of civil servants, thereby eliminating Jews.[436] Before Jews lost their citizenship by government order, medical doctors' degrees were granted only to Jews who renounced their citizenship. That restriction eliminated the new doctors from competing with Aryans because foreigners were not allowed to practice medicine in Germany.[437] A visitor to Germany aptly summarized the situation of Jewish medical professionals in 1933: "They are not forbidden to practise. But the Government has seen to it that their practises, in so far as possible, are taken away."[438]

As always, we should remember that Nazis defined "Jew" more broadly than many persons today realize. When a Kassel physician was harmed by the agreement between the city and the local medical association to exclude Jewish doctors from National Health Service practice, he went to court seeking relief from the sanction. The court ruled against him: "Plaintiff is a baptized Protestant, son-in-law of a Protestant clergyman, and was awarded the Iron Cross of the first and second class in the war; but he is of Semitic origin."[439]

Restrictions extended beyond physicians to allied professions. In August 1934 pharmacists had to prove their Aryan identity.[440] "In view of their lack of character, Jews are unsuited to the calling of a chemist," said *Der Stürmer* in February 1935.[441] Two months later Jews and spouses of Jews were no longer able to meet Prussian licensing requirements for pharmacists.[442] As a practical matter, by December Jews could no longer own or lease drug stores,[443] and after March 1936 Jews across the Reich were officially forbidden to lease pharmacies.[444] The previous year Jews could no longer take exams to become masseurs, masseuses, midwives, or nurses,[445] and in September 1938, Jewish nurses were expelled from the profession.[446] Even nonmedical segments of society joined the cause. Landlords of medical offices were expected to evict Jewish tenants by September 30, 1938.[447]

The head of Brandenburg's Medical Society declared in May 1933, "We German physicians demand that Jews be excluded from practicing on our fellow-countrymen, for a Jew is the incarnation of lies and deceit."[448] That declaration came a few months after the chief of Munich's public schools announced an end to Jewish school physicians being "let loose on German children."[449] In July 1935 the Nazi party news bulletin said any Jewish physicians who treated Aryan patients should be put to death.[450] Berlin's practitioners, in the words of a scholarly study of their conduct, "used a particularly repellent combination of anti-Semitism and pornography . . . to bring about the removal of their Jewish 'colleagues' and competitors. . . . The attitude of Jews towards 'German women' revealed in 'filthy erotic literature', apparently justified the dismissal of Jewish gynaecologists."[451] A Munich Public Health Service office displayed a sign, "German women, do not trust your body to a Jewish doctor."[452] In August 1935 a Jewish physician in Konstanz was sent to a concentration camp upon accusation of improper conduct with dozens of females.[453] That same year the same fate befell a Jewish doctor in Niederlungwitz when Aryan practitioners competing with his practice denounced him for race defilement.[454] In 1937 a Berlin resident wrote about a physician who "had a flourishing practice. He was denounced by a Nazi doctor, who wanted his practice, and disappeared one night." Relatives and friends got him released from Buchenwald after almost a year, with a promise to the Gestapo that he would leave Germany.[455] Such tactics were seen from the beginning of the Nazi regime. A diplomat in Berlin said he could not confirm that one Jewish doctor was intimidated into letting the Nazi party use his car and driver without compensation, but the diplomat was convinced that when another Jewish doctor showed reluctance to resign from a hospital he "was thereupon taken into a room, made to sit in a receptacle containing cold water and given a large dose of castor oil. Incidents of rough and maltreatment of physicians come to me so frequently and from such good sources that there is no possibility of doubt."[456] In March 1933 the *New York Times* wrote of battered Jewish doctors arriving in Czechoslovakia after being expelled from Berlin hospital staffs.[457] A later student of the situation wrote, "The essential violence in hard-core Nazi doctors' attitudes toward Jewish colleagues . . . was expressed . . . during an anti-Jewish boycott campaign. In Berlin, on 1 April 1933, they used such tactics as contacting Jewish colleagues for ostensible consultations and having them picked up by car (sometimes supplied by the same German doctors), in which they were taken to remote places and beaten and left bleeding—or else threatened and humiliated them by making them run the gauntlet, hitting them with sticks, and exposing them to the sound of rifle fire."[458] In July 1933 Nazi physicians in Berlin obtained a list of colleagues, mostly Jews, who had formed a committee to help Jewish panel doctors who had lost their practices. The Nazi doctors not only gave the list to police but accompanied police on raids to committee members' homes where they were arrested on charges of communist activity.[459] When a Jewish physician dismissed from Berlin's Charité hospital offered a farewell handshake to his successor, the Aryan refused it.[460]

Citing the September 1935 Nuremberg decree on citizenship, a summer 1938 decree revoked appointments and medical licenses of all Jewish physicians. Upon payment of a special tax, some (but not all) the former physicians might be allowed to treat Jews, under the new professional title "sick attendant."[461] These practitioners also lost all retirement and pension benefits they had accrued through their work as physicians.[462] Some Jewish physicians had still been making a good living from Aryan patients who were willing to forego reimbursement from insurance.[463] Boycott exhortations were not enough to divert that business to Aryan doctors, so the regime finally outlawed medical consultation between Jewish practitioner and Aryan patient. News item from 1938: "Some 50 Aryan doctors already have been sent from the Old Reich to Vienna to take the place of the Jewish practitioners."[464]

Aryan physicians profited from anti-Jewish measures. Disappearance of Jewish competitors allowed Aryan practitioners to treat more patients for higher fees.

The average taxable income of a doctor in 1933 was RM 9,280. Five years later it was RM 14,940.[465] Aryan doctors also moved into thousands of university, institute, and clinic appointments vacated by Jews. Observers who regard Jews as ordinary people may view Nazi actions against Jewish medical professionals as self-serving discrimination. Such was not the view of Germans who accepted the fantasy of a "Jewish threat." Around 1935 German medical journals said that anti-Jewish measures served to "maintain moral standards."[466] A 1942 German medical textbook declared, "Today, however, one can already see what a blessing it has been that the Jews were forcibly excluded from the vital professions and the offices of the state."[467] Nazis convinced themselves they were performing a public service by removing "dangerous" persons from assorted professions.

Aryan lawyers were eager to eliminate business competition from Jewish colleagues.[468] "In Breslau at noon to-day a strong troop of S.A. men forced their way into the Law Courts. Amid shouts of 'Out with the Jews!' all offices and conference rooms were opened and all the Jewish lawyers, judges, and public prosecutors were forced to leave the building forthwith. There were exciting scenes in the corridors and court rooms. . . . Many cases that were proceeding in the Courts had to be interrupted."[469] That was in March 1933. Similar courthouse incidents occurred elsewhere that month and continued into the summer.[470] A week after the Breslau disruption the Federation of National Socialist Jurists demanded that Jews be forbidden as notaries, lawyers, and judges.[471] By month's end criminal defendants could refuse to have their cases heard by Jewish judges, many of whom were no longer sitting in court anyway, and instead were sitting in protective custody.[472] April brought a decree allowing attorneys to be disbarred if they were Jews.[473] A few days later another decree suspended admission of Jews to the bar until September 30 and authorized the fascist law guild to prohibit Jews from joining.[474] Party discipline required members to avoid legal consultation with Jews,[475] thereby eliminating many clients from practices of Jewish lawyers. The expectation placed upon party members soon expanded to all Aryans; even the Union of German Professional Boxers ordered its members to avoid using Jewish lawyers.[476] Aryans began finding their names published as defilers of their race if they used Jewish lawyers.[477] Ostracism worked in the other direction as well; Aryan lawyers stopped representing Jewish clients,[478] and eventually the law forbade anyone to perform legal services for a Jew without explicitly announcing the client's "race."[479] Those actions inconvenienced urban Jews, but in provincial areas legal representation became impossible for Jews to obtain, forcing them to represent themselves against highly trained Aryan legal counsel.[480] By midspring in 1933, conditions for Jewish attorneys had become intolerable. Their attempts to retain nonlawyer positions in the profession were thwarted, demonstrated by excerpts from a circular to members of the Düsseldorf bar, May 15, 1933:

> 4. It is unprofessional to employ non-Aryan former advocates as managing clerks or in any other capacity. . . .

8. It seems no longer advisable for non-Aryan advocates, even though they are still admitted, to remain members of local bar associations or to be permitted to take part or be represented in professional conferences, where these take place.[481]

About the same time, Prussian minister of justice Hans Kerrl asked judges "urgently to recommend to all Jewish notaries in their own interest to refrain from practicing their profession for the time being," otherwise, "maintenance of public order and safety will be seriously endangered."[482] Kerrl warned, "Should they refuse to comply with this recommendation they will expose themselves to serious danger in view of the excited state of public opinion."[483] ("Prominent Jewish Lawyer Slain," read one headline.)[484] Eventually Jewish notaries were banned.[485] Earlier Kerrl had ousted Jewish judges[486] and revoked commissions of all Jewish assessors.[487] Position wanted: "Lady Assessor (Jewish), more than seven years engaged as magistrate, excellent testimonials and references, familiar with official and public business, very industrious, perfect stenography and typewriting, seeks engagement, possibly as secretary or stenographer. Terms moderate. Write, R.T. 62729 care of *Frankfurter Zeitung*."[488]

Even lawyers who merely had Jewish ancestry, but were not classified as Jews, faced harassment. When one complained to the bar association about racial ancestry slurs used by an opposing lawyer in court, the court sentenced the complainer to a month's imprisonment.[489] German Academy of Law president Hans Frank told an academic conference, "The elimination of the Jews from German jurisprudence is in no way due to hatred or envy but to the understanding that the influence of the Jew on German life is essentially a pernicious and harmful one and that in the interests of the German people and to protect its future an unequivocal boundary must be drawn between us and the Jews."[490] In 1936 the Ministry of Justice ruled that anyone seeking admission to the bar must be eligible to become a judge someday; no Jews could become judges, so Jews could no longer be admitted to the bar.[491] A decree of September 1938 made disbarment of Jewish lawyers mandatory,[492] although a supplemental decree in October allowed a quota of 175 former Jewish attorneys to represent Jewish clients in legal matters.[493] These legal representatives were called "consultants" rather than lawyers,[494] and in a distinct touch, the regime ordered the consultants to contribute a percentage of their fees, on a sliding scale of 10 to 70 percent, to a fund for relief of former Jewish lawyers.[495] To draw upon this fund, approval was required from the regime. How many Jews received approval is unclear.

One of the most far-reaching job dismissal measures was the Law for the Restoration of the Professional Civil Service, April 7, 1933.[496] Hitler had long—and incorrectly—contended that the Weimar Republic generally hired civil service employees on the basis of politics rather than professional competence.[497] One of the Restoration Act's major provisions dismissed so-called "party-made" officials.[498] In the Nazi view those unworthy employees tended to be non-Aryans, and the act's so-called "Aryan Paragraph" expanded the purge of non-Aryans from the civil service. That purge was already underway: Judges were removed from the bench; Jewish burgomasters and town officials in the Palatinate were under arrest; Jewish city workers in Breslau were on unpaid leave; those in Frankfurt had been fired.[499] The nationwide purge was so vigorous that a week before the decree a U.S. diplomat reported almost all Jews had been eliminated from all levels of government.[500] That impression was incorrect. Not only did the act stretch the definition of "government official" to the limit of its logic, it also expanded the definition of non-Aryan to sweep up many more victims than the purge had previously been able to touch. All civil servants, from architects to judges, were subject to the Aryan Paragraph. The paragraph not only covered national employees but those of local government, of public corporations (such as the assorted fascist industrial associations) and public institutions (such as the Reichsbank and German State Railway Company), and social insurance operations (such as the National Health Service). Any private enterprise was covered if the government had a 50 percent ownership.[501] Public utilities in Germany were typically government-owned, so even telephone workers and streetcar conductors were covered.[502] So, too, were "teachers in the public school system, teachers at scientific universities, and also the full and assistant professors who have been relieved of their official duties. In addition, honorary professors, non-official assistant professors and privatdozenten at universities are to be considered officers within the scope of this law. Likewise former court (royal) officials and the notaries, even when they only draw fees, have the status of public officers. Officials of the old and new military forces and the members of the protective police of the states are public officers." Also "the public-legal religious societies and the confederations are empowered to decree similar regulations."[503] For example, in September the General Synod of the Evangelical Church of the Old Prussian Union directed that persons who were non-Aryan or spouses of non-Aryans could no longer be clergy.[504] Eventually the Interior Ministry defined "public official" as anyone with "authoritative or dignified duties to fulfill."[505]

An observer in 1934 described the effect of civil service "reforms" on productivity: "Old feuds among colleagues as well as between superiors and subordinates were renewed. A wave of denunciations swept the desks of personnel officers. . . . Many a chronic failure in the service scented a new era of promise. The fear of removal, in the midst of a time of widespread unemployment, engendered cowaradice."[506]

At the insistence of German president von Hindenburg, employees were exempted from dismissal if they were world war veterans or their fathers or sons died in action. A decree of March 1934[507] extended the Hindenburg Exception to Jews who fought with German forces in postwar Baltic adventures, who fought against communists in 1920, or against Rhine separatists. The Exception also appeared in many measures relating to Jewish employment in various professions. Hindenburg died in August 1934, and the Hindenburg Exception declined as the president's health did. From *Völkischer Beobachter*, April 25, 1933: "A general concession to 'Jewish ex-service men' would be entirely unjustified. Let us rather think of the millions of unemployed German ex-service men, of the thousands of German Assessors and Jurists who cannot marry, cannot bring children into the world, but have to wait until all the 'old Jewish ex-service men' have lived their life of luxury to the full, added still more to the riches they have extracted from the German people and taken their wealth abroad."[508] A clause in the Civil Service Act itself, permitting dismissals "for the simplification of administration" served to evade the Hindenburg Exception on a large-scale basis.[509] Later the Nuremberg Decrees of September 1935 served to eliminate the Hindenburg Exception in public and private uses of the Aryan Paragraph.[510] For example, upon issuance of the Nuremberg Decrees German Railways immediately invalidated the Hindenburg Exception for all remaining Jewish workers and fired them.[511]

In 1933 editors of periodicals had to be Aryan, as did their spouses,[512] Aryan requirements were extended to other media employees as well.[513] "I received my first Nazi blow," wrote a Jewish journalist in June. "The *Reichsverband* of the German Sport Press advised me that I had been eliminated from their membership list, 'because of the new order stipulated by the National Revolution.'"[514] Six months later the reporter's work was crippled by a verbal order banning her byline. "What a devilish blow! The latest regulation requires the signature of the author to every article. No editor in Berlin would dare to print anything without my signature. Just where does that leave me?"[515] The journalist switched occupations and became a wine merchant to the Berlin diplomatic corps. In 1938, however, wine merchant permits were refused to Jews.[516]

One occupation after another was closed to Jews. A May 1933 decree outlawed new retail shops and expansion of old ones by Jews, with the intention of limiting the ability of skilled Jewish professionals to earn a living through entrepreneurship.[517] In spring 1933 blue-collar workers had to join the German Labor Front, but membership was denied to Jews, who thereupon lost their jobs.[518] That procedure was extended to white-collar employees in the summer.[519] A complementary measure limited any company's total number of Jewish employees, blue-collar or otherwise, to 3 percent of the company's work force.[520] An April 1933 decree forbade Jews from being patent agents.[521] In autumn 1938 they could no longer be patent lawyers.[522] A May 1933 decree forbid Jews from being tax consultants.[523] In July 1933 mercantile and retail fascist fronts required members to prove Aryan genealogy, endangering Jewish employment.[524] From July onward Jews could no longer be swimming instructors or lifeguards in Breslau, a ban extended nationwide to the Union of Life-Savers in December.[525] That same month Jews could no longer be jockeys in horse races.[526] Also in July Jews were expelled from all aspects of movie production.[527] By 1934 Jews could not be stage actors or cabaret performers.[528] In 1933 and 1934 most Jews who sold government lottery tickets lost their licenses to do so. The remainder covered by the Hindenburg Exception lost that protection and their licenses by 1936.[529] In September 1933 the Berlin Stock Exchange announced that reduced business dictated reduced membership: All Jewish brokers would be expelled as an efficiency move.[530] Antique dealing was forbidden to Jews in 1935,[531] as were manual crafts (though not unskilled labor).[532] Jews could no longer be archivists for photo agencies in 1935,[533] nor be motion picture distributors,[534] nor art dealers,[535] and that year Jews even lost permission to have concessions renting chairs in parks.[536] Jews could theoretically still be real estate managers, but tax authorities refused to deal with Jewish real estate managers, leaving few property owners interested in employing a Jew for that position.[537] In February 1936 Jewish literary agents were banned,[538] and after June, Jews could no longer be currency dealers.[539] Also that summer Jewish engineers were banned from construction projects.[540] A December 1937 decree prevented Jews from opening any more clothes businesses in Berlin, and at the same time Aryan clothiers promoted a boycott of Jewish competitors.[541] Also in December Jew-tainted businesses were thereafter limited to 90 percent of their former purchases of manufactured goods,[542] starting a merchandise squeeze on any Jew-tainted enterprise that had remained popular with customers. By next summer sugar was cut off entirely to Jewish bakers and candy makers,[543] effectively closing those businesses even though they were permitted by law. The same tactic had long been used by wholesale suppliers of retail merchandise: Three years earlier Aryan publishers directed their distributors to withhold magazines and newspapers from Berlin's Jewish newsstands, crippling those entrepreneurs.[544] The tactic went even further up the line of production; by February 1938 Jewish textile manufacturers found themselves unable to obtain full orders of raw materials.[545] The litany of restrictions went on and on. In February 1938 the fascist movers and warehousers guild decided to expel Jewish brokers and agents.[546] After March 1938 Jews could no longer be gun dealers.[547] That summer the occupations of detective, private guard, credit agency worker, accountant, marriage broker (except for Jewish clients), tourist guide, and traveling salesman were closed to Jews.[548] Peddling and one-person sales agencies had become popular occupations for Jews who had been fired from other jobs,[549] so the peddling ban attacked the livelihoods of persons previously rendered jobless by the boycott. One estimate said 30,000 Jewish traveling salesmen were fired that summer,[550] but the number who lost their jobs through license revocation rather than outright dismissal may have been far higher; in 1938 the Institute for the Study of the Jewish Question (a Nazi academic research group) said 110,000 traveling salesmen were full Jews; all their occupational licenses expired at the end of September.[551] That expiration terminated efforts Jewish entrepreneurs had made to support themselves without employees or shops, by taking orders for shoes, clothing, textiles, wine, and insurance.[552] Decrees of 1938 also prohibited Jews from occupations of auctioneer, real estate agent, and manager of industrial plants, houses, estates, or land.[553] In the dwindling number of Jewish businesses permitted, Nazi regulations limited control that a Jewish employer had over workers. For example, during a nationwide contest on window dressing in 1935, Jewish shopkeepers had to let their workers do displays in windows of Aryan competitors.[554] Another example, if a Jewish store's revenue dropped, Jewish employees normally had to be dismissed before any Aryans were let go.[555] Thus Jewish employees suffered from a boycott before Aryans did, and store owners probably sold out before Aryans were dismissed. After sale to an Aryan, the boycott would lift; renewed prosperity allowed hiring of Aryans to replace Jewish employees dismissed during boycott.

Jew-free agriculture was another Nazi goal. In the mid-1920s nearly a third of Germany's working non-Jewish population made its living from agriculture, but less than 2 percent of the working Jewish population did so. By summer 1934 the figure was about one percent, and that included forest workers.[556] The minuscule Jewish involvement in agriculture was declining well before Schotten's city council declared the following:

(1) Jews will henceforth be prohibited from moving to Schotten.
(2) The sale of real estate and houses to Jews is forbidden.
(3) Jews are excluded from the use of all municipal establishments such as the hospital, the cattle scales, etc.
(4) Jews are not admitted to any municipal auction—hay, lumber, fruit, etc.[557]

Brunswick's peasant leader forbade farmers to deal with Jews.[558] Königsdorf officials ordered that "cows purchased either directly or indirectly from Jews are not allowed to be served by the community bull."[559] Anyone who purchased cattle from Jews could no longer insure the animals with a company issuing such coverage in Dettingen.[560] A Nuremberg city councilor called for Aryan and Jewish zones in stockyards to determine which butchers bought from Jews.[561] Rural areas began establishing Jew-free livestock markets in 1933.[562] In late summer 1934 a Jewish community newspaper reported Jewish cattle traders were going out of business in Baden.[563] Dortmund even forbade Jews from meat markets.[564] Peasants liked to deal with Jewish cattle traders because Aryans offered less satisfactory terms,[565] but wrath descended upon Jews or Aryans who broke the boycott. One mayor was removed from office for selling his cattle to a Jewish trader.[566] In 1935 the SS menaced Jewish traders in one swine market.[567] Jews were also excluded from trade in commodities,[568] an exclusion already underway by November 1933 with a decree banning Jews from grain markets.[569] Within a year after that decree, Jews in Pomerania's cereal trade found their businesses threatened with extinction.[570] Jews in the hops trade were an early target of the regime; in the Hersbruck district those traders were eliminated by literally running them out of town.[571] When some Middle Franconia hop growers sold crops to Jewish traders in 1935, the Aryans were rounded up and forced to walk through villages while wearing signs confessing their race treason.[572] Jews were prohibited from agricultural cooperatives, and organizers of fairs forbade Jews from even attending, let alone exhibiting. Such prohibitions excluded them from rural life.[573] By April 1933 operations involving the Food Ministry had eliminated all "Jewish and Marxist elements," with replacements being chosen by the Nazi Country Traders' League.[574] A September 1933 decree forbade Jews from owning certain farms or undertaking production agriculture on someone else's property.[575] This could be disastrous for farmers if genealogists discovered a Jew among the farmers' ancestors.[576] Nonetheless, because so few known Jews were farmers, the measure had little effect on their current livelihood. It did, however, affect future livelihood. Some Jewish craftsmen who lost their living decided to try farming. When *Der Angriff* learned of this, the Nazi newspaper declared the purchase agreement for the land should be cancelled, and the peasant land sellers penalized.[577] When a Waldenberg Nazi official learned that Jews had leased a meadow he growled that the land owners would be held legally accountable.[578]

Starting in 1933 many companies decided to drop Jewish employees, without giving notice and in defiance of contracts guaranteeing employment during good performance.[579] A Reich Labor Court said that Jewish workers could be dismissed if their presence caused labor disturbances, and the National Socialist Organization of Factory Cells made a point of disrupting work until a particular Jewish worker was fired.[580] Their disruptions caused even big Jewish companies such as Fromm, Leiser, Osram, and Orenstein & Koppel to discharge Jewish employees.[581] In April 1933 a court upheld a café's termination of a Jewish employee on grounds that a customer boycott might otherwise occur.[582] Around mid-1933 the Berlin department store Rudolf Karstadt A.G. fired Jewish employees on grounds that "members of the Jewish race in Germany are to-day no longer citizens with full status and with equal rights" and "only a citizen of full status can render in full the services" which Karstadt required.[583] A court upheld the store's action, saying that being a Jew was cause for dismissal.[584] Also in the summer of 1933 Dresdner Bank fired 150 non-Aryan workers even though many had given the bank devoted service for years.[585] That autumn the Berlin Labor Court ruled that employers could fire anyone found to be Jewish.[586] In 1934 an observer noted, "Very many industrial and commercial firms controlled by non-Jews have dismissed their Jewish employees. Jewish executives and clerks are a serious liability to which business organizations are loathe to subject themselves."[587] Municipalities dealt only with companies certified as Aryan.[588] "A large rubber goods manufacturer," said a U.S. diplomat, "was informed that, in order to have his bids considered by the municipal authorities, he must submit evidence that he employed no Jews (several Jews were dismissed as a result)."[589] The Labor Court of Saalfeld ruled that public opinion justified a textile factory's dismissal of a Jewish employee, because retention would have been interpreted as lack of confidence in the Nazi program.[590] Such an interpretation could be disastrous. A Jewish worker recalled, "One of our customers from Munich showed up and saw me working there. I overheard him talking to the company owner. 'Since you continue to employ Jews, we can no longer do business with you,' he said. . . . The company let me stay until December, but then the boss told me, 'I'm sorry, but you will have to go.'"[591] In 1935 a court said a cigar store could fire a Jewish manager in order to display a "German Business" sign "at a time when this designation is a condition of business success."[592] Even

German branches of United States firms, such as Woolworth's, displayed such signs.[593] Aryan business slogans were common. A trademark on one line of clothing products said, "Adefa, the sign of merchandise made by Aryan hands."[594] By April 1933 newspaper ads from merchants proclaimed, "Purely Christian family-enterprise," "Economic Independence—The Pride of Our Firm," and "German Merchant." In June 1936 Germany's supreme court in questions of Aryan business and employment, the *Reichsgericht*, examined a movie company contract allowing a stage manager's dismissal upon "sickness, death or similar causes rendering the stage manager's work impossible." A dismissed Jewish stage manager sought relief under that clause, arguing that he was capable of performing the work, only to be told by the court that Jews were denied so many rights that in civil law they were dead; therefore, the movie company was entitled to remove the dead person from its payroll.[595] Such a decision did not penetrate new legal ground. Three years earlier a court used the same reasoning to allow the Ufa motion picture company to fire a Jewish director—and to recover salary already paid to him for a film project.[596] A Jew had the legal rights of a corpse.

Workplace boycotts could also work the other way around, with Aryan employees disrupting commercial activity of firms owned or managed by Jews. In May 1933 all Epa dime stores in Berlin had to close when Aryan workers refused to do their jobs "under Jewish management."[597] The Epa boycott spread nationwide, with employees demanding resignations from Jewish directors.[598] Nazi thugs roamed the Ullstein printing plant that same month, ordering Jews off the premises.[599] That practice was common; Ullstein was not singled out.[600] Such disruptions promoted Aryanization sales described in the next chapter.

As with other discriminatory measures, job dismissals could affect Aryans. For example, one of the Nuremberg decrees passed soon thereafter was the Law for the Protection of the German Blood and of the German Honor.[601] That law declared, "Jews may not employ female citizens of German and similar blood under 45 years of age in their households." The decree's ostensible purpose was to halt the allegedly widespread impregnation of Aryan female servants by lustful Jewish employers. The decree was passed in the super-heated atmosphere of the Nuremberg party rally, but cooler heads soon realized the practical difficulties of implementing such a decree—60,000 Aryan females would lose their jobs,[602] a prospect relished by Aryan men interested in such employment.[603] The legal definition of "servant" was broader than Americans might think. Jewish girls persuaded their father to let their unemployed Aryan female friend stay in the home, where she occasionally helped with household chores. The father was convicted of violating the Blood and Honor law.[604] Female cooks, seamstresses, typists, and secretaries became maidservants if they belonged to the household. For example, a doctor's female assistant could make herself tea in the doctor's lab, but if she did it in the kitchen of the doctor's adjoining residence she would belong to the household and could be transformed into a maidservant.[605] Under a supreme court ruling from Leipzig, a female employee of a male Jew became a "servant" if any of the following tasks were performed: "Carrying milk and butter from a proprietor's establishment to his residence; transportation of coffee from a proprietor's dwelling to his place of business; purchase of cake or rolls for Jewish business proprietors; removal of garbage from a Jewish business man's dwelling; taking a Jewish business man's children for a walk if his dwelling must be visited; purchase and delivery of foodstuffs to a Jewish employer's dwelling."[606] Given such customs of the era, through the war on Jews many jobs held by Aryan women suddenly became available to Aryan men. Categories of commercial jobs that Aryan women had to give up for protection of their honor regardless of assigned tasks included Jewish clothing company clerks, messengers, and models (even in store windows).[607] Police intervened when an unnamed citizen reported two females, aged forty and seventeen, working for a Jewish butcher. Even though their jobs had Employment Bureau permission, their employment violated the Blood and Honor decree.[608] In November 1935 a compromise reduced the "female servant" age limit by ten years if the maid were already employed in a Jewish household, and waived the age restriction entirely if no males were in the household.[609] Even with this compromise, the supposed beneficiaries of this protection reacted with one of the few mass protests documented under the Nazi regime:

> Indignant maid-servants crowded the Labour Exchanges in Berlin to-day, to protest against the new Nazi racial laws, which deprive the women of their livelihood by forcing them to leave Jewish households.
>
> In Berlin alone, it is estimated, close on 30,000 maids under thirty-five years of age will be out of work on January 1st.
>
> Some will be able to return home, but the vast majority must either go to labour camps or try to find some other kind of work, for the domestic labour market is overcrowded.
>
> Some of these women have tried to present petitions to Herr Hitler personally.
>
> Several thousand letters of protest have reached the Chancellery from servants now under notice.
>
> Meanwhile, the German Press is forbidden to make any reference to the desperate plight of these women.[610]

An estimated 30,000 Aryan female servants had lost their jobs by year's end.[611] Their desperation was intensified because such workers had been explicitly excluded from receiving unemployment benefits since 1933.[612] The women had few employment options, and the sudden glut on the labor market left those options unavailable to most. Some with rural relatives went to the countryside; others may have gone to job training camps—where the regime charged them for an opportunity to learn new job skills,[613] training made necessary by the regime's actions in the first place.

As when we discussed the revocation of legal rights, our discussion of job dismissals now reaches the arbitrary dividing line of Crystal Night, November 9–10, 1938. As before, we should consider whether job dismissal policy after

Crystal Night inherently differed from what happened before. If not, then the Holocaust was already well underway by that date.

A decree of November 12, 1938, stated that as of January 1 "operation of retail shops, mail order houses, [and] independent exercise of handicrafts is forbidden to Jews. . . . Moreover it is forbidden . . . to offer goods or services in the markets of all kinds, fairs, or exhibitions, or to advertise such or accept orders therefor. . . . Jewish shops operated in violation of this order will be closed by police." The decree also removed Jews as business executives and as members of cooperatives.[614] In the spirit of civic duty police shut down Jewish businesses immediately despite the decree's grace period, but closed businesses had to continue paying Aryan employees at least until January 1; some Aryans collected salaries from their former Jewish employers for six months.[615] Inventories could not be liquidated in going-out-of-business sales lest bargain-seeking customers be enticed from Aryan merchants. Instead inventories were bought in wholesale lots by government commissioners, at whatever price the Nazis decided to pay.[616] That merchandise was then made available to Aryan business people.

Although the closing of Jewish commercial enterprises was ostensibly directed against Jewish owners, the measure was also enacted with their Aryan employees in mind. German industry was experiencing a labor shortage that hindered war preparedness. The demise of Jewish businesses threw their Aryan employees into a suddenly expanded labor pool that could never absorb the Aryans into jobs comparable to their old ones. The only alternative was factory work.[617]

A December decree provided additional regulations to remove Jews from industry.[618] Also that month Vienna Jews could no longer be stamp dealers,[619] Cologne Jews could no longer be peddlers,[620] and across Germany Jews could no longer be midwives.[621] A decree of 1939 forbade Jewish dentists.[622] A decree of May 1939 forbade Jewish travel agents.[623] Some of these decrees may seem redundant; the regime routinely announced "new" measures to focus public attention on some aspect of the war on Jews.

By July 1933 a senior U.S. diplomat in Germany told Washington, D.C., "Consistently and relentlessly the Jews are being eliminated from practically all walks of life."[624] Jews who lost their jobs could not get new ones because hiring could only be done through Nazi-controlled labor exchanges and professional groups.[625] In September 1933 one observer reported that violent "outrages, brutal as they are, are less serious than the systematic attempt to deprive Jews of any means of subsistence. . . . [Nazis have] openly declared that if the Jews are tolerated at all, it will ultimately be only as helots without civil rights, condemned to hard manual labor."[626] Reinhard Heydrich stated to colleagues, "Jewry will become unemployed. The remaining Jews [who have not emigrated] gradually become proletarians."[627] As early as 1933 one visitor to Germany reported, "It was rather pathetic when I rang up Jewish professional men to whom I had been given introductions that I always found them at home and ready to talk at any length, for they had nothing else to do."[628] A survivor wrote, "By the middle of

1937, nearly every Jewish professional my parents knew was out of work."[629] Even two years earlier a newspaper reporter noted, "Formerly well-to-do Jews may be seen digging ditches to earn food and shelter and are subject to jeers from the Nazi press."[630] A Berlin resident recalled the Jewish employment scene in 1938, "You saw street sweepers who used to be judges, doctors, lawyers, teachers, and so on."[631] Municipal governments saved money by hiring desperate Jews at low wages for projects requiring physical labor.[632] Many Jewish professionals were shipped to Austria's Mur valley for labor battalion work.[633] By February 1939 private companies could draft Jews for unskilled labor if they could be segregated from the company's Aryan workforce.[634] Normally Jews were conscripted for loathsome tasks: "rubbish disposal, public toilets and sewage plants, quarries and gravel pits, coal merchants and rag and bone works were regarded as suitable" for Jews.[635] Wages were about RM 24 a week (under $5),[636] pay that did not allow the Jews to support themselves. In February 1939 an American observer noted that "no Jew—save for a few officials of Jewish organizations—may earn a living. For these reasons there are want and misery today among many, and the spread of destitution in the circumstances is bound to be rapid."[637] In 1938 one observer reported "men with wives and families . . . sobbing in a state of complete nervous collapse at the hopeless prospect."[638] Strapped by lack of job income, Jewish families sold household articles to generate cash,[639] a vicious dovetail between jobs policy and the Aryanization policy examined in the next chapter. Pawnshops, a traditional source of cash for persons who cannot get money from banks, could neither receive property from Jews nor redeem their pawn tickets.[640] That restriction limited the market for Jew-tainted personal goods, driving down the price. By autumn of 1939 Jews remaining in Germany were hounded in so many ways that they lived as outlaws have to live; survival depended on street savvy. When Goering drafted restless youths and unemployed former breadwinners into war industry work, not all complained. "For many," said a secret U.S. government report, "this was the first opportunity in years to work, to earn a petty livelihood and to fill out the endless hours of their empty days."[641]

In evaluating the elimination of Jews from German economic life, we should remember that their lost jobs did not disappear. Instead they were taken over by Aryans. Unemployment was a factor in the Nazi rise to power. In July 1933 an American diplomat noted a conversation with Hans Luther, German ambassador to the United States: "He thought the plains of East Africa or the highlands of Brazil ought to be opened to all German unemployed who are willing to emigrate (he thought there would be a considerable number)."[642] The Nazi regime responded to demands for jobs by taking them from "unworthy" Jews and giving them to "worthy" Aryans. The economic effect of such a tradeoff should have been nil, but the payoff in popular support for the regime was tremendous. "It was a sure way of finding jobs for all the Nazis," said an American who watched the process. "There were thousands, even hundreds of thousands, of jobs open and waiting for the National Socialist."[643] In 1931 a British student attending a

German university wrote, "Not one-third of the students at present in Heidelberg or any of the other German universities can hope to find an appointment equivalent to their education."[644] Another contemporary observer noted that university students included "thousands of sons of an impoverished middle class, all aspiring to civil service posts or medical and legal practice, all aware that these careers were hopelessly overcrowded. To them the doctrine which involved the forcible elimination of the Jewish competitor became a gospel."[645] Historians Michael Burleigh and Wolfgang Wippermann note, "People became rich and made careers, often at the expense of Jews who were discriminated against, pauperised, and persecuted."[646] This factor surely helped promote Austrian enthusiasm for the *Anschluss* with Germany. Restrictions on Jewish livelihoods that had taken five years to evolve in Germany became applicable overnight in Austria:[647] "Heart breaking scenes today at almost 10,000 Jewish-owned commercial and industrial enterprises when the employers announced to some 30,000 Jewish employes their immediate dismissal on orders from various Nazi organizations. . . . Many Jewish employers were informed that their dismissed employes would be replaced tomorrow by 'Aryans' sent by Nazi organizations."[648] Throughout the Greater Reich supporters of a Jew-free economy ranged from Aryan university graduates seeking professional positions to debt-ridden farmers delighted to pay off debts to Jewish creditors at a fraction of par. The latter process involved the organized theft of Jewish property through confiscation proceedings, and that is the topic of our next chapter.

3

CONFISCATION

A dictionary defines "expropriation" as a state's seizure of property without permission of the owner, accompanied by equitable financial compensation for the loss. Seizure of Jews' property in Nazi Germany, however, lacked equitable compensation. Even though the procedure is sometimes called "expropriation," it was actually outright confiscation. At first, Nazis described the activity as "Aryanization" of the economy. Later, they called the process "de-Judaization" of economic assets. Prosecutors at the Nuremberg Military Tribunal simply described the activity as "theft."

Property confiscation is a key element of the destruction process. Via confiscation, victims who survive ostracism can be denied houses to live in, be denied personal property that can be sold for food, and be reduced to wretchedness. Moreover, confiscated property does not disappear. Persons or agencies acquiring the property quickly develop a vested interest in promoting the destruction process.

Nazi confiscation actions against Jews occurred within a larger project to realign the nation's economic power structure according to fascist principles. Fascism eliminates antitrust laws and encourages growth of trusts and cartels. In order to grow, these economic entities must either destroy or absorb competitors. Nazi confiscation policy allowed trusts and cartels to make bargain purchases of businesses owned or managed by Jews. Germany's corporate power structure thus had a strong economic incentive to support the war on Jews. Smaller entrepreneurs had the same incentive. Others benefited as well. For example, subsidiaries of United States corporations in Germany could use the Aryanization program to buy out Jewish-owned competitors.[1] Individual Americans could also benefit; a New York lawyer was identified as the main stockholder in the parent company of a German Aryan firm that took over the Nathan Israel retail business in Berlin.[2] Although Aryanization could be used to strengthen American interests in the German economy, that element of Aryanization was a historical curiosity. Aryanization was an expression of Nazi greed.

NAZI PROPERTY CONFISCATION DECREES

Confiscation decrees were an early feature of the Nazi regime. The Reichstag Fire decree of February 28, 1933, supposedly directed against communist activity, stated in part that "orders for confiscations as well as restrictions on property, are also permissible beyond the legal limits otherwise prescribed."[3] The term "communist" was elastic enough to cover a broad scope of activity. Under that anticommunist measure the Nazi regime seized church property of Jehovah's Witnesses and Christian Scientists.[4] Whole commercial enterprises were forfeited on grounds that they had aided enemies of the state.[5] The Reichstag Fire measure was soon followed by a decree authorizing confiscation of property "used or destined for the promotion of communistic activities."[6] Such confiscations had already been underway; in March the communist headquarters Karl Liebknecht Haus in Berlin was seized by Nazis and converted to headquarters for the SA and SS, and the next month Albert Einstein's bank account was seized to prevent its "treasonable" use.[7] When taking property of Masonic lodges, the regime cited the decree against communist property.[8] Jews might be coerced to confess "communist" affiliation, thereby subjecting their property to forfeiture.[9] A July 1933 decree was even more sweeping, authorizing confiscation of property "used or destined to be used to promote . . . activities found by the Reich Minister of the Interior to be subversive to people and state."[10]

These confiscations were what American lawyers would call civil forfeitures. By using a civil action the state did not have to prove the property owners guilty of any crime. The state merely had to certify the property had been used in a prohibited manner, regardless of whether the owner even knew about the use. Such a confiscation technique has important practical consequences. Because these Nazi forfeitures were directed against property, not against persons who owned the property, children could lose their property.[11] Forfeitures could be run against estates of dead persons—who were unlikely to object.[12] Forfeitures could even be run against property owned by loyal Aryans if it was used by enemies of the state, such as by dissidents who operated from a rented building. The two "subversive property" decrees protected innocent landlords, however. If a landlord did not know that a tenant was using a building to promote subversive activity, the building would not be forfeited. In contrast, innocent owners or lienholders lost all interests in other confiscated property. For example, if a car used in subversive activity were forfeited to the state, the state did not have to pay off the remainder of an outstanding loan on the car. Other kinds of property were also subject to seizure. Although Goering was famed for looting art works in countries defeated by the Nazis in World War II, before the war Munich's National Museum built the state collection through art objects seized from Jews in Germany.[13] Not all forfeitures targeted treasures; seized objects could be petty. Radios could be forfeited if Aryans used them for listening to Soviet broadcasts.[14] In May 1933 confiscation was decreed for products vaguely described as harming the dignity of German or Nazi symbols; targets included candies or sausages molded into a swastika shape.[15] "All products of this kind are subject to confiscation without any compensation."[16] Moreover, if a product was eventually certified as permissible and the confiscation as erroneous, any damages suffered by the innocent owner were nonrecoverable.

Such seizures were more than harassment; they expressed the totalitarian nature of the Nazi regime, for the right to own property is closely linked to other civil rights. It was not a coincidence that a Prussian court used a property seizure appeal to establish that courts had no power to interfere with Gestapo actions.[17]

Regarding property seizures the Nazi government had broad power and little accountability. In August 1933 the noted American financial lawyer Samuel Untermeyer predicted that university and other charitable endowments established in Germany by American Jews would be confiscated by the regime.[18] The preceding month the U.S. ambassador to Germany attended a conference where he was told, "All Jewish property is being confiscated."[19] The scope of property confiscations was understood worldwide six months after the Nazis took power.

The Aryan business community allied itself with the Nazi government in this effort. A man who owned a store selling electrical appliances and phonograph records confessed, "I was pinning all my hopes on the Nazis, because our business was on the verge of collapse. . . . They had a program that sounded perfect. . . . They called it 'breaking the tyranny of investment capital,' which meant expropriating the department stores and renting out the space at low rates to small businessmen. . . . How could we compete with Oppenheim Electric, with their big store downtown and two branches in the suburbs? It was a Jewish company, and it did such a large volume of business that it could buy cheap and spend a lot on advertising. And the Nazis promised they would get rid of our Jewish competition."[20]

Although our examination of Nazi confiscations will focus on Jewish victims, we should remember that similar measures were applied to Aryans who ran afoul of the Nazi regime. The 1933 confiscation decrees were used to forfeit the property of Aryan industrialist Fritz Thyssen after he broke with the Nazi regime in 1939.[21] Commercial property such as newspapers, printing plants, buildings, and land owned by the German Socialist Party and the *Reichsbanner* (the Social Democrat Party's old military arm) were forfeited in May 1933.[22] A 1936 decree announced, "A German citizen who deliberately and unscrupulously, for his own gain or for other low motives, contrary to legal provisions smuggles property abroad or leaves property abroad and thus inflicts serious damage to German economy is to be punished by death. His property will be confiscated. The perpetrator is also punishable, if he commits the act abroad."[23] For German tourists returning home, passage through Nazi customs inspection could be tense. So was outward passage. A boy leaving Germany decided it was too dangerous to take any postage stamps for correspondence. "Perhaps they would consider them valuables at the border, confiscate them, and arrest me."[24] A woman recalled hearing the 1936 decree proclamation. "A friend was listening at the radio beside me and exclaimed, 'By such measures do the Nazis acquire control of more and yet more money with which to substantiate their power! When all property is brought home and registered they can seize it at their leisure."[25] Two years later a manufacturer confided to a visitor, "The people are not ignorant of the fact that ever since the Nazis came into office they have taken as forfeit the money in the treasury of every club and organization, large and small, which they have ordered to be closed. They know of private fortunes—'Aryan fortunes'—forfeit to the state."[26] One Aryan example was the seizure of property owned by *Stahlhelm* units.[27] News item, August 1939: "A list of 10,000 associations and organizations in AUSTRIA which have been dissolved by order of the Government is published in the Vienna *Gazette*. The property of the organizations has been confiscated."[28] Forfeited property could be offered for bargain prices at public auction, and a Gestapo man claimed that acquisitive Aryans denounced fellow citizens in hopes of gaining their jewels, automobiles, or even garden plots.[29] Nonetheless, although forfeitures could be run against Aryans, the primary targets were Jews.

Nazis applied two basic types of property confiscation against Jews. One type was Aryanization, comprised of forced sale of property to private individuals or businesses. The other type was forfeiture, in which property went to the government. The two methods tended to blur: Government officials might expedite Aryanization, and private individuals might benefit by buying forfeited property from the government. Nonetheless, although the private sector was the primary beneficiary of Aryanization, and the government sector was the primary beneficiary of forfeiture, we should remember that both sectors profited from the same source: Jew-tainted property.

The term "Jew-tainted property" probably communicates the situation more clearly than the Nazi term of "Jewish property." Instead of attempting to find something Jewish in the nature of property itself, Nazis looked to the nature of persons associated with the property. Personal property might be "Jewish" because it was tainted by genealogical status of the owner's grandparents. The Nazi concept of "Jewish business" raised the meaning of "Jewish property" to an even higher level of abstraction. Jewish shopkeepers dealt in the same commodities and services as non-Jews. The same business principles guided both Aryan and Jew. Until ostracism was organized they even had the same customers. No observable difference distinguished an Aryan establishment from a Jewish one. With large corporate concerns such as factories and steel mills, detecting a difference between Jewish and Aryan enterprises became even more problematical. Just as Jewish humans were inherently indistinguishable from Aryan humans, so too were Jewish and Aryan business enterprises indistinguishable. The only way to tell them apart was through some arbitrary classification scheme: For humans Nazis used genealogy; for business they used owners' racial status. If question arose about a property owner's ancestry, the questioner did not necessarily have the burden of proof. People who were unable to document Aryan ancestry could be defined as Jews, even though no proof existed that they were

Jews.[30] People could lose their property not because anyone could prove they were Jews, but because they were unable to prove they were not Jews. The treacherous nature of such a policy, and the desperation of its victims, was illustrated in 1934 when the wife of a German diplomat asked the U.S. ambassador to Germany for help in proving that neither she nor her husband had Jewish forebears![31]

At first the regime defined a business as Jewish if a proprietor or managing officer were Jewish.[32] That provided a loophole; hiring Aryans to run a business made it Aryan even if the owner were Jewish. A decree of June 1938, however, closed that loophole. Thereafter if an individual owner were Jewish (keeping in mind that such a person could be a Christian since baptism at birth), so was the business. If even one of the partners who owned a business were Jewish, so was the business. If one corporation director were Jewish, so was the business. If one lawyer with power to represent a firm were Jewish, so was the business. If one-half the stockholders were Jewish, so was the business.[33] If more than one-fourth of a firm's capital were Jewish (by genealogy of the capital's owners), so was the business. If even a branch manager of an otherwise Aryan enterprise were Jewish, so was the branch.[34] If a steel plant obtained 26 percent of its capital on loan from a bank and the bank attorney who signed the deal were Jewish, the steel plant became Jewish. A single human's status as Jew could taint a huge industrial property, regardless of the status of everyone else involved with the property.

All those persons could lose their interest in the property through Aryanization or forfeiture, let alone lose money through damage by customer boycott. Consequently Aryanization and forfeiture strengthened ostracism, for example by giving Aryan corporation directors strong motive to expel a Jewish director.[35] Such purging could certify a formerly Jewish business as Aryan.[36] The same consideration encouraged Aryan share holders to buy out Jews who owned shares in a stock company.[37] For example, starting in April 1935 newspapers had to certify that all company stock owners had Aryan pedigrees back to 1800. Jews could legally own newspaper company stock, but any newspaper company that allowed Jews to own its stock could no longer publish a newspaper. Publishers who wanted to stay in business had to find ways to take away shares from Jews who owned them.[38] In those circumstances Aryanization was actually compulsory for Aryans.

Although we are emphasizing effects of Aryanization and forfeiture on property owners, they were not the only persons harmed. Through liens and mortgages third parties could hold an interest in properties. Aryanizations operated within perimeters of ordinary commercial law, perimeters protecting those third parties. Forfeiture, however, was not bound by such limits. Nazis ruled that "the state shall not be responsible for the claims which have arisen against the former owner of the seized property" if the property was forfeited before December 9, 1937.[39] Third party interests in such property "are deemed expired with the seizure."[40] For example, if a loan were secured by a mortgage on a house seized from a Jew, the Jew's obligation to the lender did not necessarily cease, but the government had no obligation to make the lender whole if any loss were suffered after the loan became unsecured. The government might, as an act of grace, compensate such third parties but had no obligation to do so. If property were seized after December 9, 1937, however, third party claims were recognized. Compensation could not exceed sale value (as opposed to replacement cost) of the property. Nor did compensation have to be in cash: A mortgage held by the Reich might be transferred to the third party, or a lien might be given on some land. Alternatively, the government might order anyone who bought forfeited property from the state to pay the sales value to the third party. The purchaser might thereby have to buy forfeited property twice, once from the government and again from the lienholder. As another alternative, the government might order the purchaser to pay to the government whatever compensation sum the government gave the third party. Third parties with interests in corporate property, however, lost everything; not only did seizure automatically dissolve the corporation,[41] seizure cancelled any third party claims to the corporation property.[42] Nazi law termed *third parties* to be forfeiture "victims," but property *owners* lacked that legal status. In no case could a former owner of forfeited property receive compensation.[43] For example, in October 1938 the government was seeking property to use for a youth camp and seized the country estate of cigarette manufacturer Eugene Garbaty. A knowledgeable observer valued the estate in excess of RM 2 million. Garbaty received nothing.[44]

Local individual Nazis might be interested in specific Jew-tainted properties, but the regime did not have to depend upon piecemeal research to determine confiscation targets: A decree of April 26, 1938, required registration of Jewish property.[45] Much information about Jewish property was already available through tax records, but the new decree gave the regime an exhaustive inventory of everything possessed by Jews, an inventory having no apparent connection to tax revenue. This decree was issued soon after the *Anschluss*, quickly providing the regime with information about Austrian property that had been thus far untouched by Germany's Aryanization program. In 1941 a Ministry of Economics official frankly described registration of Jewish property as a key step in confiscating it.[46] A confiscation order of February 1939 was even based on the registration decree.[47] That meaning of registration was instantly recognized in April 1938. The day after the decree's issuance *Der Angriff* declared, "All Jewish fortunes of 5,000 marks or more will now be seized. We can assume with complete certainty that a large proportion of this wealth was earned by improper methods, and the Commissioner for the Four-Year Plan has therefore ordered that the Jewish capital be applied to the service of the business and industry of the Germany people."[48] The *New York Times* announcement of the measure said it was obviously aimed at elimination of Jewish property,[49] and in a June 1938 report to President Franklin Roosevelt, the U.S. ambassador to Germany saw the decree as a prelude to confiscation.[50] In May 1938 one observer in America "referred to the four-year plan of the Nazi Government to liquidate all Jewish property"[51] (the decree was signed by Goering in his role as head of the so-called Four Year Plan to revitalize Germany's economy).

The measure required Jews and their non-Jewish spouses to inventory, appraise, and register all their property with the government. A supplemental decree required separate reports by the couple's children.[52] Property to be registered included intangibles such as stocks and insurance.[53] Only "nonluxury" household items were exempt, although no registration at all was required if total property value was RM 5,000 or less. (That was gross value, not net equity. Debt could not be subtracted from the official statement of wealth.)[54] Police kept the files,[55] and Jews had to update those records when any major change in property occurred. Nazi authorities thus had a fairly current idea of exactly what could be found in a particular residence or business. What authorities intended to do with this knowledge was implied by Article 7 of the decree: "The Deputy for the Four Year Plan [Goering] is empowered to take such necessary measures as may be necessary to guarantee the use of the reported property in accord with the necessities of Germany economy." In other words, what the government wanted, the government would take. Recognizing that the intention would be widely suspected, and that property owners might therefore try to evade registration, the decree authorized fines and ten years of imprisonment at hard labor for failure to register all property covered by the decree. "The offender is punishable notwithstanding that the action was in a foreign country." Under Article 1, that class of offenders included Jewish foreign citizens who failed to register property they owned in Germany. For example, Jewish United States citizens who failed to register their German property would be subject to imprisonment if they visited Germany. In this decree Germany claimed jurisdiction over foreigners living abroad. "In addition to the imposition of the penalties," the decree concluded, "the property may be confiscated, insofar as it was involved in the criminal action." In other words unregistered property was criminally tainted, and subject to forfeiture.[56]

Jews could thwart property seizures by transferring ownership to friendly Aryans. For example, Jewish spouses might turn over property to their Aryan partners or *Mischlinge* children. By December 1938 such closely held family transactions became common enough to attract Hitler's personal attention. He allowed continuation of transfers to *Mischlinge* children "for the time being" but limited transactions between spouses. A Jewish wife could turn over her property to an Aryan husband, but a Jewish husband could not give his property to an Aryan wife. Moreover, if a couple was childless, both spouses would be treated as full Jews for property purposes.[57] Another approach was for spouses to make a formal legal division of marital property, so that part of a couple's assets could be salvaged if officials moved against the Jewish partner.[58] Apparently to help track such property, a summer 1938 regulation forbade Aryan husbands of Jewish wives to open their bank safe deposits boxes without the presence of a policeman.[59] If the regime had particular interest in property protected through marriage, a court might simply declare the marriage invalid.[60] A statement from

Minister of Justice Franz Gürtner indicated the regime even considered property angles when couples applied for marriage licenses: "Marriage licenses can be refused when it is evident that the parties have no real intention to contract marriage in the usual way, but merely to secure some external advantage that might be derived from marrying."[61]

Although registration of Jews' property expedited seizures in Germany, lack of registration in Nazi-occupied areas did not deter Reich officials. An official in France reported on acquisition of household goods: "Confiscation officials went from house to house when no records were available of the addresses of Jews who had departed or fled. . . . They drew up inventories of these homes and subsequently sealed them. . . . Goods are dispatched first, to large collecting camps from where they are turned over, sorted out and loaded for Germany."[62] The system did not always work smoothly. In 1941 Alfred Rosenberg told Hitler, "A great number of Jewish dwellings remained unguarded. Consequently, many furnishings have disappeared. . . . I beg the Fuehrer to permit the seizure of all Jewish home furnishings of Jews in Paris, who have fled, or will leave shortly, and that of Jews living in all parts of the occupied West, to relieve the shortage of furnishings in the administration in the East [Ostland]."[63] Thousands of railway cars full of such furnishings, enough to outfit completely almost 70,000 houses, were dispatched from France to worthy Aryans in Germany and Ostland.[64] Recipients of such household goods had good reason to support the war on Jews.

Through a decree of November 1941 the German government seized property owned by Jews who lost their German nationality.[65] (Although Jews could not be citizens, they could be German nationals.) Loss of nationality occurred if a German Jew emigrated from the country. Refugees now lost any property they had left in Germany (although in practice this had happened since 1933).[66] For example, an exile who still owned a house in Germany now forfeited the house. A Dresdner Bank official estimated that RM 1 billion in Jew-tainted real estate would thereby come into government hands. Some was sold; some was given to war veterans (providing foot soldiers with a tangible reason to support the war on Jews). Government pensions to any Jewish emigre covered by a Hindenburg exception stopped. Private pensions also stopped, although companies had to pay a settlement fee to the government lest they profit at the expense of the regime.[67] Jews who lost German nationality were also forbidden to inherit property from German nationals, altering the earlier rule that Aryan relatives had preference over any Jew named in a German national's will.[68] Those Aryan relatives were now cut out. Any such legacy left to a Jew who lost Germany nationality was forfeited to the state, as was any property that would have gone to the Jew if the German national died intestate. Refugees of course were not the only class of Jews to which this decree applied. Jews shipped out of Germany for slave labor or immediate extermination were also covered by the decree.

A July 1943 decree announced "the property of a Jew shall be confiscated by the Reich after his death."[69] Confiscation of personal effects at death camps is well known. In theory all items went to the state, but in practice seepage occurred. After the war Mauthausen commandant Franz Ziereis admitted in disgust, "Everybody in that camp got at once a big car. Obersturmfueher Hackmann drove out in a Mercedes, with stolen diamonds on the fingers, and his subordinate, Untersturmfuehrer Meyer, imitated like a monkey all these manners."[70] Confiscation from inmates also applied to intangible property. For example, any cash value from life insurance policies went to the government (although companies were excused from paying death benefits lest extermination activities become too public).[71] Securities payable to "bearer" were processed by the Reichsbank's securities division. Savings bank accounts of deceased Jews were also acquired.[72] Not even Aryans could inherit property from Jews any more. The government got it all. The government also collected any debts owed to deceased Jews.[73]

SEIZURE AS PROTECTIVE CUSTODY

In the previous chapter we saw a court declare that Aryan identity was crucial for commercial success of a business. An attorney promoting an Aryanization refined that court decision: "It is in the interests of the enterprise itself, of its employees, and of its stockholders . . . that the transfer of the Jewish property to Aryans be required, against the will of the present owners, if necessary."[74] Seizure was justified to protect the property's value and productivity. Greed was transformed into altruism that protected the community's economic health. Just as Nazi doctrine held that individuals no longer had a right to control their physical bodies, but instead had a higher duty to protect the Aryan race, so too we find that property owners no longer had a right to use property in ways that might diminish its value to the larger community (whether value be measured by number of employees or size of tax base). Just as citizens could be taken into protective custody (protective for the state), property could be taken into protective custody.

Protection was in Goering's mind when he promoted sweeping seizure laws during 1938. He was alarmed at destruction of property in pogroms: "It's insane to clean out and burn a Jewish warehouse then have a German insurance company make good the loss. And the goods which I need desperately, whole bales of clothing and what-not, are being burned; I miss them everywhere. I may as well burn the raw materials before they arrive. The people of course, do not understand that; therefore we must make laws which will show the people once and for all, that something is being done."[75] Rather than restrain the people, Goering's plan was to grab Jew-tainted property before Aryan mobs could.

Nazi officials may have taken an indulgent attitude toward rioters who destroyed Jew-tainted property in misguided displays of civic duty, but looting provoked a different response. Theft proved rioters were motivated by selfishness rather than patriotism; Nazi officials could become indignant if Aryans took Jew-tainted property without government authorization. On Crystal Night SS Lt. General (and commander of the SD and the Gestapo) Reinhard Heydrich sent urgent teletype messages across the Reich: "Business and private apartments of Jews may be destroyed but not looted. The police is instructed to supervise the execution of this order and to arrest looters." "Looters are to be arrested." "Inform me by 11 November 1938, at 8 AM, by telegram, all cases of looting known to you." "Proceed ruthlessly, by intensive interrogations, to establish the persons guilty and to secure the objects of the looting."[76] An amazed eyewitness remembered, "Something really strange had been happening all over, but particularly at the bigger, more elegant Jewish stores around the Kurfuersten-damm. The S.S. were arresting store owners by the dozen—but both the S.S. and the police stood guard at the stores. 'They stopped the looters, would you believe?'"[77] When reading a transcript of a Nazi leadership meeting held after Crystal Night, one can almost hear fists pounding on the table when a report is made about looting from the Margraf Jewish jewelry store in Berlin:

> *Goering:* Daluege and Heydrich, you'll have to get me this jewelry through raids, staged on a tremendous scale!
>
> *[SS Lt. Gen. and commander of the Reich's urban police Kurt] Daluege:* The order has already been given. The people are being controlled all the time. According to reports, 150 were arrested by yesterday afternoon.
>
> *Goering:* These things will otherwise be hidden. If somebody comes to a store with jewels and claims that he has bought them, they'll be confiscated at once. He has stolen them or traded them in all right.
>
> *Heydrich:* . . . We have already several hundred people who were plundering, and we are trying to get the loot back.
>
> *Goering:* And the jewels?
>
> *Heydrich:* That is very difficult to say. They were partly thrown into the street and picked up there. . . .
>
> *Daluege:* The Party should issue an order to the effect that the police will immediately receive a report in case the neighbor's wife, (everybody knows his neighbor) . . . appears wearing new rings or bracelets. . . .
>
> *Goering:* Now for the damage the Jew has had. At Margraf's the jewels disappeared, etc. Well, they are gone, and he won't get them refunded. He is the one who has to suffer the damage. As far as the jewels may be returned again by the police, they belong to the State.[78]

Citizens who picked up jewelry from a street were thieves. Government agents who confiscated the same jewelry were law enforcers. The difference was clear to Nazi officials, less so to postwar Nuremberg Military Tribunal prosecutors.

Top Nazis met right after Crystal Night to determine how to use the momentum that the violence had gained for the war on Jews. Goering opened the meeting.

> Gentlemen! Today's meeting is of a decisive nature. I have received a letter written on the Fuehrer's orders by the Stabsleiter of the Fuehrer's deputy Bormann, requesting that the Jewish question be now, once and for all,

coordinated and solved one way or another. And yesterday once again did the Fuehrer request by phone for me to take coordinated action in the matter.

Since the problem is mainly an economic one, it is from the economic angle that it shall have to be tackled.[79]

Goering announced a mass closure of Jewish stores. His announcement was sudden but his decision was not. Referring to the murder that Nazis used as the excuse for Crystal Night, the November 18 issue of *Berliner Börsenzeitung* (a newspaper considered close to Goering) declared "the shots fired in Paris at an aide of the German Ambassador did indeed prematurely set in motion measures."[80] In other words Crystal Night merely accelerated and concentrated previous plans. The *Berliner Börsenzeitung* also declared, "Long before the measures now instituted, the attentive reader could have seen the impending utilization of Jewish property in the economic process coming. The registration decree issued earlier this year by the government was such a hint." Hints had long been coming; closing Jewish retailing was but an extrapolation from earlier measures forbidding Jews from owning certain types of property. For example in 1933 Jews were forbidden to own hereditary manors, farms that passed from father to son.[81] That ban operated as a property confiscation. Christian farmers could find themselves transformed into Jews through genealogical research by covetous neighbors or others. Such transformation would cost them their farms.[82] After Crystal Night such transformation would close any business.

After Crystal Night many Jew-tainted businesses were no longer to be Aryanized, but liquidated. Moreover, owners could not sell their retail and wholesale stocks of goods to customers in the free market. Goering explained, "Their stocks are to be made available for sale in other stores; what cannot be sold, shall be processed through the 'Winterhilfe' [a Nazi charity] or taken care of otherwise."[83] Goering continued, "The trustee of the State will estimate the value of the property and decide what amount the Jew shall receive. Naturally, this amount is to be set as low as possible." Jews normally received the assessed value of a business's physical equipment, nothing more.[84] Under Goering's scheme the state would then sell the property to Aryan business people "according to its real value," thereby making a windfall profit. This scheme was formally decreed on November 23.[85]

No problem was expected on finding buyers. A report on Berlin's economy noted, "For every Jewish retail shop there were usually three or four applicants—various trade organizations split into factions to back up individual applicants."[86] At the meeting of Nazi leaders after Crystal Night, Goering noted, "Strong attempts will be made to get all these stores to party-members and to let them have some kind of compensations. I have witnessed terrible things in the past; little chauffeurs of Gauleiters have profited so much by these transactions that they have now about half a million. You, gentlemen, know it."[87] Goering was adamant that any monetary benefit this time would go to the state, not to private individuals.[88] On December 10, Goering declared that henceforth neither individuals nor private enterprises nor Nazi party enterprises could retain any economic windfall from Aryanizations. "Transactions which were made since 1 Nov 1938 contradictory thereto, will be cancelled. Only the Reich is entitled to the benefit from the elimination of the Jews from the German economic life. Persons and agencies which have illegally benefited from the transfer of Jewish businesses or other fortunes from Jewish possession, may therefore be ordered to pay a compensation tax in favor of the Reich."[89] The tax recovered 70 percent of windfall profits made on purchase of businesses and 100 percent on real estate, "windfall" being defined as the difference between normal market value and price paid.[90] A decree of 1940 pushed the cutoff date backward to January 30, 1933, allowing the regime to collect compensation for any Aryanization profiteering.[91]

Under the December 3, 1938, decree on "Utilization of Jewish Property,"[92] the government took steps to protect its interests in Aryanizations. Owners of Jewish "industrial enterprises as well as organizations, foundations, institutions, and other enterprises which are not industrial, insofar as they are to be considered Jewish" could be compelled to "sell or liquidate" at any time. That decree was confirmed by one of February 6, 1939, which approved "use of force" in transactions. Such transactions were called de-Judaization (in distinction from "voluntary" Aryanization). Force was approved for industrial properties and agricultural or forestry lands. Although agitation was underway for an end to "excessive" Jewish ownership of houses and apartment buildings,[93] "for the time being" compulsory means would not be used in de-Judaization of general real estate.[94] (The pace in Aryanization of real estate fell behind other types of property because so many Aryans held mortgages on Jewish-owned real estate;[95] a Jewish house carrying as much debt as one already owned by a prospective Aryan purchaser was often no bargain.) A government-appointed trustee could take over a Jewish business until sale or liquidation was completed, with the owner having to cover the trustee's expenses. While the business operated under a trusteeship the owner had no authority to sell or liquidate; the trustee, however, could not only make a decision to sell but set the price. Cutting out the owner simplified Aryanization negotiations, particularly if the owner resisted the deal or was in a concentration camp and unavailable for negotiating.[96] Sometimes trustees were business competitors against the Jewish firm; in one publicized instance a Jewish firm and its trustee were fighting in a major lawsuit.[97]

Jews could continue to own real estate properties or mortgages unless ordered to sell, but could not obtain new ones. A Jew could no longer sell real estate or mortgages without government permission. This allowed the state to determine who could purchase the property at what price. The practice was already underway with Aryanization of businesses. A Jewish jeweler reached agreement on selling the business to an Aryan. Local officials approved the sale, but higher ones said the business was overpriced and refused to authorize the sale unless the price came down. The Jew accepted a lower amount.[98] Under the December 3 decree a high bidder did not necessarily have the priority claim. Nor could "little chauffeurs of Gauleiters" necessarily profit from slick deals any more. The decree also ordered Jews to deposit their stocks and bonds at a foreign exchange bank, where they would be listed as Jewish assets. Such assets could not be freed or transferred without government permission. One effect of this measure was to protect the stability of stock markets from panic selling by Jews.[99] Aryan stock market traders thereby benefited from the war on Jews. Big corporations were another beneficiary of the order depositing Jewish-owned stocks in banks, because the corporations were allowed to buy back their own securities from those private accounts regardless of whether the Jew wanted to sell.[100] Any immediate financial gain aside, the corporation gained by reducing Jewish taint in its ownership.

For several years already, regular banks immediately notified the Gestapo if a Jewish depositor withdrew more than RM 1,500 from an account.[101] The Gestapo quickly ascertained whether the depositor was attempting to protect cash assets by transferring them abroad. Jews faced other limits on access to their bank accounts as well.[102] As early as March 1933, Jews in Pirmasens could not withdraw money from their bank accounts until all their debts to Aryan creditors were paid.[103] By summer 1938 Jews across Germany were limited to withdrawing a weekly allowance from their own funds.[104] Some restraints on accounts were mandated by the state; others were imposed by individual banks as an expression of civic duty.[105] In December 1938 restrictions were so stringent that one Jew had to ask permission to withdraw money to buy new clothes; permission was denied on grounds that such use of funds was wasteful and for no good purpose.[106]

In addition to bank regulations the December 1938 "utilization" decree stated, "Jews are forbidden to acquire, pawn or sell objects of gold, platinum or silver as well as precious stones and pearls.[107] Such objects, except in the case of existence of attachments on behalf of a non-Jewish creditor at the time when this decree goes into effect[108] may only be acquired by public purchasing offices, established by the Reich. The same applies to other jewels and objects of art insofar as the price of the individual objects exceeds one thousand Reichs-marks."[109] A decree of February 21, 1939, required Jews to turn in such items to government purchasing agencies, which appraised and bought them.[110] Again the "little chauffeurs" were deprived of profit. More importantly, as with stocks and bonds, Jews were hindered in converting assets into cash that could be used to leave Germany or to pay the Crystal Night fine, which is discussed below.

And even if the government gave permission for a Jew to sell, payment need not be in legal tender. The Jewish Orenstein and Koppel locomotive works was purchased with Argentine shares.[111] Jews who sold property to the government might be paid in shares of Reichswerke Hermann Göring A.G. ironworks or other government companies.[112] One observer noted rules allowing Jews to receive payment in "securities, the possession of which gives them no economic influence," that is, "payment" in worthless paper.[113] If payment were offered in Reich bonds, apparently they might be nonnegotiable, with the Jewish bondholder receiving only interest payments.[114] And if payment were in cash, it might be deposited in an account where the Jew could not withdraw the principal but merely receive interest earned.[115] Moreover, payment of principal might be through installments over a long period of time.[116] Whether compensation was small or large, Jewish recipients received a stipend sufficient only to buy bare necessities.[117]

To emigrate, Jews not only had to raise enough cash for travel but enough to satisfy the receiving country that they would not become a welfare burden. Substantial sums were then confiscated by the Nazi regime as Jews paid their way through the emigration bureaucracy. For example, a "flight of capital" tax had to be paid on their property—which was assessed at a high value for this purpose, and which was assessed on gross value rather than net (debts owed on property were not deducted when calculating flight tax). Before the Nazis took power all emigrants, Jewish or not, had to pay an emigration tax on their property if its value exceeded RM 200,000 or if the emigrant's annual income exceeded RM 20,000. The purpose was to discourage wealthy and talented citizens from leaving. The Nazis, however, modified the tax in May 1934 to confiscate property from emigrants of ordinary means—more particularly, from Jewish emigrants being hounded out of the country. The new tax was designed to exploit Jewish emigration, not discourage it.[118] For example, Nazi laws requiring Jewish emigrants to leave most of their property behind accomplished the tax's original fiscal goal—preventing flight of property from Germany—more efficiently than the tax itself did. Yet Jewish emigrants still had to pay the tax on what they left behind, not just on what they took with them. Even Jews without plans to emigrate could face a bill for this tax on the excuse that they would emigrate someday.[119] Sudden demand for a tax payment equivalent to 25 percent of their property, payable on a few days' notice, forced many business people to liquidate their enterprises in order to raise the tax payment,[120] and thereby helped promote Aryanizations. Perimeters of the flight tax were extended to include Jews who earned RM 20,000 in any calendar year from 1931 forward or who owned property exceeding RM 50,000 in value at any time after January 31, 1931. Emigrants who passed either threshold had to pay a flat 25 percent impost on all their property; interest on any unpaid amount accrued at a rate of 120 percent a year.[121] Aryan emigrants were normally exempt from the tax, on grounds they were promoting Nazi goals abroad.[122] Potential Jewish emigrants, however, also paid an additional sum that the regime could use "to promote the emigration of the Jews."[123] Another tax ranging from 0.5 percent to 10 percent on gross value of property was collected from emigrants for a Nazi fund allegedly devoted to care of elderly Jews in Germany.[124] And of course there were the usual bribes for passports, visas, and border crossings. All these steps were property seizures, even though some proceeds went directly to government officials rather than government coffers.

Jewish emigrants could take furniture and other personal belongings approved by the government (valuable items would be blocked), RM 1,000 worth of any other goods, and RM 10 in cash.[125] Everything else stayed behind. Emigrants did not necessarily lose ownership of those assets, but recovering them after leaving the country was a challenge. One method was to sell property to Aryans, normally at sacrifice prices. If an owner tried to realize maximum price through auction, goods had to be called "non-Aryan property" and professional dealers were forbidden to bid.[126] Permission for auction sale could be tedious to obtain; one Jew was able to auction household furniture only after getting a court's approval.[127] Sale proceeds went to blocked accounts. Emigrants could then purchase German goods abroad and pay for them from the blocked accounts back in Germany—one more way by which Aryan business people profited from the war on Jews.[128] A variation exploited the severe limitation on cash that an emigrant could take. Although almost no cash could be taken, emigrants could buy hundreds of marks of coupons redeemable for merchandise from ship's stores on the German emigration vessel. Jews were free to resell those goods on board or after disembarking. A brisk trade ensued on the high seas as refugees offered goods to foreign passengers in hopes of acquiring foreign exchange. Wise foreigners exercised patience; prices declined as the voyage progressed.[129]

Eventually the government or its assigned agents acquired assets that emigrants had not transferred to private individuals.[130] Before Crystal Night a contemporary observer estimated that fortunate Jewish emigrants left 90 percent of their property behind;[131] those with less skill or luck left more.[132] After Crystal Night Jewish emigrants could no longer take any property at all.[133]

The flight tax dovetailed with other elements of confiscation. For example, Jewish property owners might be arrested to soften their stance in Aryanization negotiations. Upon accepting an offer they could no longer refuse, victims were typically forced to pledge they would emigrate within a month. Before leaving, however, they had to pay a flight tax of 25 percent on the property they had just sold to Aryan buyers. The tax was figured on capital value of the property, not the bargain purchase price. Thus sale proceeds might not cover the tax. To pay the tax such Jews might have to sell foreign property they owned.[134] In that way the regime was able, in effect, to confiscate foreign property theoretically beyond the reach of Nazi law. Jews in this position were highly motivated to raise enough funds to pay the flight tax. Without paying they could not emigrate, and if they violated their pledge to emigrate, they were subject to arrest.

We should not leave the topic of emigration without considering the influence of property confiscation on immigration. Normally we hear of people striving to leave Nazi Germany, but some were striving to enter. These were mainly German expatriates who had left the Weimar Republic in disgust. With a regime more to their liking in power, they eagerly sought to return. The regime welcomed and promoted their return. To that end the Central Office for Property and Goods Exchange matched expatriate Aryans with Jews seeking to trade their German property for foreign property. These were Aryanizations by barter rather than cash, but terms were still outstanding for expatriate Aryans. "For well-known reasons," said the Office in 1935, "many well-going businesses, factories, and so forth are being sold off at present far below their true value."[135] Expatriate Aryans could substantially increase their wealth by trading their small businesses abroad for larger ones in Germany, an opportunity luring them back to the Reich.

The Jews were trading down, but the trade increased their chances of being accepted as immigrants by the country hosting the old Aryan businesses they now owned. An Aryan expatriate who had lived for years in the United States traded his New Jersey house for one owned by a Jewish family in Germany, who were not only promised the American residence but were also promised the Aryan's ice business.[136]

The working of assorted emigration principles in real life can be illustrated with a case study. This case also demonstrates interests that foreign business people had in the war on Jews, and how foreign courts protected those interests. A wealthy Jew from Dresden took out insurance with Lloyd's of London against confiscation or destruction of his property. While he was abroad on a business trip in spring 1933, Nazis took possession of his house, alleging the victim had been aiding communists and promoting corruption. The regime made free use of the premises and contents; for example, Nazis exploited the wine cellar while hosting a party there. Lloyd's resisted the insured's claim for compensation on grounds that the regime had not confiscated the property but was simply collecting a flight tax of RM 800,000. A British judge ruled that the insured had not lost his property because German authorities, through their willingness to discuss the matter, recognized his continued ownership. The judge was particularly swayed by a letter the victim's representative sent to Nazi authorities, in which the victim refused to recognize the regime's claim to his property—evidence, the judge said, that the victim himself did not believe his property had been taken by the regime. Nonetheless, the judge ruled, government occupation of the insured's house limited the insured's use of his property, thereby causing a partial loss, and Lloyd's had to pay for that partial loss.[137]

A case from Sweden is also worth consideration. In 1939 a Swedish court ruled that when both the exiled Jewish owner and the Reich commissioner of the same business submitted a bill for the same transaction, the Jewish owner would be paid rather than the Reich commissioner.[138] An observer noted, however, that money owed to the Jew had to be paid through a debt-clearing arrangement between Sweden and Germany, an arrangement requiring the money to go through Germany, leaving the regime in control of the funds.[139] In effect, the court awarded moral high ground to the Jew and awarded his money to the Nazis.

Such cases demonstrate support given to Aryanization mechanisms by foreign courts. International legal support cloaked the Holocaust with international legal credibility. Illegality of Nazi measures may have been apparent to judges at the Nuremberg Military Tribunal, but was less apparent to their colleagues who had opportunity to evaluate the Holocaust when it was underway. Their refusal to recognize its illegality not only demonstrated that judges may experience fundamental ignorance of law despite their erudition; their stance also helped Nazis see the war on Jews as consistent with international legal standards, and helped defendants at the Nuremberg Military Tribunal to portray those postwar proceedings incorrectly as mere victors' vengeance.

Not all foreign courts supported the Holocaust. A Yugoslav court refused to register the appointment of a Nazi trustee running the Austrian home office of a Sarajevo branch firm. The court held Aryanization to be illegal under Yugoslav law and refused assistance that Nazis had sought in taking over the Sarajevo branch.[140] We can speculate about what might have happened if such understandings of law been more prevalent, but such speculation would be idle.

The Nazi regime eventually eased its limits on trade in Jew-tainted property, with municipal pawn shops allowed to purchase jewels and silverware from Jews.[141] In February 1939 a decree ordered Jews to turn in personal property to "appropriate organizations." Items were then sold, with national or local governments getting the money. The Reichsbank received coins and gold bullion thusly confiscated.[142]

If property was not required by government agencies, those agencies could sell it at public auction and take the proceeds.[143] Sales were not limited to household goods of Jews. Crystal Night operations yielded large quantities of store merchandise. As one Nazi official put it, "There is no question of returning the goods which were taken away from the Jews because one does not know their original owners. . . . Goods will be checked, and shall be sold to [Aryan] retail-shops."[144]

When Aryan purchasers made unfair offers to Jewish property owners, the Jews knew they would receive no compensation at all if the government took the property through forfeiture and sold it to the Aryans; such interlock of government forfeitures with private Aryanizations was broad and deliberate. Threat of forfeiture was an engine that powered Aryanization. For example, by June of 1938 police were pulling over Jewish drivers for minor traffic violations and confiscating the cars.[145] Austrian Nazis applied a distinct touch to that practice; taking possession of the cars but forcing Jewish victims to continue paying for upkeep.[146] That summer Old Reich Jews had to obtain new license plates that identified their cars as Jew-tainted property.[147] To avoid possible forfeiture to police (or other mishap promoted by new license plates), one automobile owner recalled, "I drove to a car rental firm. 'Do you want this car for five hundred marks?' I asked. The salesman was speechless. My current 'Mucki' was a 1938 model of far greater value. It did not take long before we came to terms."[148] The wisdom of such action was demonstrated in December, when the government confiscated all automobiles and motorcycles owned by Jews.[149]

PRIVATE BENEFITS FROM CONFISCATIONS

Having examined principles of forfeiture and Aryanization, let us more closely examine benefits received by Aryans who participated in the Holocaust.

One benefit was business advice from the regime. Assistance was available to Aryans who did not understand the Aryanization process. The Reich League of Medium and Large Retail Enterprises published information on how to take best advantage of Aryanization opportunities, emphasizing ways to avoid paying too much for a Jew-tainted enterprise and ways to exploit goodwill that the old owner had built up with customers.[150]

Advice on how to avoid paying too much was hardly needed. Fear permeated Aryanizations; even in 1935 an observer noted Jewish business people frantically selling out at any price.[151] In April 1938 an Aryan merchant from Munich said, "I was so disgusted by the brutal . . . and extortionary methods employed against the Jews that, from now on, I refuse to be involved in any way in connection with Aryanizations, although this means losing a handsome fee. . . . As an old, honest and upstanding businessman, I [can] no longer stand by and countenance the way many 'Aryan' businessmen, entrepreneurs and the like . . . are shamelessly attempting to grab up Jewish shops and factories, etc. as cheap as possible and for a ridiculous price. These people are like vultures swarming down, their eyes bleary, their tongues hanging out with greed, to feed upon the Jewish carcass."[152]

Bargain prices were typical. In 1933 the Jewish owner of a Mannheim shipping enterprise offered to sell it for RM 1,000 (about $300).[153] That same year a Jewish doctor offered his practice, all medical equipment and furnishings, an office with rent paid through March 1935, and the family home for RM 5,000.[154] Lawyers and judges offered legal libraries at fire sale prices.[155] In 1934 an Aryan publishing firm spent RM 6 million to acquire the Jew-tainted Ullstein firm valued between RM 50 and 60 million.[156] Tax authorities assessed the Mosse publishing company at over RM 40 million, but an Aryan buyer acquired it in 1934 for RM 5 million.[157] An observer in 1936 reported, "I heard of one merchant, a typical case, who was forced to sell a million-mark business to an Aryan for 100,000 marks."[158] Another observer noted in July 1938, "A Jewish business enterprise of an agreed net value of 6,000,000 marks was recently 'Aryanized' for 200,000 marks in foreign exchange."[159] Still another observer reported in December 1938, "A Jew in North Germany, who owned a factory worth 1,300,000 marks, was forced to sell it for 800,000 marks—relatively a much higher price than many get. Then he had to give 100,000 marks to the Nazi Labor Front and then pay 175,000 marks as an emigration tax, 140,000 marks as his share of the [Crystal Night fine] . . . and 50,000 marks as a 100 per cent tax on his purchases since 1933. Of the 335,000 marks remaining he could transfer only 7 per cent, which gave him a net of 23,450 marks in foreign currency for his factory worth 1,300,000 marks."[160] After Crystal Night the standard price for a Jewish business in Nuremberg was 10 percent of its ordinary market value.[161] A victim's net receipts could be lower than these figures suggest; if the Aryan buyer needed to spend money to restore a deteriorated Jewish business, that expense would be deducted from the agreed price.[162]

Even small transactions were bargains for Aryans. For RM 700 in 1935 a Franconia farmer acquired a synagogue to use for grain storage.[163] In the 1930s a Jewish family decided to emigrate; a family member recalled an Aryan friend's visit to their house one night. "He wanted to buy it. The house was valued at 21,000 marks, but he told father that since it was a Jewish house, he had to pay only 13,000 marks for it."[164] Franconia *Gau* official Fritz Schoeller purchased a house from a Jew. A Nazi report noted, "The house has a nominal value of RM 43,300 and an exchange value of RM 50,000. The buying price was fixed at RM 5,000."[165] That price was more favorable than terms received by Jews in Vienna, whose houses and businesses were Aryanized during Crystal Night for RM 10 apiece.[166] Austrian Nazis were particularly aggressive; within a few weeks of the *Anschluss* an official announcement said Aryans had acquired a third of Jewish property in Austria. Surveying the Austrian scene the *New York Times* said "thousands of 'Aryans' are eager to acquire confiscated businesses";[167] at that time 60,000 Jewish businesses in Austria were available to Aryan applicants.[168] A few days after Crystal Night *The Times* of London reported that "Jewish businesses are changing hands with great rapidity and at extremely low prices. At least one case is known of a large industrial concern which was finally sold at one five-hundredth part of its value."[169] Far earlier, in October 1935 the *Westdeutscher Beobachter* said so many Jews were trying to sell their businesses that not enough buyers were available.[170]

Aryan buyers did not need to possess the purchase price themselves. Even today most banks would gladly make loans backed by mortgages on property exceeding the loan value by 1,000 percent. Aryan banks found such business so lucrative that they acted as matchmakers between Jewish firms and Aryan buyers,[171] a service for which banks collected a fee equal to 2 percent of the purchase price. Banks made still more money by requiring purchasers to bank with them.[172] In addition to providing capital for Aryan purchasers, banks also encouraged Aryanization by denying capital to credit-worthy Jewish businesses (either by calling old loans or refusing new ones), thereby forcing them to sell out to Aryans.[173] One victimized department store sold out to a bank for under 1 percent of the store's worth.[174] In such transactions banks could make fortunes even if acquired businesses were resold at bargain prices to Aryans; banks took over Jewish businesses on speculation and then looked for Aryan buyers.[175] Profits from financing Aryanization were so good that entrepreneurs established private banks devoted to that business.[176] Banks themselves, of course, were subject to Aryanization if Jewish; the Aryan Merk and Finck private bank in Munich apparently became Germany's largest through that means,[177] and Burkhardt & Co. was established specifically to Aryanize the Hirschland Bank.[178] Moreover, whenever a Jewish bank was Aryanized, factories and other commercial enterprises controlled by that Jewish bank automatically came under control of Aryans who acquired the bank.[179] For example, when the Jewish Bleichroeder and Arnhold banks were acquired by the Aryan Hardy bank, Hardy specialized in their brewery and ceramics businesses, with Dresdner Bank taking up their other interests.[180] Bank control over commercial enterprises is probably one reason why so many banks were Aryanized by industrial groups rather than by Aryan bankers.[181] For example, purchasers of the M.M. Warburg and Co. bank in Hamburg included Siemens-Schuckert Werke A.G. and Siemens and Halske A.G.[182]

Apparently the regime eventually noticed the bonanza income that banks were mining from Aryanization and decided to set up its own middleman. In autumn 1935 the Nazi Economics Information Agency announced plans for a new central corporation that would either buy Jew-tainted businesses outright and sell them to Aryans, or else make loans to Aryans who could not arrange ordinary bank financing.[183] Plans to establish an institution for helping "business people" unable to meet bankers' standards demonstrated that a significant number of Aryans who sought Jew-tainted enterprises lacked financial and entrepreneurial resources needed for business success. The regime was replacing competent Jewish business owners with incompetent Aryan ones. Admittedly management can be more important to mercantile success than ownership, but the regime was even forcing Jews to give up management of concerns they were still permitted to own.[184] Small wonder that consumer goods and services declined in quality during the Third Reich.

The scope of confiscation went beyond purchase of Jew-tainted property. Ostracism, for example, promoted confiscation of pensions. Companies had no obligation to pay pension benefits to dismissed Jewish executives;[185] Jews forfeited those pensions to their employers. Charitable organizations, too, profited from such confiscations; when the Central Organization of German Deaf dropped Jewish members in 1933 they lost pensions which they had bought through subscription in earlier years.[186] The April 1933 Civil Service Law limited the government's pension obligations to Jews dismissed from public employment.[187] Subsequent regulations under the Civil Service Law eliminated pensions received by many Jews, surviving spouses, or children.[188]

Nazi seizures were so thorough as to cover classes of property unfamiliar to many Americans. Americans normally do not think of debt as property, but a U.S. diplomat in Berlin noted "innumerable instances in which Nazis used their positions in the Party to void debts" owed to Jewish creditors.[189] Rural debtors failed to pay Jewish cattle dealers, helping to run them out of business.[190] The practice was seen in urban areas as well. After a Nazi beer hall operator became tardy in paying commercial rent for a year and then outright stopped paying, he received an eviction notice. The tenant visited the Jewish landlord and warned, "I care nothing about the law; we are now in power, remember that." The landlord called the police. Not long afterward four Nazis roused him from his bed in the dead of night. "I had to sign the order to the Sheriff cancelling the order of eviction, and had to sign another letter to the tenant Zink, stating that the order of eviction was called off. I hesitated to sign and they drew their revolvers on me, and my wife in terror fell to her knees, and then I signed."[191] This was in March 1933. Publicity awarded to such incidents had a gratifying effect. In 1934 when a landlord was taken into protective custody after filing a civil suit to evict a tenant, about 800 such court actions were quickly dropped by Berlin landlords.[192] Nazi debtors received forgiveness of cash loans under threat of violence to Jewish lenders.[193] Nazis even extorted refunds of debts already paid: Due to flaws in merchandise, in 1931 a Chemnitz glove manufacturer consented to a discount of RM 3,400 in a bill to a St. Louis textile importer. In 1933 the manufacturer told the importer to refund the money, or the importer's Jewish agent in Germany would be murdered. The Jew fled the country.[194] As years passed and Nazis acquired more expertise in such matters, strong arm tactics were less needed. In a 1938 meeting of high Nazi officials, one explained,

> In Austria, individuals, not institutions, owe the Jews 184 billion Reichsmarks. This way the Jews certainly have invested money in a way we don't like. . . . A dependency of the Aryan artisan from the Jewish creditor is created which we do not want. Now the question arises, and I would answer yes. Should trustees not be created to administer these debts. . . . Therefore it does not have to be paid. . . . We won't simply pay but leave the decision for payment up to the trusteeship.[195]

We may be confident that Nazi trustees were not fastidious about protecting Jewish creditors. Relying on civic duty and the educational nature of law, Aryan debtors cited decrees issued after Crystal Night as grounds for refusing to pay debts owed to Jews.[196]

Cancelling debts owed to Jews could extend to the most petty transactions. Soon after Nazis took power, Dortmund's mayor declared that Jews could not redeem municipal pawn tickets they held.[197] SA members would make purchases on credit from Jewish merchants and refuse to pay, or intimidate merchants into accepting a heavy discount for cash transactions.[198] In 1937 a court ruled that husbands were not responsible for debts incurred at Jewish stores by wives.[199] The short-term effect of this ruling was a windfall for Aryan households where wives had run up bills with Jewish merchants. The long-term effect was to discourage those business people from granting credit to wives of Aryan households, thereby reducing sales. Wives were willing to defy the boycott because in that era German wives had an allowance for household shopping. They could keep any surplus, so they had a personal financial motive for patronizing Jewish merchants who offered prices lower than those at Aryan stores. Some housewives may have depended on safety in numbers to avoid pillory danger; *Der Angriff* was horrified at the number who thronged to 1938 midsummer sales offered by Berlin's Jewish merchants.[200] Wives were not the only Aryans who appreciated savings provided by Jewish merchants: "Jewish shops . . . sell brown shirts at reduced prices. Outside one emporium a Nazi in uniform was seen asking a passing boy to go and buy one for him."[201] In 1934 Frankfurt citizens were irked about boycott picketers hindering them from shopping at stores with the best prices.[202] A Nazi economic press service reminded Aryan merchants that they needed to deliver good merchandise at good prices in order to succeed; business success could not be assured simply by suppressing Jewish competitors.[203]

HOW SEIZURES WERE CONDUCTED

Power corrupts, and money is power. Profits in confiscations were so vast that transactions swirled violently in an atmosphere of wickedness. Samples of that atmosphere merit examination.

Government administrators in Berlin became alarmed that provincial Nazi party leaders and organizations were not only skimming Aryanization profits but requiring bribes in order for transactions to be completed. An April 1938 law invited corruption by requiring Aryanizations to be approved by Nazi party *Gauleiter*.[204] On April 26 a reform decree required Aryanizations to have government approval as well,[205] thereby monitoring what Nazi party organizations were doing. In September 1938 the Reich Chancellor of the Exchequer forbade party organizations from accepting any sort of compensation for assistance in Aryanizations.[206] Subsequent attention to obedience of this order documented the atmosphere of Aryanization.

> Shares of the Mars-Werke, Nurnberg, with a face value of Reichsmark 112,500, were acquired through publishing house manager Fink for the Gauleiter [Streicher] according to the latter's instructions. . . . These shares were in the possession of the Jewish banking house Kohn, the proprieter of which was at that time in protective custody. Verlagsdirecktor Fink, as agent for the Gauleiter, acquired the parcel of Mars-Werke shares from this Jew at 5 per cent of the face value, i.e., the sum of Reichsmark 5,600.
>
> . . . The Gauleiter . . . gave the order to transfer the parcel of shares from the account of the banking firm Kohn to the account of Fink at the Dresdner Bank. He further ordered that his name should not be mentioned at all in connection with the transaction.
>
> By order of the Gauleiter, Fink withdrew Reichsmark 5,600 from a Stuermer account.[207]

The preceding narration is from Nazi archives, but the coercive nature of Aryanization is also documented elsewhere. Raymond H. Geist, a senior American diplomat in Berlin, stated,

> I knew well the leading German cigarette manufacturer, Eugene Garbaty. . . . He was compelled to sell his factory, worth between seven and ten million marks for the sum of one million marks. . . . Garbaty applied for a passport and received one only after paying a bribe of 500,000 marks to the corrupt Count Heldorf [*sic*], Chief of Police in Berlin, and enough other fines to equal the million marks that he had received for his factory. . . .
>
> Another instance of the same nature occurred with respect to my landlord, Mr. Franz Rinkel. . . . One Dr. Lilienthal, a fanatical Nazi lawyer practicing in Berlin, coveted Rinkel's house. . . . My landlord was approached by Dr. Lilienthal and told the price the latter desired to pay, a mere fraction of the value of the estate. . . . He sold because he knew that if he did not, he would be accused of some trumped-up crime and taken away to the concentration

camp. . . . I know that on many occasions where it was thought necessary to increase the pressure, the prospective purchaser or his agent would be accompanied by a uniformed S.A. or S.S. man. I know because I lived in the immediate neighborhood and know the individuals concerned, that Baron von Neurath, one time Foreign Minister of Germany, got his house from a Jew in this manner. Indeed, he was my next door neighbor. . . . Alfred Rosenburg [*sic*], who lived in the same street with me, purloined a house from a Jew in a similar fashion.[208]

When von Ribbentrop spotted a country home he wanted, he had the owner dispatched to a concentration camp and took over the estate.[209] When Goebbels offered RM 300,000 for Jakob Goldschmidt's magnificent villa near Berlin the Jewish banker accepted the offer. Goebbels, however, never paid.[210] When banker August von Finck Aryanized J. Dreyfus and Company he also took Dreyfus's 7,500-acre Bavarian estate—but without paying for it.[211] In February 1938 the Gestapo harassed a young man for days, saying harassment would end if the man's father would sell his store. His father finally agreed. The Gestapo approved a purchase price of RM 500,000, which the father considered to be fair market value. He only received RM 130,000, however. The rest was retained by the Gestapo.[212] Such tactics were not limited to persons of high wealth or high office. An observer in 1933 described an environment in which "an enterprising Storm Trooper put his National Socialist card in his pocket, his swastika emblem in his buttonhole and presented himself at the office of a prosperous business as its commissar. Thousands of such officials were never authorized by the authorities. The proprietor or manager might telephone to headquarters, of course, but he seldom did; he had read too much about concentration camps."[213] Five years later another observer noted that such a mode of operation was still typical; any Jew who "still owns a business has more reason to tremble than the rest. Some fine day a party functionary appears and reveals that the *Arbeitsfront* . . . intends to purchase the business; it will set a price and determine the method of payment; a word of opposition means the concentration camp."[214] After the *Anschluss* a man in Nazi uniform stopped the midnight performance at Vienna's Femina Cabaret by walking on stage, announcing that the cabaret owners had failed to accept an Aryanization purchase offer, and therefore the business was Jewish and hereby closed until an Aryan trustee could take over management. "The speaker was heard in silence and he departed in silence, and the waiters had scarcely grasped the implication of his statement in time to present the bills before the more nervous Austrian clients fled from the building. Similar scenes were enacted the same night in two other Vienna cabaret houses."[215]

Aryanizations proceeded with a rude vigor from the start: In 1933 three gun-wielding Cologne Nazis burst into a Jew's residence, forced him to open a safe, and took RM 800 found inside. Apparently the party, not the police, disciplined the three; the act was not considered a criminal matter.[216] In July 1933 Herbert L. W. Goering complained to Heydrich about scams in which Aryans who coveted a Jewish business would collude with SS men who arrested the Jewish owner briefly. Upon release the victim would be visited by the Aryans, who claimed responsibility for getting the SS to relent, and suggested that the Jewish business person show thanks: Either give them money or let the Aryans into influential positions in the business where their connections would "protect" the enterprise.[217] Also in 1933 two employees of an 800-person Berlin clothing firm denounced their Jewish employer for having *Reichsbanner* pennants in the store's basement. The two workers accompanied four Nazis who demanded an explanation. The merchant said the items were obviously old stock that had not been discarded and that he could hardly be expected to know about every item on the premises. The Nazis thereupon beat him, took his passport, and relieved him of RM 450. He was hardly in a position to fire the two employees and decided to avoid returning to his store while they continued to work there.[218] On a summer day in that same year hundreds of Nuremberg's Jewish merchants, lawyers, and doctors were marched to barracks after storm troopers seized bonds, cash, and banking documents found in the Jews' houses (receipts were given only occasionally, and not always for everything taken).[219] Also that summer, thousands of Munich's Jewish merchants had been given a taste of Dachau.[220] The connection between such arrests and property acquisitions by Nazis was noticed and publicly commented upon at the time.[221] Similar tactics were used in Austria during consolidation of the *Anschluss*: SA men routinely pushed into homes of Jewish professionals and left with cash and jewelry;[222] business owners who resisted Aryanization were arrested and held until they agreed to sale terms and signed a statement that the agreement was voluntary.[223] Sometimes customers of a Jewish business, instead of owners, were targeted for intimidation. In June 1938 police raids on Jewish cafés in Berlin's fashionable Kurfürstendamm district frightened customers, thereby discouraging business and promoting Aryanization of the cafés.[224] In 1938 a Nazi actor wanted the Munich apartment of an elderly Jewish woman; he simply denounced her to authorities who ordered her to vacate. Faced with loss of her home she committed suicide.[225] A Jew recalled the autumn 1938 atmosphere in Middle Franconia, "Through terror acts or by being compelled to sign, people were forced to sell all their belongings for a bargain price."[226] The U.S. ambassador privately reported to Washington, D.C. about Nazi success at simply urging individual Jewish business persons "to sell out at a price named arbitrarily by the prospective 'Aryan' purchaser."[227] Sometimes the SS provided an Aryan buyer and dictated the price.[228] Tax authorities could aid Aryanization by putting a business under "tax examination," halting sale of any goods under examination until tax inspectors were satisfied.[229] Jews who were nonetheless bold enough to hold out might receive a government order directing them to turn over operation of the business to Aryans. In autumn 1936 Jewish drug store owners were given one week to find Aryans to run their stores; the Jews could continue as owners but would have no say in the business.[230] The chief of the Nazi druggists association declared that the law made hundreds of pharmacies available for lease by Aryan druggists.[231] After the Austrian *Anschluss* even the formalities were disregarded. The Nazi Party expropriated Vienna's Zwieback department store, along with hotels, restaurants, and shops in the city. Nazis who wanted Vienna's Kraus & Schober department store arrested the store's officials and seized the business.[232] In Burgenland province Nazis made Jewish shopkeepers close up and attempted to push thousands of Jews into Hungary, but Hungarians closed the border to them. "The Jews," said a contemporary account, "including many women and hundreds of children, were then driven in trucks to Vienna and left in the city's Jewish quarters. They had been forced to leave their homes without an opportunity to remove any of their belongings, and they arrived penniless and without overcoats although the weather was unusually cold. The children were half-frozen and starving."[233] They fared better than Vienna's stamp dealers; when police confiscated philatelic inventories in December 1938 owners were sent to concentration camps.[234] From the very beginning brutality was used in property confiscations: In July 1933 Nazis ousted Eutin's mayor and put him under protective custody until he agreed to forego salary owed, plus pay RM 3,000 to the government after release. In this case authorities announced, "Plaintiff and his counsel declare that all their statements and agreements were made of their own free will and that no duress of any kind was exercised."[235] Still, he fared better than some. As part of Aryanization, in May 1933 the regime forced the Mosse publishing firm to spend an amount equivalent to the previous fifteen years' earnings to endow a war veterans fund.[236] Mosse was not singled out for such treatment either. When the Jew-tainted Simson Company was expropriated in 1935 the regime took several million marks from the firm as a penalty for alleged profiteering during the Weimar Republic.[237]

Streicher's minions applied a clever twist to Aryanizations: Aryan merchants were forced to help finance Aryanization of properties desired by Franconia's Nazi party. For example the party and the Nazi Smallholders Association (the Hago) formed a stock company to take over a Nuremberg department store. All Aryan merchants in Nuremberg had to buy at least RM 500 of shares as a show of civic duty.[238] Offices of other *Gauleiter* suggested establishment of funds where Aryan business people would contribute to help other Aryans buy Jewish businesses,[239] but Streicher's associates crossed the fuzzy line between civic duty and shake down.

Property could even go to the government by Aryanization rather than forfeiture. In 1938 the city of Fürth paid RM 180 for one real estate parcel valued at RM 20,000, and paid RM 100 for other property valued at RM 100,000.[240] Minister of Justice Franz Gürtner delicately noted, "Rights individual owners of real estate might have in respect of adjoining property, have suffered a certain curtailment in favour of institutions that are of particular importance to the community."[241] For example, a state university quarreled with an adjacent synagogue about abutment rights; after Crystal Night the synagogue agreed to sell its wrecked property to the university. A historian who examined the contract found it indistinguishable from any standard real estate transaction. "What makes it part and parcel of mass murder is something invisible": The synagogue official who signed the contract was let out of Buchenwald expressly for the purpose of making the contract.[242] After Crystal Night Goering recognized development potential in prime real estate lots occupied by damaged synagogues. "All these not completely intact, shall be razed by the Jews. The Jews shall pay for it. . . . We shall build parking lots in their places or new buildings. . . . The Jews shall have to remove the damaged or burned synagogues, and shall have to provide us with ready free space."[243] That practice was already underway. Back in the spring Nazis announced that Munich's main synagogue was occupying space urgently needed for a parking lot. For tax purposes the structure was assessed at RM 700,000 (and of course the normal market value would have been far greater). When the Jewish community declined a Nazi offer of RM 100,000 for the property, the Nazis demolished the building anyway.[244]

In addition to intimidation, Nazis could knock down prices by other methods. One method was to refuse advertising to Jewish firms, even refuse commercial directory listings,[245] so as to cripple sales and reduce market value of a basically sound firm (which would likely recover its profitability once boycott actions were lifted). Another method was the general customer boycott described in the previous chapter; *Deutsche Justiz* reassured citizens that temporary hardship suffered by Aryan employees of a boycotted enterprise would end when the Jewish owner submitted to Aryanization.[246] Compassionate authorities in Schwerin reduced suffering of Aryan employees by closing Jewish businesses while ordering the owners to pay the Aryans two months' wages.[247] Still another peaceful method of encouraging Aryanization was to issue "job security" regulations virtually forbidding a Jewish store owner from dismissing Aryan employees.[248] Thus if boycott action against the store reduced revenues below the amount needed to meet the payroll, the owner either had to go broke paying unneeded Aryan workers, or else sell out. The situation gave potential Aryan buyers a strong bargaining position. After Hitler Youth looted a jewelry store in June 1938 the Jewish proprietor said, "We have been starving for a long time. Business was dead. The law prevents us from getting out of a lease or dismissing an employee as long as a penny can be squeezed out."[249] Government also promoted Aryanization by revoking business licenses held by Jews unless they sold out to Aryans.[250] Another type of government intervention was illustrated in Magdeburg when three executives of the Bachrach Brothers department store were arrested for alleged race defilement, an event which prompted police to close the Jewish store.[251] The closed store produced no revenue, and owners then had an economic reason to sell the business. Threats of government intervention were a routine bargaining technique to drive down the price in Aryanizations.[252]

Not all Jewish businesses disappeared through Aryanization. Many simply vanished. Aryanization was not only intended to transfer successful Jewish businesses to Aryan owners but to reduce competition;[253] many Jewish businesses were liquidated rather than transferred. Those selling candy, tobacco, wine, or fabrics were special targets for closure rather than transfer to Aryans.[254] Other shops were targeted for closure because of their geographical location rather than their merchandise.[255] A secret wartime U.S. government report noted, "Of 3,750 Jewish retail establishments in Berlin on August 1, 1938, only 700 were transferred to 'Aryan' hands; 3,050 disappeared."[256] Two careful historians later put the total of Germany's Jewish businesses in April 1938 at 39,532. A year later half those firms had either been Aryanized or were in the process. The rest had disappeared.[257] A contemporary report declared that two-thirds of Jewish businesses had been closed rather than Aryanized.[258] At the completion of Aryanization in Vienna only 20 percent of old Jewish businesses were open under Aryans; the other 80 percent had been closed permanently.[259] Jew-tainted inventories and other business property did not vanish if a Jewish business disappeared. Most likely they were acquired at bargain prices by Aryan business competitors. Even before Crystal Night Aryan trade associations would go to a Jewish shop engaged in some trade, buy its inventory, and close down the Jewish competitor forthwith.[260] Note the interplay between Aryanization and the social ostracism described in our previous chapter. Steps to ostracize Jews by forbidding them to pursue various businesses and employment opened the assets involved in such work to covetous Aryans. Those assets ranged from factory equipment, to medical office supplies, to sample cases belonging to traveling salesmen. Ostracism not only gave jobs to Aryans; it presented them with wealth. Even identification of victims promoted property seizures. Supposedly all Jews were criminals, therefore all their property had been acquired criminally and could be rightly confiscated by the government without compensation.[261] Eventually an SS order said that henceforth all official discussion of Jewish possessions would simply refer to them as "goods originating from thefts."[262]

The Aryanization program was a key element in creating the business community's support for the Holocaust. Participants of course did not admit this. Goering termed Aryanizations of business enterprises as "an ordinary business transaction . . . one merchant selling, the other one buying."[263] He explained, "We shall try to induce them through slight, and then through stronger pressure, and through clever maneuvering—to let themselves be pushed out voluntarily."[264] If the property transfer was not a forfeiture to the state, the transfer was considered voluntary—the property owner had a free choice between receiving money or receiving imprisonment. After careful study of life in one German town, a historian found that intimidation was less in some Aryanizations than in others, and purchase prices were more fair in some than in others. Nonetheless, "with few exceptions, and with a truth which finally became absolute, all liquidations of Jewish property between 1933 and 1945 were forced."[265]

CRYSTAL NIGHT FINE

In our discussion of property confiscation we have thus far considered Aryanization and forfeiture, and we have also seen how the emigrant "flight tax" was used to confiscate property. One specific confiscation measure was so prominent, however, that it deserves special mention. That measure was the fine imposed on all Jews as "atonement" for the murder of a German diplomat by a Jew in France, the murder which served as the Nazis' excuse for Crystal Night.

On November 10, 1938, Hitler conferred with Goering and Goebbels. Goebbels said Jews should be fined as part of the Crystal Night attack, with proceeds going to each *Gau*. Goering considered the whole matter impossible, and suspected Berlin *Gauleiter* Goebbels was pushing it for his own *Gau*'s financial benefit. But Hitler agreed to a RM 1 billion fine.[266] When Nazi leaders met at the Air Ministry two days later, they already knew that decision. Their discussion on the fine was limited to finding a good way to implement it.[267] A few hours after the Air Ministry meeting, Goering decreed the Crystal Night fine.[268] As punishment for their "hostile attitude" Germany's Jews were to forfeit RM 1 billion to the government, payable in four installments due December 15, February 15, May 15, and August 15. Using property registration figures, the Finance Ministry imposed a flat 20 percent levy on all property owned by Jews (foreign nationals exempted). The fine was figured on the value of property shown in the most recent registration documents prior to November 12, not on value after Crystal Night destruction or as realized in a post-Crystal Night sacrifice sale.[269] Jews who protested the Finance Ministry figures risked prosecution for having falsified the value of their property in registration documents.[270] After Crystal Night a Munich Jew sold real estate supposedly worth RM 100,000 but only realized RM 18,000, an amount insufficient to pay the fine assessed against the property.[271] The regime quickly realized that "little chauffeurs" were profiting from such deals at the expense of the state. In response, fine collectors were authorized to accept real estate at the value it held in the most recent property registration forms prior to Crystal Night.[272] The Jew lost the real estate regardless of whether it went to a chauffeur or the government; the barter arrangement simply helped the government by cutting out the chauffeurs. Indeed, soon after the barter system began, Aryans had to buy official permits to acquire real estate from Jews; the amount paid for the permit allowed the regime to recover any windfall profit the buyer might make.[273] As an alternative to transferring real estate when paying the fine, Jews could transfer corporation stock. Because Jews could not sell stock to raise cash, such transfers were an opportunity for Jews to salvage something from those blocked assets.[274] Although circumstances of such stock and real estate transactions were hideous, those transfers were exceptions to the normal undervaluing of Jewish property. Real estate values were set by property registration forms that declared values much higher than post-Crystal Night market prices, and stock prices were determined by the stock market. When paying the Crystal Night fine, Jews who bartered real estate and stocks were cheated less than Jews who sold property to generate cash for paying the fine. That economic reality encouraged Jews to give up their stocks and real estate, expediting the regime's goal of removing those particular assets from Jewish hands as soon as possible. The government was careful to protect the value of property received in this way; when the fine's second installment came due in February 1939 much real estate received in the first installment remained unsold,[275] apparently to avoid a market glut that would depress prices. Securities given in fine payment by Jews were delivered to the *Preussische Seehandlungsbank*, which then sold them in small enough lots to avoid depressing the market.[276] Talk arose about those sales giving corporations an opportunity to Aryanize their finances in a package deal by buying back their own securities while purchasing government bonds.[277] In addition to the *Preussische Seehandlungsbank* other German banks were involved. For example, to pay the fine a concentration camp inmate told a U.S. bank to turn over his American cash assets to the *Deutsche Golddiscontbank* of Berlin while turning over mortgages on U.S. real estate to *Deutsche Bank Filiale München*.[278]

Although no Jew was allowed to collect insurance settlements for Crystal Night damages, insurers paid those settlements to the government, which credited them to the amount a Jew owed for the fine.[279] That procedure may have permitted some Jews to pay the fine without having to sell assets. A major goal of the fine, however, was to make Jews turn over items that the regime could convert into foreign exchange (foreign purchases of Nazi bonds were less robust than the regime wished). For example, Jews could deliver jewelry, precious metals, and art objects to fine payment offices.[280] Some Jews turned over insurance policies which had cash values,[281] cash values that remained undiminished by Aryanization pressures.

If a Jew was unable to pay the fine, the owed sum was added to fines paid by other Jews.[282] When total receipts appeared insufficient to reach RM 1 billion, Jews were ordered to pay an additional 5 percent of their wealth in the autumn of 1939.[283] In theory only the Jewish partner in a mixed marriage was liable for the fine,[284] and Jews who lacked enough wealth to file a property registration form were exempt,[285] but Nazi legal principles did not assure exemption. The Minister of Finance did rule, however, that capital value of pensions and allowances be excluded in calculating a Jew's share of the fine.[286] In addition to the Crystal Night fine, which all Jews had to pay, some Jews were assessed personal fines on top of the general one.[287]

Simultaneous with the Crystal Night fine decree, another decree said "operation of retail shops, mail order houses, independent exercise of handicrafts is forbidden to Jews" as of January 1, 1939. It was also illegal for "Jews from the same date to offer goods or services in the markets of all kinds, fairs, or exhibitions or to advertise such or accept orders therefor."[288] We have already noted this post-Crystal Night mass closure of Jewish business enterprise, but now we see how effects of the fine and closure decrees combined to put more force behind the Aryanization drive—store closures curbed incomes of Jews and thereby compelled them to sell off yet more property in order to pay the fine. Ensuing bargains may have contributed to sentiments expressed in confidential Nazi reports from Speyer and Munich, that citizens were delighted with the fine and the ban on Jew-tainted business.[289] At the time a Nazi official noted that Jews could only sell at an "amount that is far below the value,"[290] thereby assuring that many Jews would be wiped out financially by the fine. And indeed, a careful contemporary observer found that to be the case.[291] The fine even pushed forfeitures deep into home life. As of January 1, 1939, Jews had to turn in "typewriters, adding machines, electric household appliances, binoculars, cameras, radios." Officials put a valuation on those items and credited that amount to the Jew's Crystal Night fine account.[292]

Crystal Night insurance claims provided another source of confiscation income for the government. A Berlin insurance broker reported Crystal Night claims from Jews totaling RM 500 million; a Rhineland broker reported RM 700 million.[293] Still another estimate put losses at RM 1 billion.[294] Insurance companies asked if they were liable to compensate Jewish policy holders for losses in the state-sanctioned Crystal Night riots. "The companies are liable," Goering declared, but "the [insurance settlement] money belongs to the State. That's quite clear."[295] Goering thereby found a way to make money from Jewish property even if it was destroyed. The more vandalism by government agents, the more income for the government. That government stance gave insurers strong incentive to drop Jewish policy holders, adding to their ostracism. Moreover, the November 12 decree for the Restoration of the Street Scene in Relation to Jewish Business not only confiscated property insurance settlements but ordered Jewish business owners to repair Crystal Night damages.[296] After the Crystal Night loss, Jewish business owners suffered an equivalent loss as they paid for repairs to premises they could no longer operate and had to turn over in good condition to Aryans who gave inadequate compensation.

We have seen how property confiscations benefited the government, business people, and well-connected persons. We have also seen how turbulent SA men could extort assets from victims. We have yet to consider, however, ways in which ordinary, peaceful, law-abiding citizens benefited from Holocaust forfeitures.

Some benefits were indirect. The Jew-tainted Simson Company was perhaps best known as an armaments manufacturer, but also made bicycles and baby carriages. In celebration of the firm's confiscation in 1935, the regime distributed 1,000 baby carriages to families with four or more children, thus giving ordinary citizens a stake in industrial seizures.[297]

Another class of benefits, however, was direct. When Jews were rounded up for transport to camps, victims could take only a small amount of hand luggage. The remainder of personal possessions stayed behind. Those were distributed to neighbors in two ways.

The first way was informal. Victims typically had advance notice of transport. On their own initiative they might offer possessions to friends, or might be willing to give possessions to Aryans who asked for them. An acquaintance went to a Jew whose mother had just been transported and asked, "Now that your mother'll no longer need them, how about letting me have her two fur coats?"[298] A Jew facing imminent transport gave the family silverware to an Aryan. Someone else asked, "Do you have a suit for me, maybe?" The victim regretfully replied that his suits were registered with the government, but introduced the person to a Jew scheduled to leave in the same transport, who had an un-registered suit that would not be missed at the public auction of the Jews' property after their transport.[299] The matter-of-fact atmosphere and lack of animosity in such property transfers was striking: "You're leaving? Can I have this?" "I'm leaving. You want this?" All such arrangements were private and unpublicized.

The second way of distributing transported Jews' personal possessions was public and very publicized. Government officials would post a notice at the entrance of a victim's residence, declaring that the contents were forfeited to the Reich and would be sold at public auction. These auctions were festive occasions where neighbors acquired household furnishings, fine clothing, and assorted personal luxuries at bargain prices. Everything left behind was sold—even children's garments and toys.[300] The government got the auction proceeds, and Jews' neighbors got the property. It was a win-win scenario for everyone.

This practice was already underway well before mass shipments of Jews to death camps. After Polish Jews who had long lived in Germany were deported, the Saxonian Minister of the Interior wrote to Himmler in 1938:

> I ordered the sealing of residences and of some business premises of the expelled Jews in order to spare the *Reich* avoidable damage claims from the evicted Jews and the Polish government. . . . Securing of these premises . . . results in increased damages for the Aryan creditors of the evicted Jews, damages which I can no longer justify. The Police and I are faced by growing mountains of very urgent complaints. The simple cases, where debts of expelled Jews were unknown or barely known, grow more complicated daily, often because the expellees naturally do not pay regular rents, but on the other hand, rent taxes must still be paid by the landlords. . . . Until now, I have not considered myself empowered to empty the apartments. . . .
>
> However, . . . I can no longer justify current conditions and intend to release police officials as of 10th January 1939, to settle questions raised by the expulsion. I am assuming that none of the evicted Jews will return to Germany. . . . I will permit court bailiffs to decontrol and sell off the property of the evicted Jews, in so far as the owners wish.[301]

Although such a letter does not reveal how closely the regime followed wishes of expelled Jewish property owners, the letter's concern for Aryan creditor and landlord "victims" is an interesting rationale for distributing household goods. Sometimes local officials used their influence to preview items in sealed premises. "As the functionary moved from room to room, his excitement mounted visibly. At the end he burst out 'All my life I have always dreamt of furniture like this!'"[302] Another pleased recipient of Jew-tainted property wrote, "I have a cozy apartment. . . . One bedroom and a living room with all of the accessories. Practically nothing is missing."[303] Spouses of such officials were also allowed previews, giving them opportunity to determine whether desired clothing would fit them properly. Nazi officials were known to skim choice items prior to public offering. Apartment building custodians, also, might use their keys for surreptitious visits that skimmed items for black market sale. Certain classes of property, such as jewels and precious metals, might be excluded from the neighborhood sale and sent to central depots. An SS officer at one depot politely asked the wife of Hitler Youth leader Baldur von Schirach, "Do you want any diamonds? They go at a ridiculous price."[304] A Swedish newspaper correspondent said his wife watched a vacated Jewish residence as an official crew removed property excluded from auction. "The men did not speak to her. They worked calmly and methodically; everything was catalogued, packed and taken away."[305] Disposition of skimmed property occasionally generated ill feelings between the SS and other government agencies.[306] Institutions and individuals asked the SS to reserve items ranging from baby carriages to suitcases.[307] An SS policy directive gave front-line soldiers priority in purchase (via post exchanges) of confiscated "watches and clocks of all kinds, alarm clocks, fountain pens, mechanical pencils, hand and electrical razors, pocket knives, scissors, flashlights, wallets and purses."[308] Other items were available to troops as well. Enclosing an outline of her foot, a woman wrote to a soldier friend, "This is my foot size! The high boots just arrived, [they are] first class. Tell me, could you not procure women's boots, lined inside?"[309] SS policy held that "women's clothing and women's underwear . . . have to be handed over to the office for ethnic Germans against payment. Underwear of pure silk is to be handed over to the Reich Ministry of Economics."[310] Police who handled forfeited property in their community sometimes got first choice in purchases.[311] In late October 1942 Himmler directed that warehouse stocks of confiscated Jew-tainted property be delivered to ethnic Germans. Recipients, he said, were "to be provided each with a dress or suit and, as far as available, with a coat and hat, 3 shirts, appropriate underclothing, and other items of daily use as well as a suitcase. Needy persons are also to be given feather beds, blankets, and bed linen. . . . The matter is very urgent, the things must be at our disposal by Christmas!"[312] "It has to be strictly observed," said another directive, "that the Jewish star is removed from all garments and outer garments which are to be delivered."[313] One Nazi charity protested vehemently that it had received hundreds of garments with Jewish stars sewed on them; moreover many were spoiled by bloodstains.[314] Large supplies of such garments were no secret. A Strasbourg company specialized in processing bloodstained clothing marred by holes and sought a large credit line from Dresdner Bank to expedite business.[315] One wonders what impression such shipments made on recipients.

Enough clothing to fill hundreds of railroad cars was sent to Germans made needy by air bombardment of cities. These shipments were called *Liebesgaben*, love's presents.[316] Eventually Aryans became disgruntled that there were not enough Jewish personal belongings to go around. Tenants of an apartment block in Fürth were disturbed that so much Jewish property was tied up by tax authorities in 1942. "Where is the justice and *Volksgemeinschaft* in that?" they asked.[317] In 1943 a provincial German judge wrote, "Since air-raid victims often arrive here poorly dressed and without their possessions, people ask 'What happened to the property of the Jews? Their belongings would suffice to meet the need of all evacuated air-raid victims.' It is wrong that people who in those days acquired the property of the Jews for little money or without compelling reason should now remain in undisturbed possession of their loot."[318] Fifty years later historians debated whether Aryans knew what happened to Jews who left their property behind. A more relevant question is whether the Aryans cared.

Despite official and unofficial skimming of Jew-tainted property, personal possessions in vast quantities remained for official auctions attended by neighbors of departed Jews. American news correspondent Howard K. Smith witnessed such sales.

> Belongings were sold at public auctions, and good Aryans fought like jackals over a carcase. . . . Auctioneers were ordered to work in conjunction with plain clothes men who stood in the background at each auction to bid prices up. The auctions were carried out in the abandoned homes themselves. The doors were unsealed for the first time after the midnight raid, and the auctioneers, accompanied by policemen, elbowed their way through little crowds, called together by newspaper announcements of the auctions, outside the former Jewish homes. . . . The auctions were ugly spectacles, with ill-tempered citizens crying curses at one another and at the auctioneer, threatening with all the standard threats to have one another arrested and to call friends "high in the party" into their squabbles. One woman was arrested for calling the official bid-up man a "lousy white-Jew."[319]

Many years later an Aryan recalled what he had seen as a boy.

> I overtook Frau Lachmann and another woman, who were carrying a rolled-up rug. . . . Their faces were covered with sweat as they stopped for a moment to breathe. Frau Lachmann shouted that I should tell my mother that genuine Persian rugs were being auctioned off for next to nothing at the Hotel Bavarian Court. She shouted, Tell her to hurry, the best things were already gone!
>
> But my mother knew already about the Persian rugs. Frau Beyer was there, talking to her. Frau Beyer had bought three of them "cheap as dirt"; she said over and over again in a firm voice that they had been bought "legally, very legally, everything was in the open!"—that the government itself had sold them, "therefore there was nothing to worry about."
>
> . . . Nobody explained anything to me; my eyes and ears gathered innuendoes from the air. The rugs, the silver, the furs had a dark origin. Nevertheless, they made everybody happy! The objects had fallen "out of the blue," a fantasy come true. They made Frau Beyer stutter and perspire with excitement, yet on the streets one didn't talk about them. . . .
>
> All around me in other homes that winter there were ghosts: they had slipped in with certain objects that made the apartments shine. These objects had a suspect character to them—my mother said so. I was afraid to touch them. The objects belonged to mysterious "others." They radiated something I could not understand.[320]

Ghosts may have haunted one other class of property. Police offered rewards to anyone revealing property that could be confiscated, an opportunity to turn a profit while settling private grudges.[321] Citizens who betrayed a hiding Jew might receive one-third of the Jew's property. Himmler noted that such rewards could total thousands of Reichsmarks for the informer.[322]

We should not conclude our examination of property confiscation without recalling one of the most enduring images of the war on Jews, removal of hair and dental gold from death camp victims. Those grisly confiscations, however, were but an extrapolation from prewar policies. Felt and carpet industries had long sought men's hair, and women's hair was used for making hair nets and cosmetic hair pieces.[323] The Nazi regime discouraged dental gold work, and in July 1937 a report appeared that dental gold was being recovered in "exceptional cases."[324] The announcement did not specify details of recovery. A decree of February 1939 said Jews could retain gold tooth fillings "in personal use," language which led one contemporary observer to ask whether dental gold was being removed from Jewish corpses.[325]

HOW MUCH PROPERTY WAS STOLEN FROM THE JEWS?

"Reliable estimates" in October 1935 put Jewish capital property at RM 12 billion, a figure excluding personal property.[326] That figure was for replacement cost, not the actual cash value which was far lower in the Aryanization market. About the same time Jews in Geneva who were promoting an emigration plan put the total of German Jewish property between RM 1 billion and RM 3 billion,[327] a figure surely far too low. Until the property registration decrees provided definitive figures, Jews were assumed to have RM 12 billion to RM 20 billion in German property alone.[328] Registration showed total property holdings of Jews to be half that amount. One Berlin banker valued total seizures of Jewish property at RM 7 billion to RM 8 billion.[329] That private estimate, considered accurate by a U.S. diplomat who witnessed the Aryanization process, is consistent with public statements by Nazi officials. In April 1938 State Secretary Rudolf Brinkmann of the Economics Ministry put Jewish property in Greater Germany (which in April 1938 was the old Reich plus Austria and Saar) at RM 7 billion.[330] On November 15, 1938, Goebbels totaled Jewish wealth in Greater Germany at RM 8 billion,[331] but his figure appears to have been out of date. Minister of Economic Affairs Walther Funk clarified the Goebbels figure, saying that before Crystal Night Aryans had acquired RM 2 billion of Jewish property, with RM 5 billion remaining in Jewish hands according to official property registrations.[332] The RM 5 billion figure, however, did not reflect current depressed market value of Jews' property.[333] One contemporary authority reported Crystal Night destroyed between RM 1 billion and RM 2 billion of property for which Jews received no compensation.[334] Another authority estimated physical damages at RM 1.3 billion.[335] Still another contemporary authority put loss of market value in commercial property at RM 4 billion, plus another RM 1 billion physically destroyed.[336] By government order Jewish businesses wrecked during Crystal Night had to repair and restock their premises, which shortly afterward were lost to owners through compulsory Aryanization. On top of that was the RM 1 billion Crystal Night fine. Crystal Night probably eliminated at least 60 percent of Jewish wealth that had existed the day before. Moreover, some Nazis who claimed knowledge of Jewish wealth believed Funk's RM 5 billion figure to be grossly inflated, that Jewish holdings were barely half that amount.[337] A "distinguished banker" in Berlin felt even that estimate was too high, putting the maximum at RM 2 billion.[338] If these lower figures were correct, the impact of Crystal Night would be correspondingly greater. Nazi statistical methods unquestionably inflated Jewish wealth: for example, pensions and allowances were capitalized.[339] An elderly impoverished man who owned no property but received a monthly pension of RM 60 would be counted as owning capital equivalent to seven times his annual pension, RM 5,040, even though he had not a pfennig to his name.[340] The same principle worked for private family arrangements. If children of an elderly woman pooled their resources to support her with RM 72 a month, that sum was multiplied by 100 months to give her capital property of RM 7,200. Considering Nazi methods of calculating Jewish wealth, we can hardly be surprised to learn that while collection of the Crystal Night fine was underway, observers found that Jewish property totaled closer to RM 4 billion rather than RM 8 billion.[341] In addition, during the fiscal year starting April 1, 1938, the regime acquired RM 342 million through the flight tax collected from emigrants, probably mostly from Jews.[342] (Total flight tax receipts from April 1933 to April 1940 are estimated at RM 900 million.)[343] Whatever set of figures one chooses to believe, however, almost all Jewish property that existed in April 1938 was confiscated by year's end. Soon after World War II one authority reported an estimate that during the Third Reich's twelve years the regime had confiscated $8 billion from Jews.[344]

Nuremberg Military Tribunal prosecutors noted that Jews' "property was seized and confiscated, and they were deprived of means of earning a livelihood, by the State, by Party organizations, and by individual members of the Party." Prosecutors characterized those actions as crimes against humanity, and maintained that perpetrators bore criminal liability.[345] Prosecutors declared such crimes against humanity had been occurring since January 1936, while Germany was at peace with all other countries. Thus the offenses were separate from wartime atrocities, and Nuremberg tribunal judges decided they had no jurisdiction.[346] The Flick case judgment on industrial Aryanizations, however, had this proviso: "A sale compelled by pressure or duress may be questioned in a court of equity, but . . . such use of pressure, even on racial or religious grounds, has never been thought to be a crime against humanity. A distinction could be made between industrial property and the dwellings, household furnishings, and food supplies of a persecuted people. In this case, however, we are only concerned with industrial property."[347] The court thus left open the question of whether forfeiture of personal property (as opposed to industrial property) was a crime against humanity. In the Ministries Case the court once again emphasized the narrowness of its holding on this issue, declaring that an act could be a crime against humanity yet still fall outside the Nuremberg tribunal's jurisdiction if the crime against humanity violated no international law.[348]

We have now considered three steps in the destruction process: identification, ostracism, and confiscation. Our next chapter discusses the penultimate step: concentration.

4

CONCENTRATION

We have seen how some ordinary people are identified as different from others. Members of the targeted group can then be ostracized. Ostracism creates a climate in which confiscation of their property gains public support. Ostracism leads to loss of income; confiscation leads to loss of capital. Victims thus lose means to pay rent or mortgages and thereby lose their living accommodations. Such people have little choice as they are shunted into particular geographical locations. There they can be watched closely by authorities and ignored by citizens who neither want to witness nor contemplate what happens to victims. We have called that step in the destruction process "concentration," and it is the topic examined in this chapter.

Concentration involves excluding victims from some areas while gathering them in others. Soon after the Nazis took power they began expelling Jews from rural districts. By 1936 that policy had emptied virtually all Jews from Silesia, Anhalt, Upper Bavaria, Mecklenburg, and the state of Bremen.[1] In May 1938 the American Jewish Joint Distribution Committee reported that "many smaller Jewish communities disappeared entirely in the last five years."[2] One consequence was that except in cities, fewer and fewer Germans had contact with Jews. For those Germans who no longer encountered Jews, the Holocaust was mere background music accompanying more urgent matters, and what happened to Jews was hardly noticed.[3]

Another consequence, to which Nazis seem to have given no thought, was the migration of rural Jews to urban areas where they were still tolerated. By 1939 over 80 percent of Greater Germany's Jews lived in cities, mostly Berlin and Vienna.[4] Despite that migration the urban population of Jews may not have increased in numbers because so many were leaving Germany. Berlin's Jewish population, for example, declined by about 4,000 from August 1, 1935, to August 1, 1936,[5] and two years later huge declines in urban Jewish populations had been measured across Germany.[6] Regardless of numbers, however, the proportion of Jews in cities grew because of exclusion from the countryside. This development was not welcomed by Nazi authorities. Frankfurt's mayor asked whether rural Jews could be prevented from migrating to the city, but Frankfurt's police chief could devise no lawful method.[7] By spring 1938 Nazi officials were pondering whether incoming rural Jews should be banned from settling in certain Berlin neighborhoods, thereby further concentrating the city's Jewish population.[8] Concentration allowed measures to be directed against victims more efficiently. Moreover, as Jews got shifted to housing in certain areas, the quality of that housing began to deteriorate; by June 1933 Jewish homeowners were no longer allowed to receive standard government subsidies for house repairs and remodeling.[9]

Earlier we saw Jews forbidden to acquire ownership of real estate, whether by purchase or inheritance. Not only did that policy transfer Jewish wealth to Aryans, it gradually pushed Jews out of neighborhoods lacking rental property. Given enough time, such a policy would have assured that Jews could no longer own their residences. Jews would have to depend on Aryan landlords for shelter. By 1935, however, Aryan landlords had begun turning away Jews who sought to rent apartments.[10] Jews renting houses in real estate developments financed in part with government funds found that developers were cancelling leases.[11] Building societies outright evicted Jewish renters from apartments.[12] "Hundreds of house owners in the fashionable suburbs have been ordered by National Socialist organizations to give notice immediately to Jewish tenants to vacate their apartments within a fortnight. Despite the fact that the minimum legal notice is three months."[13] As with property confiscations, Aryans were ever alert to turn a profit from concentration: Jews facing eviction received visits from Aryan furniture movers.[14]

Jews occupying government-funded housing were evicted. President Paul von Hindenburg had succeeded in providing low-cost public housing for Jewish World War veterans and their families, but in 1935 the Nazis kicked them out.[15] The same happened with housing owned by Jewish organizations. On April 22, 1937, the Gestapo confiscated thirty-three B'nai B'rith homes for children, the aged, and the infirm, throwing out residents forthwith. One observer noted that hundreds of "aged Jews who had contracted with the fraternal order for support during the rest of their lives were reduced to a condition of wandering beggary."[16] After the *Anschluss* Jewish occupants of municipal housing in Vienna were ordered to leave on two weeks' notice.[17] By 1935 occasional drives evicted Jewish tenants from entire residential blocks.[18] For example, "In celebration of the 'Hitler victory over Czechoslovakia' a large number of men and women wearing official Nazi badges are calling at night at the homes of Jews in the Doebling District [of Vienna] ordering them to evacuate their homes within 24 hours and threatening them with 'Dachau, or worse.'" Police stood aloof from the situation.[19] That was in October 1938. A few months earlier the Reich house owners' guild sought the right to evict any Jewish tenant, arguing that Aryans should not have to live in the same building with Jews. Noting that principle, an observer commented, "Scarcity of houses caused by the rebuilding of the city [Berlin] provides a strong incentive to put this principle into practice."[20] A court ruling that same year held that Aryan house tenants could withhold rent if a Jewish tenant lived in the same house, a ruling motivating Aryan landlords to make their rental property Jew-free.[21] By summer's end any Aryan resident of an apartment block had legal power to force eviction of all Jewish residents in the block.[22] Through custom, if not through law, Aryan hotel guests had obtained the same right by summer 1935, being able to cause eviction of any Jewish guest.[23] Munich's Königshof and Vierjahreszeiten hotels even evicted Jews who were permanent residential guests.[24] Landlords who lacked enough civic duty to remove Jewish tenants were eventually compelled to act; in summer 1938 the regime ordered landlords to evict all Jewish physicians from their residences.[25] One contemporary critic decried "notice to Jewish tenants to evacuate the apartments which they hold under lease. The threat of homelessness hangs on the Jewish people in every town in Germany."[26]

"The time is rapidly coming," said another observer, "when Jews will find no flats except in houses where only Jews reside."[27] By May 1939 that time had come; Jews were prohibited from living in the same building with Aryans.[28] Also by May 1939 Jews could no longer live in housing owned by Aryans;[29] at the end of the month Berlin's mayor ordered all such residents to get out and move into housing owned by Jews.[30] Because Jews could not live in housing owned by Aryans, and could no longer acquire ownership of real estate, the number of housing units available to Jews inexorably shrank. By 1938 Jews resisted selling homes, from fear of having no place to live.[31] That was one reason brutality was used to Aryanize houses, to produce fear greater than fear of homelessness.

Courts took judicial notice of ostracism, and expressed civic duty by citing it as legal grounds for geographical concentration of victims. In March 1938 Charlottenburg's municipal court declared that exclusion of Jews from the social community was reason enough to exclude them from apartments constructed with tax money.[32] No Jew could benefit from the government's push to expand housing. A September ruling from Berlin-Schöneberg's municipal court went further, holding that Jews could not be part of residential communities.[33]

That possibility began to congeal that same month when the German Labor Front urged Jewish landlords to sell their boarding houses by month's end. A contemporary observer reported, "Berlin Jews were thrown into consternation by this measure. As more and more Jewish tenants are receiving notice from non-Jewish real estate owners to leave their residences, allegedly because other non-Jewish tenants object to their presence, Jews increasingly have been engaging rooms in Jewish boarding houses. If these boarding houses also are to be liquidated many Jews will face a problem in finding places to live."[34] In addition to Jewish residents, Jewish landlords were also victims in the Labor Front campaign; renting out rooms was one of the few ways for Jews to obtain a legal income.[35]

Crystal Night started a new level of harshness in housing restrictions, perhaps best exemplified by the short-lived order for all Jewish families in Munich to depart the city within forty-eight hours. They were to leave their cars behind and inform the Gestapo by 6:00 P.M. on November 10 on when they would be delivering residential and garage keys. The order was rescinded but illustrated what was considered reasonable.[36] Some of Munich's Jews left anyway; one was told to list his house with an Aryan real estate agent or suffer the consequences.[37]

Soon after Crystal Night, Franconia's deputy *Gauleiter* Karl Holz told Streicher, "In view of the great existing lack of housing, the best thing would be to put the Jews into a kind of *internment camp*. Then the houses would become free in a twinkling, and the housing shortage would be relieved." Streicher had little concern about feelings in Berlin, but even he recognized that such a move would be countermanded as unacceptable. "Thereupon," Holz recalled, "I said to him *that I considered it unthinkable that, after the Jews had had their property smashed they should continue to be able to own houses and land*. I proposed that these houses and this land ought to be taken away from them, and declared myself ready to carry through such an action. I declared that by the Aryanisation of Jewish land and houses *a large sum could accrue to the Gau out of the proceeds*. I named some millions of marks." Streicher told Holz to proceed.[38] After Jewish landlords were forced to do hours of rigorous physical exercise while chanting demeaning slogans, they were given opportunity to sign over their property.[39] An official Nazi report on this matter stated, "The Aryanisation was accomplished by the alienation of properties, the surrender of claims, especially mortgage claims, and reductions in buying price. The payment allowed the Jews was basically 10% of the nominal value."[40] The implication here is that the *Gau* of Franconia then sold the houses and real estate to Aryans for a higher price and pocketed the difference. The higher price was not necessarily normal market value—Goering noted that Aryans were far less interested in buying Jewish assets of any type if the price were fair market value.[41] Even a discount price, however, would provide a windfall for both the Aryan buyer and *Gau* seller. A Nazi report of thirty-three Aryanizations in the *Gau* of Franconia found a difference of RM 14.5 million between the property's actual value and the price paid to the *Gau* by Aryans.[42] Concern arose, however, about bargain real estate transactions depressing the market for Aryan-owned houses,[43] an example of how the war on Jews could hurt perpetrators.

A contemporary observer reported Crystal Night eviction of 30,000 Viennese from their residences (which were then looted).[44] Berlin authorities announced that at least 8,000 houses would be taken from Jews in that city and turned over to Aryans, ending circumstances where "a Jewish family of three occupy a villa with 12 or more rooms, while German parents with children have to huddle in emergency quarters or huts."[45] Jewish homeowners allowed to retain Berlin residences were forced to take in the evicted strangers.[46] By the end of November Jewish apartment dwellers on Vienna's main streets had to move into accommodations on side streets. The official excuse for these Vienna evictions demonstrated how various elements of the destruction process dovetailed: Main street apartments failing to display a swastika flag on celebration days were deemed to spoil the celebration; because Jews could not display a swastika flag, the solution was to evict them.[47] After Crystal Night landlords throughout Germany began evicting Jewish tenants forthwith.[48] "Authorities, swamped with eager non-Jewish home-seekers, pleaded with applicants today to be patient until the number of apartments eventually to be available was known."[49] Persons favored by the regime had priority for moving into rental property vacated by Jews,[50] and bureaucratic competition erupted between municipal and party authorities, vying for the privilege of determining who should get the apartments.[51] Voracious demand for former Jewish housing continued as the Holocaust cranked into full gear. In December 1941 a local party bureaucrat told the Gestapo, "Since the intention to deport the Jews from Göttingen in the near future has already become common knowledge, the district [party] administration has been flooded with applications for flats."[52] One student of the topic found that the war on Jews "put as much dwelling space on the housing market as one year of somewhat below-average building activity. In Vienna, for instance, within four years of the *Anschluss* one out of every ten inhabitants availed himself of the re-housing opportunities that followed in the train of genocide."[53] Throughout Greater Germany Aryans "moved up" to desirable housing left behind by Jews. A German judge whose approval was needed for such property transfers explained, "The question of freedom of will was perhaps dubious but . . . every action in life was governed by some influence or other."[54]

The Crystal Night decree closing all Jewish businesses also forbade Jews membership in a "cooperative society."[55] This was a housing restriction. Anyone who joined a cooperative building society gained a right to live in houses or apartments affiliated with the society. Such membership gave Jews a legal claim to reside in buildings that also sheltered Aryans. Removing Jews as members removed their claim to cooperative housing, allowing Aryan residents to have Jews evicted[56] (as had been occurring with other types of housing).

After Crystal Night, Hitler further limited Jews' access to private housing. Although German law forbidding tenant evictions except for nonpayment of rent or violation of lease[57] remained formally intact, Hitler directed that circumstances be exploited "in individual cases in such a way that Jews will live together in one house, as much as feasible under rental conditions."[58] This directive increased availability of housing for Aryans while increasing concentration of Jews. "You will know that in a particular house only Jews are living," Goering noted at the time. "That'll bring about a concentration of Jewry which may even facilitate control."[59] The idea was not to create Jewish ghettos, but to have separate Jewish houses and apartment buildings scattered through Aryan neighborhoods. Heydrich explained, "The German population, their blocks or houses, force the Jew to behave himself. The control of the Jew through the watchful eye of the whole population is better than having him by the thousands in a district where I cannot properly establish a control over his daily life."[60] Heydrich felt community policing made ghettos unnecessary.

An April 1939 decree presented Jews with new housing restrictions.[61] Through that decree (foreshadowed by earlier announcements)[62] tenant protection laws became limited in applicability to Jews, reducing the need to proceed on a case-by-case basis. If an Aryan landlord certified that shelter for a Jewish tenant was assured by local housing authorities for the remaining time period of a lease, the tenant could be evicted. (That eviction option soon became mandatory.)[63] New shelter did not have to be equivalent to premises vacated, nor did rent payments have to be the same. The decree thereby established a legal framework for an Aryan slumlord bonanza. Moreover, Jews in apartments or houses (whether rented or owner-occupied) had to accept as tenants or subtenants any Jews sent by local housing authorities. No matter how obnoxious these strangers might be, they had to be accommodated. Local housing authorities could demand a fee for their domicile finder service; bureaucrats made money by concentrating Jewish housing. A side matter was the continued applicability of tenant protection laws to Jews if their landlord was Jewish. The decree was not intended to give Jewish landlords any more power than they already had. Indeed, it took away power because they could no longer rent out premises without permission of local housing authorities. Those bureaucrats determined who would be tenants of Jewish landlords. The April 1939 decree also forbade Aryan tenants to sublease to Jews, further limiting housing opportunities for Jews. By the next month Aryan tenants had the right to break their leases with Jewish landlords.[64] Another policy promoted concentration by forbidding certain Aryans, such as armed forces personnel, to rent housing from Jews.[65] Through such policies more and more rental property owned by Jews became occupied exclusively by Jews.[66]

Such steps had been discussed at the highest levels in November 1938, with Goebbels showing particular interest.[67] Two complementary approaches were followed, excluding Jews from some neighborhoods and concentrating them in others. In spring 1939 fashionable areas in Berlin such as the Hansa Viertel, the Bayerisches Viertel, the Kurfürstendamm, the Tauentzienstrasse, the Potsdammerstrasse, the Luetzowplatz, and the Tiergarten district were proclaimed to be Aryan zones. Jews living there were forced to move.[68] Authorities in other cities received permission to specify districts where Jews would be banned.[69] That was the exclusion approach. The concentration approach was illustrated on December 5, 1938, when the authoritative Nazi newspaper *Völkischer Beobachter* predicted that Jewish residences in Berlin would be restricted to "rows of streets in the center and the north of Berlin, where the Jewish element has predominated for centuries already, as for example the Muenz- Linien-, and Grenadier-Strasse." The newspaper urged Jews to "start right now looking for another residence in one of the above-mentioned parts of Berlin, and perhaps effect an exchange of residence with one of the blood Germans [Aryans] residing there."[70] Berlin police chief von Helldorf agreed with the newspaper's recommendation.[71] The recommended locales were slums notorious for high crime rates; the grungy ambience of Grenadierstrasse was used in location shooting for the movie *Hans Westmar*.[72] A few weeks before the Berlin recommendations from news media and police, Ribbentrop told diplomatic circles that plans were afoot to concentrate Jews in neighborhoods suffering from high crime rates. Once settled there, Jews would be treated as habitual criminals.[73] Goering found the idea attractive and thought it would be well received by Aryan business people who could exploit a population unable to make purchases elsewhere: "German storekeepers would love to dwell in the ghetto if they could do some business there."[74] Indeed, Goering did not see how ghettos could be avoided as a natural outcome of ostracism, as Jews were banned from one occupation after another, resulting in lower income that limited housing choices.[75] Heydrich, however, adamantly opposed creation of ghettos.[76] He and his supporters carried the day. Jews of Greater Germany continued to live among Aryans. Admittedly, after World War II began some special barracks-type Jewish housing was constructed, and some Jews moved into existing structures such as monasteries.[77] The ghettos which became such a notorious part of Holocaust history, however, were not located in Germany, and were not established until wartime stress changed many other Nazi policies as well.

Although permanent concentration of large numbers of Jews in a particular locale was not government policy in Greater Germany, identity card records and police teletypes provided a mechanism for instant round up. On short notice, during Crystal Night operations police apprehended 26,000 Jews and sent them to concentration camps.[78] Moreover, those victims were not selected at random from the Jewish population. Arrests emphasized healthy, wealthy males.[79] Speaking of an earlier one-day mass police effort across Germany an amazed observer said, "It gave a striking demonstration of the speed and efficiency with which the Nazis can mobilize the police for any specific purpose."[80]

Regulations ostensibly having nothing to do with Jews might nonetheless interlock with the concentration policy. For example, by 1937 civil service supervisors could require government employees to reside within a particular distance from their office.[81] This requirement could provide an excuse for evicting Jews from residences in the zone around a government workplace. Government workplaces could include banks, hospitals, schools, telephone facilities, railway enterprises, lawyers' offices, and many other enterprises that gave the residency requirement sweeping power to shape the character of neighborhoods.

Note, too, how the concentration policy was but one expression of a broader Nazi approach to any lack of a civilian commodity. When schools became crowded, instead of constructing more schools the Nazis eased overcrowding by removing Jewish students. When beaches became crowded, Jewish bathers were excluded. When the concentration policy was implemented, a U.S. diplomat noted that German cities lacked enough housing and observed that Nazis in response seemed ready to promote evictions of Jews from their residences.[82] Rather than build enough housing, the Nazi answer was to remove Jewish occupants of housing and turn vacated residences over to Aryans. The population understood and adapted to the Nazi approach. Confidential Nazi reports frequently mentioned approaches to local officials by Aryans wanting Jewish tenants evicted from dwellings desired by the Aryans, who said they needed relief from housing shortages.[83] And Aryans whose homes fell to urban renewal projects in Berlin and Munich were promised housing currently rented by Jews in buildings owned by Aryans.[84] Concentration thereby allowed the regime to avoid replacing housing stock it destroyed.

The scholarship of Henry R. Huttenbach provides extraordinary documentation of what happened to Jews in Worms, a case study allowing us to see many aspects of the concentration policy in operation. Although Worms had a historic Jewish quarter, Jewish residences were distributed around town in 1938. The organized Jewish community owned two large buildings in the old Jewish quarter: an old age home and a community center. After Crystal Night authorities designated about sixty houses and apartments as *Judenhäuser* for 360 persons, six per housing unit. That was double the average habitation in the town's Aryan housing units. Evictions from familiar homes and overcrowding among strangers in unfamiliar housing heightened the continual level of anxiety experienced by victims. If Jewish homeowners moved elsewhere they had to sell their residences to Aryans. In order to drive down prices city officials threatened to withhold papers that Jews needed for permission to move away. If the house were a unit of *Judenhäuser* its remaining Jewish residents had to cram into other *Judenhäuser* when the owners sold. In January 1940 Worms had 223 Jews living in thirty-eight locations. The old Jewish quarter contained almost two-thirds of the town's Jewish population, with 6.1 persons per housing unit. One house had fifteen residents, another had eighteen. As sanitation facilities broke down under such levels of concentration, the threat of medieval diseases loomed over Jewish residents who were already stressed up to—and sometimes beyond—their ability to cope. (A *Mischling* survivor from another city recalled, "Domestic dramas were commonplace, most of our tenants being Jewish and under intense emotional pressure, so my father became a sort of unofficial divorce lawyer.")[85] The two community buildings were inundated with elderly Jews fleeing the countryside. In October Worms had 193 Jews living in twenty-five locations. The old Jewish quarter contained 70 percent of the town's Jewish population, with 19.3 persons per unit. In February 1942 Worms had 181 Jews living in nineteen locations, plus another four Jews in mixed marriages who lived in Aryan residences. By October, however, the only Jews left in town after mass deportations were the four in mixed marriages. All former Jewish housing was available for Aryanization.[86]

Steps to concentrate Jews were an important element in the war on them, yet the prewar historical record is so abbreviated that our chapter must be brief despite the topic's importance. When discussing life in Germany before World War II, survivors' accounts have comparatively little to say about concentration. Perhaps most people normally change residences often enough that one more relocation seems trivial in comparison to other sufferings of victims. Nonetheless, being able to concentrate victims promotes continuation of the destruction process into its final stage, annihilation. Note how the power to tell victims where they must live interlocks with the power to confiscate their houses, which in turn derives from the power to ignore civil liberties in which personal and property rights are intertwined, rights abdicated by citizens as they respond to propaganda of hate and fear directed against victims.

The power to tell people where they must live may seem innocuous, but when used as part of the destruction process, such power can be a prelude to telling people where they must die. And when.

5

ANNIHILATION

The final step in the destruction process is annihilation. The population of victims is eliminated through prevention of birth and infliction of death. We have noted that various elements of the destruction process can occur simultaneously, and Nazis began killing Jews in 1933 long before anyone "dreamed the dream of the gas chamber."[1] Even though we might not be surprised that perpetrators who disregarded deaths from the start welcomed deaths at the end, Nazi officials failed to recognize what they were doing. Extermination camps were not constructed in fulfillment of a master plan but were instead the outcome of bureaucratic thrust, in which reasonable persons resorted to ever-harsher measures as previous efforts failed to achieve victory in the war on Jews. Annihilation was inevitable once the process of destruction began. All elements of the process, from identification to ostracism to confiscation to concentration, build toward fulfillment through annihilation. The process can be quenched and abandoned, but no doubt exists about its outcome if it continues. Theory demands it. History proves it.

PREVENTION OF BIRTH

Limitations on marriage help prevent births. Those limitations can be regulations explicitly directed toward marriage or be side effects from other policies. Employment policies, for example, had side effects on marriage. The Jew-free workplace extended to spouses of workers. Civil servants could marry only Aryans,[2] and government workers could be fired on grounds of marriage to a Jew.[3] Those policies encouraged break up of any couple that included a Jew. Even private employers would dismiss Aryan workers who married a Jew.[4] Self-employed professionals found themselves at risk as well; an Aryan lawyer who legally married a Jew found himself disbarred for choosing a Jewish mate.[5] Failure to marry and to have babies was a firing offense for many Aryan government workers, and cause for denial of promotion to others.[6] That domestic requirement meant that a government worker and a Jew could continue an intimate relationship only through an extramarital affair, a moral burden that many Aryan-Jew couples could not endure even if they were willing to risk legal penalties for sexual contact between Aryan and Jew. By summer 1938 employability was a legal requirement for marriage,[7] preventing more and more Jewish couples from marrying as more and more occupations were banned to Jews. Legalities aside, inability to support a family deterred Jews from marriage. That inability was worsened by property confiscations. Concentration also discouraged Jews from marrying and having babies; family homes were no longer secure.

These policies produced demographic consequences that were well known at the time. Those consequences merit consideration here as the factual foundation on which Nazis constructed claims of a growing Jewish threat.

When the Nazis took power Jewish birth rates were declining and death rates were rising, a trend that became ever more pronounced under the regime.[8] In 1934 births among Jews in Frankfurt on the Main were about 60 percent of the 1933 total, and deaths among Jews outnumbered births by a factor of five.[9] The aging trend of the Jewish population accelerated during the Nazi years. From 1933 to 1939 the number of Jews from infancy to twenty-five years old declined by over 80 percent; even middle-aged Jews from forty to fifty-nine years old declined, by 51 percent. In 1938 30 percent of the Jewish population was age sixty or older.[10] In January 1934 demographers had already estimated that by 1945 Jews of childbearing age would total only one-fourth the number found in 1925,[11] a projection that would have grown ever smaller if population trends of later years had been extrapolated. From 1933 through 1939 deaths exceeded births in the Jewish population.[12] In 1936 the Palestine Foundation Fund of Germany announced that the Jewish population was four-fifths the 1933 total.[13] By summer 1938, even by including Jews acquired in the *Anschluss* with Austria, the Reich's Jewish population was only three-fifths the 1933 total.[14] Barely a year later the population was two-fifths the 1933 total.[15] Emigration had much to do with these trends; young and middle-aged Jews fled with their families whenever possible, while elderly Jews lacked heart to start new lives abroad.[16]

Formal restrictions on marriage were aimed more at reducing the *Mischlinge* birth rate than at reducing the Jewish birth rate, but they nonetheless affected Jews' ability to have children. As early as May 1933 a Dortmund official openly stated that marriage rules were intended to control childbearing.[17] Without getting into complexities of the rules,[18] in general Aryans could marry Aryans and Jews could marry Jews, but Jews could not marry Aryans. First-degree *Mischlinge* were encouraged to marry Jews or other first-degree *Mischlinge*, and second-degree *Mischlinge* had to marry Aryans. The idea was to keep "racial" lines pure, absorbing *Mischlinge* into one race or the other through "scientific" breeding principles. Cohabitation between Aryan and Jew was illegal in itself, but an unmarried Aryan-Jew couple that produced a baby was subject to especially harsh punishment.[19] As always, the governing factor was genealogy, not religion. In 1936 a Stuttgart court sentenced a Christian Jew to a year's imprisonment for a race-defiling relationship with an Aryan woman.[20]

As soon as the Nazis took over, in 1933 authorities began counseling Aryan-Jew couples against marriage, sometimes declining to issue marriage licenses even though no law prohibited such marriages.[21] In April 1933 Julius Streicher declared, "The time is not far distant when by law it will be forbidden for a Gentile to marry a Jewess or a Jew to marry a Gentile girl."[22] Prussia's Ministry of Justice recommended such a law in September.[23] By 1934 race offices were establishing whether a couple's genealogy permitted marriage.[24] In 1934 a court forbade issuing a marriage license to a Jewish man and a pregnant Aryan because "a woman who saw fit to have intercourse with a Jew in 1933, when knowledge of the significance of racial thought had taken firm root amongst the German people, is deserving of no milder treatment. She must be punished for her frivolity and lack of responsibility."[25] When Mainz Nazis demonstrated that year against nuptial plans of an Aryan and Jew, the couple found themselves in protective custody instead of in matrimony.[26] In February 1935 *Deutsche Justiz*, the Nazi jurists journal, called for a legal ban on marriage between Aryan and Jew.[27] In July a Wetzlar court ruled that regardless of any written law on the subject, officials could prevent such marriages as contrary to the regime's race policy.[28] Soon afterward authorities instructed marriage registrars to cease permitting marriages of Aryan-Jew couples.[29] When a couple asked a Bad Sulze court to order a marriage registrar to give them a license, the judge refused on grounds that such a marriage would be immoral.[30] That couple was luckier than others; some who applied for a marriage license were taken into protective custody by the SS.[31] Conscription law provided one legal rationale for action against Aryan-Jew couples. In spring 1935 civil service bureaucrats noted that no member of Germany's active or reserve military forces could marry a Jew. Because all Aryan men were active or reserve personnel, none could marry a Jew.[32] Not until the Nuremberg Blood and Honor decree of September 15, 1935, however, were such marriages outlawed by statute.[33]

Occasionally a determined couple could massage their genealogy to evade a marriage prohibition. To marry her Aryan beloved, a blond and blue-eyed first-degree *Mischling* decided to document that her mother was illegitimate, which because of the family genealogy would shift the mother from Jew to first-degree *Mischling*, in turn transforming her offspring into second-degree *Mischlinge* permitted to marry Aryans. The mother, relatives, and friends colluded in the necessary perjured statements about the mother's illegitimacy, and permission to marry was granted by the Race Investigation Office (*Rassenforschungsamt*).[34] Not all couples, however, had vague enough genealogies and brave enough friends to achieve such a feat.

Besides genealogy, another legal restriction on marriage was health. Couples could not marry without certification from a eugenics board that they were free of genetically transmitted disease.[35] Engaged couples were requested to provide data at least back to the grandparent level, and preferably on their thirty-two great-great-grandparents and all descendants and spouses of descendants.[36] Many couples found that expectation to be formidable. And as we shall later see, the

Nazi definition of genetic disease was broad enough to veto marriage plans of many couples.

Marriage regulations were the cornerstone of an edifice of criminal offenses called "race defilement." The edifice housed many offenses unrelated to marriage, ranging from friendship to sexual harassment, but all were seen as potential contaminants of the Aryan racial line. Nazis believed the biological component in these offenses meant they were based on science rather than on cultural value. "National Socialism is nothing but applied biology," said Berlin University biology professor Dr. Fritz Lenz in 1931.[37] In race defilement cases the Gestapo and other police agencies did not just enforce Reich law; they helped people avoid perils associated with violation of scientific law governing reality. If race defilement went unchecked, nature would invoke consequences far greater than judges and police could invent. "The will of nature is the will of God," declared Dr. Achim Gercke, a Reich Interior Ministry race expert.[38] Nazis saw themselves as defending not only civilization but humanity itself.

Motivated by civic duty, Nazis began punishing race defilement long before particular acts were outlawed; offenders were admonished for failing to implement the regime's racial policies regardless of absent legal obligations. In September 1933 the Prussian Ministry of Justice suggested that sex between Aryan and Jew be made a crime,[39] a clear message of disapproval. The June 1934 *Völkische Kampfblatt* printed a poem saying that Aryan women who associated with Jewish men should be beaten and branded.[40] At a December meeting in Fürth 500 Nazi physicians asked Interior Minister Frick to punish race defilement between Aryan women and Jewish men. The doctors said women should lose their German nationality and be sent to a labor camp if they attempted sex; if they achieved sex they should be sterilized. Men were to lose German nationality, all their property, and be incarcerated for attempting sex. No sanctions were asked if the males were Aryan and females Jewish[41] (although such sanctions were eventually enforced.)[42] That same month Julius Streicher went further, telling Franconia's judges, "Sexual relations of a Jew with a non-Jewess should be punished with death."[43] The next February an article by Dr. Fritz Hartmann in *Deutsche Justiz* urged harsh legal penalties for such conduct;[44] the following August an article by Dr. Ludwig Fischer in the journal of the German Law Academy suggested imprisonment,[45] and *Der Stürmer* demanded the death penalty.[46] We have already seen couples pilloried; Munich police, Breslau Gestapo, and authorities in Aurich, Berlin, Stuttgart, and elsewhere across the Reich were arresting people for race defilement in summer 1935,[47] prior to the Blood and Honor decree. No sexual component needed be present for race defilement, however; a Jew and Aryan who played a game of cards together committed race defilement.[48]

Race defilement charges created new opportunities for blackmail and revenge. Before any male Jew had sex with a female he had to obtain proof that she was Jewish; accepting her word was not good enough. A Jew was convicted of race defilement when an Aryan woman deceived him about her race.[49] After the Aryan wife of a Jew rejected the advances of an SA leader in 1934, the Nazi denounced her for defaming the regime and its Führer. Although she apparently defended herself successfully against those charges, a Nuremberg court ordered her imprisoned four months for race defilement. The *Fränkische Tageszeitung* suggested she be put in a concentration camp upon completion of her judicial sentence.[50] A Düsseldorf man sought to cast away his spouse by claiming she was sexually involved with a Jew.[51] (False denunciations of unwanted spouses, on all sorts of grounds, became so common that investigating police routinely began asking if divorce proceedings were underway or under consideration.)[52] A bold Aryan husband of a Jew managed to have her Aryan lover convicted of race defilement and imprisoned for eighteen months.[53] A mere invitation to cohabit was considered race defilement,[54] as were far more innocent invitations. In Magdeburg, where authorities zealously pursued race defilement cases,[55] a contemporary chronicler told of a young Jew "waiting for a friend one day outside the apartment building where the friend lived, when a 'German-blooded' girl appeared and began to wash the windows of the apartment on the first floor of the building. . . . The Jew asked her what she was doing that evening and if she would go to a movie with him. The girl not only rejected the invitation but also had the Jew arrested, and a court sentenced him to four weeks imprisonment."[56] Salesgirls at the Barasch department store in the same town successfully pressed race defilement charges against male Jewish coworkers.[57] In 1936 a Frankfurt court imprisoned a Jewish salesman for a year to punish his "aggressive attitude" while chatting up an Aryan woman. No sexual activity was involved, but the court said the educational nature of the Blood and Honor law required the Jew to be convicted for violating its spirit.[58]

Marriage between Aryan and Jew provided the most acute example of race defilement. Such marriages were legal before the Blood and Honor decree, and we shall consider those shortly. Even afterward, however, lawyers succeeded in establishing a nebulous zone occupied by special couples. For example a particular German woman became a Turkish citizen upon marrying a Turk. After that marriage ended she believed she married a German Jew. In December 1935 a Berlin court supported her belief halfway; the ceremony was valid enough to make her a German national again but not valid enough for her new husband to escape prosecution for violating the Blood and Honor decree's ban on marriage between Aryan and Jew. The court sentenced him to fifteen months for race defilement.[59] If German Aryans and Jews attempted to evade the Blood and Honor decree by marrying abroad, a Nazi public prosecutor could have the marriage annulled.[60]

Regarding valid Aryan-Jew marriages, which may have occurred years before the Blood and Honor decree, the regime encouraged such couples to divorce. In autumn 1933 Prussia's Ministry of Justice suggested that racial status be grounds for divorce in all Aryan-Jew marriages.[61] By the next year courts freely accepted race as grounds for divorce.[62] Said the High Court of the State of Baden at Karlsruhe, "The petitioner would not in August 1930 have married the respondent if he had then had such knowledge of the racial question as he has acquired since the National revolution,"[63] a principle followed by most Baden judges.[64] Also in 1934, a Breslau court dissolved a marriage when the Aryan husband said he had been unaware of his wife's Jewish genealogy when they married seven years earlier.[65] Even foreign courts accepted those grounds when considering divorce petitions from German nationals living within the foreign court's jurisdiction.[66] German judges began to wonder, however, about the sincerity of Aryans who suddenly discovered racial imperfections in spouses now that such considerations had become grounds for divorce: one court rejected the 1934 petition of a man who said he first realized the racial wrongness of his spouse in 1926, but he got the divorce on appeal.[67] The Reich Supreme Court then announced that no more divorces would be granted on racial grounds unless the petition had been filed by October 15, 1933.[68] The Supreme Court also declared that for racial status to be grounds for divorce, at the time of the marriage ceremony the Aryan partner had to be unaware of the Jewish partner's racial status. Aryans who knew they were marrying Jews could not divorce on racial grounds.[69] In January 1936 *Juridical Weekly* expressed the regime's dissatisfaction with that court stance, suggesting that Aryans be allowed automatic divorce of Jewish spouses during a six-month period beginning November 30, 1935.[70]

Given that the mere existence of an Aryan-Jew marriage was often legal grounds for its termination, Aryans had little defense when employers or guilds required a choice between continuing a career or continuing a marriage. News item, April 1933: "Nazis Demand Divorce of Jewish Wives By Officials if They Are to Retain Jobs."[71] A Berlin resident wrote in June 1933 about a woman married to a non-Aryan: "She had to drop him to comply with the rigorous demands of the Nazi creed."[72] An Aryan recalled his divorce from a second-degree *Mischling* wife. "We separated in the fall of '33 by mutual consent, before my admission to the Reich Press chamber. We remained good friends, and fortunately nothing happened to her. But the divorce could not be avoided under those particular circumstances. Otherwise I could not have kept my [newspaper] department and would have been fired."[73] In 1932 a Jewish woman "met a young brewery owner from Nuremberg. They fell in love, got married around the end of the year, and lived in Nuremberg. Then came the Third Reich. Slowly things began to change: she was a 'Full Jew.' Her husband managed to hold things off for a while one way and another. . . . But soon even his good connections didn't help anymore. So first they formally separated; then they officially divorced but continued to live a married life. Then at one point she said she couldn't stand it anymore; there was no sense in it." She left.[74]

Such marital break-ups were not always driven by selfishness. "A young Gentile woman Anna knew was married to a Jew. The couple owned a small, well-kept hotel in Berlin. One day the woman came to ask Anna's advice. The party had demanded that she dissolve her marriage; if she didn't, she was told, she'd be forced to give up her hotel. What should she do? . . . Aunt Martha listened to the story. Then she said, 'Divorce your husband and send him abroad.' She made it clear that the issue was not so much one of keeping a property as it was safe-guarding a human life. If he was out of the country, no harm could come to him."[75] Alas, such strategies were thwarted as the Reich's fiat spread across Europe. An Aryan-Jew couple who fled from Germany to Czechoslovakia in 1936 were arrested there by the Gestapo in July 1939 on charges of race defilement.[76]

Aside from employment security, Aryan housing, and other advantages accruing to Aryans who divorced Jewish spouses, as of December 1938 all property penalties were dropped against Aryan women who divorced Jews.[77] Later such benefits arrived upon the Jewish husband's demise as well. An Aryan woman's husband was transported to Auschwitz and death: "When she reported her changed circumstances to the local food office at the beginning of the next rationing period, the clerk informed her that she was entitled to full rations again and—in all sincerity—congratulated her on her re-Aryanization."[78]

Divorce was a major disruption in family life of course, a disruption that the regime might impose even if spouses were happy together and declined to divorce. In autumn 1933 Prussia's Ministry of Justice decreed that Jews could not intermarry with other races, and existing civil marriages of such couples were thereby annulled.[79] Inability to produce children was grounds for divorce,[80] and if an unmarried person of any race were sterilized, marriage was forbidden to that person. If such an individual nonetheless succeeded in marrying, authorities could have that marriage annulled.[81] In January 1936 a proposed law was announced, allowing prosecutors to sue for divorce of any couple who opposed the Nazi regime. Such a marriage was defined as immoral and "disordered."[82] Soon thereafter authorities received power to order compulsory divorce of any couple involved with "immoral," criminal, or communist activity.[83] Later that year a superior court in Halberstadt granted a divorce to a woman on grounds that her husband had asked her to spend more time at home and less time with Nazi activities.[84] Earlier the Reich Supreme Court ruled that a husband could divorce a wife who made insulting remarks about Hitler.[85]

Fecundity was the theoretical reason for the regime's interference with a marriage, so we can hardly be surprised at the regime's interference with a couple's children as well. In addition to physical reproduction the regime also scrutinized adoptions. By the end of 1933 couples could not adopt children of a different race.[86] Previous interracial adoptions could be voided. In August 1936 a Berlin court removed an adopted Aryan child from its Jewish parents. The court noted with disgust that despite the parents' knowledge of race laws "the father still clung to the child." The court ordered the father to provide financial maintenance for the child in its new home.[87] While such a policy may have grieved every family it touched, a far more sweeping threat to family solidarity was the regime's extensive power to determine custody of children born to a marriage.

Berlin, summer 1935:

> A fifteen-year-old Jewish schoolboy had formed a friendship with a fourteen-year-old "Aryan" girl. On the orders of the ladies of the National Socialist Welfare Organisation, district Prenzlauerberg, the girls of the upper forms organised a "raid," that is to say, on their way to school the two were systematically watched, followed and molested. One day they could endure this constant shadowing no longer and took refuge in the entrance of a house. The police were called immediately and the two terrified children dragged out. A *Stürmer* photographer was quickly on the spot and snapped the "depraved juvenile debauchee." At the instance of the National Socialist Welfare Organisation the parents of the girl were deprived of the custody of their child. Pending her removal to a reformatory she was "taken care of" by the women officials attached to the Welfare Organisation, and under persistent and suggestive cross-examination, "the girl weepingly admitted" (*The Stürmer's* phrase) to having been ravished in an indescribable manner in the home of the fifteen-year-old debauchee.[88]

Racial considerations opened new avenues for divorced parents to continue the war of their former marriage through custody disputes. A husband was held to be responsible for the break-up of a marriage in 1925, and the wife was awarded custody of their two infant children. Both parents remarried. The mother, however, chose a Christian spouse with Jewish genealogy. After the Nazis took power, the children's biological father applied for custody. In 1934 the court ruled that despite the biological father's lack of attention to his children in previous years and despite the loving atmosphere in which the children were living with their mother and stepfather, "National Socialist ideals" had to take precedence over selfish personal considerations. The children were ordered removed from their racially polluted home, and custody was awarded to their biological father.[89]

Race, however, was but one factor in custody decisions. "If the older generation cannot get accustomed to us," Hitler said in June 1933, "we shall take their children away from them and rear them as needful for the Fatherland."[90] A Waldenburg court declared in November 1937: "Whoever wakens in children opinions which bring them into conflict with . . . racial and national unity has not fulfilled the condition on which he was entrusted with their bringing up. For reasons of general policy this right must be taken from him." The court thereupon seized the children of two pacifist International Bible Students.[91] Seizing children because of parental politics was so common that a juvenile court attracted the regime's attention for failing to seize children from parents who "show signs of being opposed to the National Socialist State. They do not possess a single Swastika flag. They have not arranged for their child to join the Hitler Youth," and their "11 year old girl attracts attention by constantly refusing the Hitler salute in school." Simple parental failure to put children in the Hitler Youth had been long considered grounds for a court to put the children in foster homes.[92] In the case at hand, however, the juvenile court merely ordered protective supervision.[93] Nonetheless parents across the Reich knew that any lapse of civic duty could break up their families. An SS memo of April 1938 reported on two parents who "appeared in the voting center in Guenstedt on Sunday morning and deposited their vote, after both had been advised of their duty to vote by the police in Griefstedt and had been threatened with the removal of their child in case of non-participation."[94] Friendship between parents and Jews was a failure of civic duty that could be grounds for the regime putting children in a "politically reliable" foster home.[95] In April 1935 the Berlin-Lichterfelde municipal court declared "exposing a child to Communist or atheistic influences is adequate reason for depriving the parent of the custody of the child."[96] So was exposing a child to pacifist Christian influences, according to a Hamburg district court that took children away from their Jehovah's Witness parents in May 1936.[97] The regime was far more protective of parental rights in other contexts. Hamburg's municipal court decided in April 1935 that "the fact that the mother of the child is a prostitute is not sufficient justification for the court to deny her the custody of her children who have been placed in unobjectionable foster homes."[98]

Another Nazi attack on family life came from using parents and children to denounce each other to authorities. In Nazi Germany "the family as a collective unit is held responsible for acts of each of its members."[99] The regime not only encouraged family betrayals but sometimes required them. The January 26, 1937, Civil Service Law required civil servants to report any disloyalty observed among family members, friends, or strangers.[100] In September that year the Reich supreme court ruled that family privacy did not exist. The court held that the most intimate conversations between husband and wife or parent and child, even if the listener promised secrecy as a condition of the conversation, were subject to criminal prosecution if the family member brought forward a denunciation.[101] (Ironically, however, courts would grant a divorce to a spouse denounced to the Gestapo by a marital partner, regardless of any reason for the denunciation and even regardless of its accuracy, on grounds that the betrayer violated marital intimacy.)[102]

Betrayals could be inadvertent. A contemporary observer noted, "It is not unusual for parents to tremble in fear of their children in present-day Germany. This does not necessarily mean that the Hitler Youth leaders systematically urge the children to spy upon their parents, though they may occasionally do so. It is quite sufficient for children thoughtlessly to repeat casual talk they have heard at home so that it comes to the attention of some Party office. The fear that such childish prattle will lead to trouble has definitely thrown a pall over the relationship between parents and children."[103] Decades later a man recalled childhood questions to his father about concentration camps in 1933. The father explained and then added, "'Fred, look . . . don't talk about this to anyone else . . . outside the family I mean. Don't talk about anything we say about these things to anybody outside. Not even to your best friends. It's dangerous for all of us. You understand?' I didn't but nodded."[104] Another man recalled a dangerous childhood lapse. "The day after the Reichstag burned, I, like a dumb kid, said in school, 'That wasn't a communist that burnt it.' One hour later I went home for lunch and there was an SS man at the door who said to my father, 'Mr. Miller, your son said such and so at school.'" The SS man "frightened the hell out of all of us."[105] A *Mischling* child was unaware that his mother was Jewish. She later mused about her son's primary school days, where he learned "Jews should be struck whenever one came across them. He communicated this advice to us at supper one evening. The blood rushed to my head, I was so appalled by the enormity of the moment and my inability to say, 'Look, here's a Jew sitting right in front of you—your own mother!' But the boy was still so childish and naïve and so inclined to blurt out everything he knew that we didn't dare enlighten him."[106] Another mother watched in horror as her happy child declared in public, "Do you know, Mummy, Werner says his mother listens to the radio just the way you do, with your ear right up against it." The mother said, "I held my breath. . . . Listening to foreign broadcasts was punishable by a minimum of five years imprisonment, and the maximum penalty was death. . . . I had never met Werner's mother, but as from now she and I were bound to each other as if we had committed murder together. 'Well, she's probably deaf,' I said firmly, . . . 'deaf as a post in one ear, same as I am.'"[107] The same mother noted, "When we first arrived in Berlin in 1939, we knew of neither a good doctor nor a good dentist. Both had to be politically reliable because they would be able to talk to the children and could also listen in to whatever one might have to say whilst under an anaesthetic."[108] Such concern was not theoretical. A nurse denounced a patient "to win him back again for the Führer."[109] Doctors also faced risks from patients. An American student consulted a Jewish doctor in Berlin, who joked to her that studying was "not in good taste" today. She mentioned the joke outside the office. The jest got back to the regime, and the doctor fled. He was tracked down and put under protective custody.[110]

A middle ground between innocent and deliberate betrayal was court-ordered betrayal. For example in race defilement cases the Aryan member of an engaged Aryan-Jew couple could be compelled to testify against the betrothed.[111]

Deliberate betrayal of family members, however, may have been the most notorious element of the Nazi denunciation system. Sometimes the motive was revenge over a long-held grievance. Sometimes the motive was sudden anger from a quarrel, transferring routine family squabbles to the police system through a moment of anger that was later sorely regretted. And perhaps saddest of all, sometimes the motive was civic duty through which the regime managed to convince a child, parent, or spouse that respect for a person's privacy was less important than obedience to a bureaucrat's criminal fantasies.

That process of persuasion was most effective with children, whose immaturity made them easy prey to arguments that confused even many adults and which often perverted natural adolescent rebelliousness. We have earlier seen examples of children threatening and betraying parents. Knowledge of such incidents poisoned family intimacy. "Margarete Rieck was pale, and her husband seemed upset: 'Frau Bella, we are dreadfully worried. The boys won't listen to us any more. Guenther had to join the Hitler Youth. The other two, the Young Folk. Margarete wanted Guenther to take a bunch of roses from our garden to you. He refused. When Margarete insisted that he obey, he drew his dagger from its sheath and assaulted her, his own mother! He shouted: 'I belong to the Fuehrer first! The family comes second. If you want to continue your friendship with Aunt Bella, I shall have to report you to the party!'"[112] An American living in Berlin during the regime's early days noted, "Espionage is carried on in intimate family circles. One intellectual once told my father that since his young son had joined the Party there was no longer peace in the home. The parents were afraid to express themselves openly in front of him and his friends, and were also fearful for the older friends they entertained who might talk frankly in front of the boy."[113] A survivor of that era wrote, "Frau Brettschneider was crying in my aunt's store. Her son, in the Hitler Youth, denounced his father to the S. S. for listening to foreign radio stations. Herr Brettschneider was arrested and had been missing for over two weeks. No word from him or about him. Most of the neighbors were avoiding her. And she was living in dreadful silence with her 15-year-old son, who was smugly proud of himself."[114] A Hitler Youth officer later remembered those days: "Walter Hess, a minor Hitler Youth leader, acquired a certain amount of fame and a promotion for reporting his own father directly to the *Gestapo*. It appeared *Herr* Hess, once a Communist, had called the *Führer* a blood-crazed maniac and scolded his son for his allegiance. *Herr* Hess was arrested the same night and sent to Dachau, where he died of sudden 'heart failure,' at a healthy age 40."[115] During Crystal Night a nine-year-old boy excitedly asked his father for a hatchet so he could join his young friends: "We're going to smash everything the Jews have got." His father refused to entrust the little boy with a hatchet, but was afraid to forbid the lad's partic-ipation.[116] A former Gestapo officer recalled a father disciplining two teenage daughters for returning pregnant from a *Bund Deutscher Mädel* camp (the female version of Hitler Youth). They complained to the Gestapo, which sent him to Buchenwald.[117] A contemporary observer despaired, "Among people I know, I have heard of more than one case of children denouncing their parents politically, and thereby delivering them to the ax."[118]

Consequences were not always so dreadful, but even lesser ones darkened family and neighborhood spontaneity. Around late 1935 a balloon peddler told a visiting American about a four-day jail stay. "I was grumbling about the butter shortage to some neighbors. A Hitler Youth girl of sixteen heard me. For-tunately, my documents were in order, so they released me."[119] In 1934 a pharmacist's wife

> met a friend on the street who had asked, "How is business?" and she had an-swered, "Bad—practically nonexistent." This conversation had been overheard

by a boy of fifteen, son of her nearest neighbor. He had reported it at the next meeting of his Hitler Youth Group.

"They have a weekly confessional," she enlightened my puzzlement. "We have these confessionals in all our National Socialist Groups. . . . The adult or child who is most diligent in protection of the state stands highest in favor. . . .

"My neighbor's son meant me no harm. He did what he thought was right in repeating my words at his little group. *'Klagen und Klatchen verboten!'*—grumbling and gossiping are forbidden. We had a two months' campaign of education on this in the spring. His report was forwarded to the Party official of this district. I am now being taught to remember not to grumble. My punishment is light, really."[120]

Betrayals of adults by children may have received the most notoriety, but betrayals went the other direction as well. In spring 1933 a young Jewish male fell in love with an Aryan female. Her father disapproved, and when she refused to abandon her beloved, the father went to the SA (storm troopers). They put the daughter's boyfriend in a concentration camp for six weeks. Upon emergence he looked like "raw, lacerated meat. He will probably never regain his health."[121] After a race defilement case in which the Jewish man was deported to Poland, the Aryan woman's mother learned in May 1937 of the daughter's intention to repeat the offense by traveling to Poland to be with her beloved. The mother alerted authorities who then prevented her daughter from obtaining a passport, thwarting the daughter's plan.[122]

Fear of betrayal was not the only pressure on family coherence. A young boy preparing for *Jungvolk* (junior branch of Hitler Youth) became distraught when he was denied graduation with his *Pimpf* troop because his father's Nazism was not enthusiastic enough. "I found him a few nights ago on the kitchen floor unconscious," the father confided to a visitor. "While his mother and I were attending an anti-air-raid rehearsal, he stuffed newspapers under the door and turned on the gas. We barely saved his life. I have now signed a paper that I will join the Arbeitsfront, and become active in the Party. After all—my life is lived. I was in the last war and all that. But the boy—he must have his chance. He took the signed paper to his Gruppenleiter. They are going to promote him now."[123]

Nazi policies examined so far in this chapter disrupted family life, a disruption often intended as indirect limitation on childbearing. Nazis were not coy about pursuing goals, however, and the regime did not hesitate to introduce direct limits on bearing "unfit" children.

Tax breaks and marriage allowances were manipulated to encourage certain couples to have babies and to discourage other couples from having offspring. Aryan newlyweds could receive a zero interest loan totaling up to RM 1,000 and issued in the form of scrip redeemable for household goods at approved stores. The average loan from 1933 to 1937 was RM 610. One-fourth of the loan was forgiven for each child born to the marriage. Jews, however, were ineligible for marriage loans and thus did not receive that financial incentive to have children. About 28 percent of couples who married in 1936 received such loans. Nazi authorities believed the loans had considerable impact on birth rates, crediting the loans with increasing Prussia's birth rate from 16.0 per 1,000 to 18.3 per 1,000 (comparing the first quarters of 1933 and 1934). Marriage loans were financed through a bachelor's tax paid by all unmarried adults, including Jews even though Jews could not receive the loans they financed. In addition to marriage loans, outright one-time grants were made to Aryan families with more than four children. From autumn 1935 to summer 1937 the average grant was RM 340.[124] Aid in children's school expense was also offered.[125]

Couples with children also received reductions in income tax. Not only did married couples with children pay a lower rate than childless couples, unmarried Aryan mothers paid a lower rate than unmarried childless women.[126] Aryan couples were excused entirely from income tax liability if they had four or more children. After February 1938 all these income tax breaks were denied if the children were Jews.[127] A November decree further announced that widowed or divorced persons having custody of Jewish minors would be taxed as bachelors.[128] Elimination of tax breaks depended on race of the children, not the parents. A Jew could be the parent of a *Mischling* and keep the tax benefit, but if an Aryan-Jew marriage produced a Jewish child, the tax benefit disappeared even though the Aryan parent was penalized.[129] Tax regulations anchored in race of offspring were clearly aimed at manipulating fecundity.

We have noted the supposed biological basis of Nazi marriage regulations; indeed many were classified as health law.[130] Doctors could decide if someone would be allowed to marry.[131] Anyone living in Nazi Germany who exhibited "severe bad humor, depression, fear, disgust with life" was considered medically unfit for marriage, as was anyone suffering from diseases listed in the sterilization law discussed below.[132] "There will be borderline cases," authorities acknowledged, "whose judgment requires great expert knowledge and a strong sense of responsibility on the part of the examining physician."[133] As we shall see, this meant that physicians, nurses, and other medical professionals became law enforcement personnel whose primary concern was the well-being of the community rather than the well-being of individual patients. "We university teachers," said Nazi medical writer Hanns Löhr in 1935, "are obliged to teach the student that the health of the *Volk* stands above the health of the individual as the ultimate aim of the art of medicine."[134] Persons classified as both criminal and sick had no right to refuse involuntary treatment allegedly intended to help either them or the community. Once such a treatment philosophy is accepted, circumstances such as those which turned medical healers into criminal defendants at the Nuremberg Military Tribunal become assured.

We should not be surprised if a regime that supervised sexual and fertility decisions of citizens could also require Germans to obey other rules governing their physical bodies. Just as Jews had no right to hold their property and thereby lessen its usefulness to the community, persons in Germany had no right to use their bodies in ways that might reduce their value to the community. Germans were told to seek good health not for selfish personal benefit but because healthy persons were more useful to the community; "Your health does not belong to you!" said one slogan.[135]

Such attitudes were focused at the workplace.[136] Reich Labor Front leader Robert Ley called on Germans to give up alcohol and tobacco,[137] a call moderated by Goering, who ordered air force personnel simply to avoid "misuse" of alcohol and tobacco.[138] Once the European war started, party functionaries identified workers who spent "too much" money on beverage alcohol; they were then apprehended for dispatch to "institutes of welfare," labor gangs, or concentration camps.[139] Even poor productivity in the workplace was interpreted in a medical context, indicating the worker was biologically inferior.[140]

The worker health campaign was directed particularly at women. In August 1933 women who used cosmetics could not attend Nazi workplace cell meetings in Lower Franconia, and were expelled from that labor group if they smoked in public.[141] Also that month restaurants were supposed to start displaying signs asking women customers not to smoke. Citizens were urged to confront women who smoked on the street and remind them of their duty to refrain, "duty as German women and German mothers," in the words of Erfurt's police president.[142] The war on women smokers became so intense that even SA Chief of Staff Ernst Röhm felt things had gone too far, declaring it was ridiculous to prohibit women from powdering or smoking in restaurants and that neither the SA nor SS would get involved with such issues any more, particularly in confronting such women on the street.[143] Authorities later announced creation of a Reich Office to combat use of alcohol and tobacco.[144] "When a woman gives herself up to the enjoyment of smoking," Julius Streicher warned, "she destroys not only her body but her soul." Streicher also called for action to limit cigarette advertisements aimed at youth.[145] One survey found that 90 percent of Hanover boys aged fourteen years had experimented with tobacco smoking, and 10 percent were regular smokers.[146] Nazis acted as if an entire generation were threatened. After the Law for the Protection of Youth was enacted in March 1940, youths under eighteen years of age could no longer be on streets after dark, nor patronize restaurants, movie theaters, and other entertainment spots after 9:00 P.M. unless chaperoned by an adult. Youths under sixteen could no longer buy liquor by the drink, and were forbidden to smoke in public.[147]

Limitations on autonomy of one's physical body went beyond alcohol and tobacco use. "Overeating, party spokesmen have declared, is a form of treason to people and state."[148] Treason was a capital crime, and that characterization of overeating was not entirely rhetorical. A regime that limits what persons can put in their own bodies can easily decide to limit what people can have in their minds. During World War II a *Luftwaffe* officer confided to his diary that he was unsure Germany would be victorious. In the confusion of an air raid, someone found his diary and reported it to authorities. The officer was thereupon charged with "military subversion of his own person," a treasonous death penalty offense.[149] Crime against one's mind is no more bizarre than crime against one's body.

If citizens can be compelled to have good health, they can be compelled to accept involuntary treatment for conditions that the state defines as unhealthy. Perhaps the most famous example of involuntary treatment, an example relating directly to annihilation through prevention of birth, was sterilization. The state "has the right to implement such measures for the benefit of the community as are scientifically proved expedient in the way of population policy or eugenics," explained Dr. Walter Gross, head of the Reich Bureau for Enlightenment on Population Policy and Racial Welfare. "It is not humane," he continued, "that among civilised peoples the standard of living of that section of the population which is fit and able to work is lowered by burdening it with the excessive levies necessary for the maintenance of and keeping within its midst the hereditarily diseased who, despite these heavy costs, can never be healed of their ailments."[150] Dr. Achim Gercke, a Reich Interior Ministry race expert, declared about 1934, "We have the negative side in our work which translated into race technique means: extinction. In its last consequence, it amounts to *sterilization of those hereditarily inferior*. . . . There is in truth only one humane idea, that is: *'furthering the good, eliminating the bad.'*. . . We simply fulfill the commandment, no more, no less."[151]

Nazis rejected any notion that involuntary sterilization was punishment.[152] Soon after the sterilization law was passed the *Hakenkreuz Banner* of Mannheim, Baden pilloried Aryan females seen in the company of male Jews and suggested that such race-defiling females be sterilized if they refused deportation to Palestine,[153] but the idea found no support from authorities involved with sterilization. Punitive use was officially rejected; instead the surgical intervention was portrayed as a "truly beneficial deed for the hereditarily sick family."[154] In the words of Dr. Gross, "How great is the mental agony of a person suffering from some hereditary disease in the pitiful knowledge that not only he himself is incurable but that his children frequently begotten in ignorance of the complications of his own trouble, are doomed to a similar or worse fate. Timely sterilisation rids the hereditarily unfit of such mental torment."[155] Nazis claimed it also ridded the state of financial torment; one semi-official publication claimed Germany had been on the verge of bankrupting itself through care of undesirables, but sterilization was halting that deadly waste of resources.[156]

The spring after the Nazi regime took power an official stated that one goal was to control childbearing through sterilization,[157] and summer 1933 saw the Law for the Prevention of Offspring with Hereditary Diseases.[158] The law required sterilization of persons suffering from mental retardation, schizophrenia, manic-depressive behavior, epilepsy, deafness, blindness, Huntington's Chorea, physical deformity, or alcoholism. Controversy existed about whether the law required sterilization of persons addicted to drugs other than alcohol,[159] but we may be confident that civic duty and the educational nature of law promoted such sterilizations. Apparently such principles also established depression as additional grounds for treatment.[160] The law applied to everyone in Germany, even foreign citizens residing there.[161] Physicians, nurses, and other medical personnel were required to inform the government about patients' hereditary defects even if professional confidences had to be violated. At first doctors who failed to do so were fined RM 150; later they were removed from their practices.[162] Physicians consulted the Gestapo when difficult questions arose, such as explaining to a child's legal guardian why a sterilization was performed on a child without the guardian's permission.[163] Hundreds of thousands of persons were sterilized before World War II, by one account two hundred thousand in 1934 alone.[164] "Unsuitable" women were sterilized wholesale. One observer watched sterilization operations at a city hospital for over an hour, and the disassembly line was running before and after he watched. At this hospital six surgeons were kept busy at the task four days a week. When the observer asked who determined which women were sterilized, his SS guide told him, "We have courts Herr Direktor Ziemer. We have courts. It is all done very legally, rest assured. We have law and order."[165]

Nazis prided themselves that sterilization decisions were based on infallible medical diagnosis which was nonetheless subject to review panels before any operation was approved. Dr. Ernst Rüdin (Professor of Psychiatry at the University of Munich, staff member of the Kaiser Wilhelm Institute of Psychiatric Research, and director of the Kaiser Wilhelm Institute for Genealogy and Demography) coauthored the Interior Ministry's 1934 commentary on eugenics law.[166] In 1938 one of Rüdin's coauthors, Arthur Gütt, M.D., assured doubters, "Special courts have been created to decide whether, in any given instance, the provisions of the Act are to be applied to it. They are composed of physicians and judges. Prior to making their decision, they carefully examine the circumstances in question. . . . The work performed by the courts is of a highly responsible nature, its ultimate object being to stamp out all hereditary diseases."[167] Nazi commentator Erich Berger noted in 1939, "In contrast to other states, the German [sterilization] laws have been administered through the large-scale mediation of genetic health courts, with the possibility of appeals to appellate genetic health courts, excluding for all time the possibility of the *abuse* of these laws. Furthermore, criteria for genetic health and sickness have been so thoroughly and clearly formulated that the possibility of error on human grounds has been completely eliminated. Countless safeguards have been built into the law and the procedures for its implementation—safeguards which, taken together, prevent improper diagnosis by a doctor and effectively protect the person to be sterilized."[168]

For example an intelligence test was administered to determine whether someone needed treatment for mental retardation. Sample questions: "What type of state do we have at present?" "Why does one build houses higher in towns than in the countryside?" "What does it mean to boil water?" "What does it cost to send a letter?"[169] An official report on sterilization said, "Among the feeble-minded there is a large number who have a certain mental agility and who answer the usual easy questions quickly and apparently with assurance" but "who only after a more searching examination betray the utter superficiality of their thinking, their inability to reason and their lack of moral judgment." The Nazi report noted, "Feeble-mindedness becomes especially clear when the disproportion is established between purely intellectual capacities—even if only superficial—on the one hand and the whole life conduct on the other."[170] The implication here is that an apparently normal person who resists the regime demonstrates retardation. Courts eventually made that implication explicit by developing the doctrine of "camouflaged" or "social feeble-mindedness," in which medically hidden retardation was revealed by deviancy from Nazi social norms.[171] A memo circulated to party leaders in January 1937 noted

> The question whether the person is an imbecile cannot be ascertained solely by carrying out an intelligence test, but requires detailed evaluation of the *whole* personality of the human being. This review shall not only take into consideration the knowledge and intellectual abilities of the presumed imbecile, but also his ethical, moral and political attitude. A number of Civil Service doctors have, up to date, attached little importance to the reviewing of the personality as a whole. They have, up to now, hardly ever called for or used information regarding the political conduct of the supposed patient with hereditary disease.
> . . . It is the task of all Gauleiters to ascertain that the law regarding hereditary health will, in fact, be used in the sense in which it was designed. School masterly examination is not to be alone decisive in judging whether a person concerned is an imbecile. It is, in fact, to be ascertained as well, how the person behaves in daily life, whether he can meet the demands which life makes on an average person, and whether he can be regarded as a full member of the community.[172]

One set of postwar legal proceedings included this exchange between an attorney and concentration camp doctor Friedrich Mennecke:

> Attorney: So, you had two kinds of cases: the mentally ill, which had to be evaluated according to medical criteria, and those which had to be evaluated according to political and racial criteria?
> Mennecke: One simply cannot distinguish the two, Herr Attorney. The two cases were simply not divided and clearly separated from one another.[173]

Nazis identified mental retardation as especially likely among Jews,[174] and after firsthand observation of sterilization policies in Germany, an American eugenicist reported that anti-Jewish measures were not an attack on Judaism but were rather "a large-scale breeding project, with the purpose of eliminating from the nation the hereditary attributes of the Semitic race."[175] Aside from mental retardation, sterilization experts were able to diagnose other genetic conditions that could have been missed by general practitioners. "I knew a Jewish woman of middle age, in the trying years of physical change, who was pronounced insane and whose son was forcibly sterilized to prevent procreation of a perfectly healthy line."[176] In another case a man with one leg was sterilized, even though his physical deformity was caused by a workplace accident, on grounds that a one-legged man could not earn an income that would properly support a family.[177] Nazi medical writer Hanns Löhr declared in 1935, "The social upheaval of the present time will help us to turn from an undue concentration on individual symptoms and organs to the consideration of the 'whole' human being."[178] Nazi medicine was holistic medicine.

Not all involuntary recipients of sterilization therapy appeared pleased. Some filed appeals, but their lawyers had no right to plead before the court.[179] The appeals process, one contemporary observer noted, was "not unduly cumbersome." For example, in 1935 a sterilization was carried out upon a Swiss citizen while he was appealing the decision.[180] "It is foolish," said Dr. Gross, "to want acquiescence from a human being who has no command over his morbid instincts or of one who is to be prevented from procreation for the very reason that he is suffering from some mental debility."[181] Dr. Gross continued, "The specialist in the sphere of hereditary transmission, both medical and legal, backed by the knowledge of biological necessities must, if called upon, take upon his shoulders the responsibility which the individual patient is unable to bear."[182] Nazis lamented that "persons lacking in understanding" failed to attend sterilization hearings and might even try to avoid compliance with court-ordered therapy. A Nazi report noted that resistance was futile; police always tracked down patients and assured their receipt of treatment.[183] In June 1937 the Gestapo told the captain of a Dutch ship in a German harbor that a German crew member was wanted for treason. They took the man away, but the Gestapo's story was a ruse to simplify seizing the man; in reality he was removed to undergo court-ordered sterilization that he had been fleeing.[184] The sterilization law said a "doctor has to request the necessary measures from the police authorities. Where other measures are insufficient, direct force may be used."[185] Victims could, however, avoid sterilization by accepting confinement in a concentration camp.[186] Prosecutors at the Nuremberg Military Tribunal grimly ridiculed Nazi claims that victims thereby had a free choice: "A person was a free agent if he had a choice between sterilization and deportation to a concentration camp."[187] Tribunal prosecutors defined the offer of those two alternatives as a crime against humanity.[188]

Some Germans did, however, welcome sterilization. Contraception among the hygienically fit was discouraged so adamantly as to be nearly a criminal offense, and was actually grounds for divorce.[189] Hereditary health law was a godsend for sexually active persons who wanted to avoid procreation. If they seemed free from genetic affliction they might claim their grandmothers suffered from hereditary disease.[190] Sterilization-on-demand was illegal; some hereditary flaw or "serious danger to the life or health of the person" preventable by sterilization had to be demonstrated.[191] Abortion-on-demand was illegal but "interception of pregnancy for hygienic reasons" was permissible;[192] abortion was legal for any pregnant woman targeted for sterilization.[193] In practice abortions for racial hygiene were mandatory.[194] Embryos believed to produce first-degree *Mischlinge* could be aborted.[195] In 1938 abortion-on-demand became legal for all Jewish women,[196] and in 1942 the regime decided to stop prosecuting any unmarried women who sought abortions.[197]

While examining limitations on birth we have seen an insidious transformation of medical professionals, from healers protecting individuals into bureaucrats protecting the state. This transformation promoted a new concept of criminal law combining medicine with law enforcement. Nazi judges paid less and less attention to specific acts that brought a defendant to court. Instead judges pondered what those acts revealed about a defendant's personality, which in turn expressed a defendant's immutable genetic make-up.[198] "No distinction is drawn between the perpetrator and the accessory, between the attempt and the consummated act."[199] The question was not whether someone committed a burglary, but whether the person was inherently a burglar—if so, the person's conduct was beyond hope of reform. It was also beyond defense; defendants might contest reports of their actions, but they could hardly deny the reality of their biological bodies. "In cases of doubt," one superior court declared, "it is becoming legal practice also to take the outstanding characteristics of the accused's clan into account."[200] Prison officials "took measurements of all the features of prisoners and if their biometric characteristics seemed to jibe with some other known criminal they were immediately ear-marked as congenital offenders. You may be sure that whenever a prisoner's nose was a little longer than that of the ordinary Aryan type he was found to be a congenital criminal and held indefinitely in preventive detention."[201] Judges discovered that relying on medicine, rather than law, gave them arbitrary and absolute power in rendering verdicts and sentences.[202]

Just as attempts to interfere with biological destiny could never produce a third leg, neither could anyone hope to turn a burglar into a productive member of the community. The combination of law and medicine easily became lethal.

INFLICTION OF DEATH

Some lethal consequences were side effects of other Nazi policies. For example identifying Jews by blood led some hospitals to keep separate Aryan and Jewish blood supplies, and those hospitals refused to let members of one race receive transfusions of alien blood from the other race.[203] Conceivably such a policy could kill a patient needing blood. Ostracism included medical care. Travel restrictions on Jews prevented Jewish physicians from attending some patients.[204] We are already familiar with bans on use of health spas by Jews, and with bans against Jewish physicians attending patients in hospitals. Schotten's city council even forbade Jewish *patients* to use the city hospital,[205] and by spring 1938 Nuremberg's Sebastian and Holy Spirit hospitals refused to admit Jewish patients.[206] Jews injured that autumn during Crystal Night were denied emergency treatment at hospitals in Cologne, Stuttgart, and Worms—denial having fatal consequences for some.[207] Near Bad Reichenhall an elderly Jewish widow lay unconscious for three days after Crystal Night, during which time no physician was willing to treat her.[208] At a meeting of top Nazi officials after Crystal Night, Reinhard Heydrich urged an official ban against Jews being patients in hospitals that admitted Aryans.[209] Eventually Jews could go only to Jewish hospitals; though beds might be available in Aryan hospitals, Jews had to wait for space at a Jewish institution even if the delay would be fatal.[210]

Another lethal element of ostracism limited food supplies to Jews. In late 1935 an observer reported, "Jewish women have been forbidden entry to dairies and to bakeries and grocers' shops. Milk cannot now be got even for tiny children. Some shops used to supply their Jewish customers secretly, taking orders on the telephone. But when this was discovered, as for example in Elbing, the second largest city in East Prussia, the local papers published the names of the shopkeepers concerned. Since then, the Jews in Elbing have not been able to buy food. To-day there are at least fifty cities and towns, amongst them Magdeburg (300,000 inhabitants), Schwerin, Marienwerder, Dessau, and Fürstenwalde (near Berlin) where milk is not supplied to Jewish children."[211] In November 1938 the United States consul in Leipzig passed along reports that food suppliers were refusing to sell to Jews in Weissenfals,[212] but across the Reich such ostracism was old news.[213]

Outside large metropolitan areas, drug stores would not sell medicine to Jews. Bakeries would not sell bread. Milk suppliers would not sell milk.[214] "In the smaller towns and villages this causes the most desperate hardship," said an observer.[215] Heydrich gloated in 1938, "No, I'd say that for the necessities in daily life, the German won't serve the Jew anymore."[216] After Crystal Night Jews could no longer serve Jews either. Jewish retail businesses in Vienna were forbidden to reopen for days, making it nearly impossible for Jews to buy food at shops or restaurants; in Munich mothers desperately sought milk for their children.[217] All Jewish businesses had to close at year's end, and Bavaria's *Gauleiter* said Aryan shops did not have to serve Jewish customers.[218] Obtaining food became a greater and greater challenge.

Unemployment also promoted death. Researchers have long known that jobless persons die at a higher rate than the gainfully employed. A cascade of events descends upon the unemployed: loss of income, loss of housing, reduced access to health care and even to food. In Germany public welfare assistance was typically unavailable to Jews; in 1938 Munich even stopped welfare benefits to Jewish children.[219] Family stress increases when breadwinners become unemployed, taking a psychological toll with physical consequences. "In 1937, after twenty-one years of employment, the [Deutsche] bank had dismissed him because he was Jewish. Prior to his dismissal Kurt had suffered a kidney ailment, which quickly worsened, and he soon died."[220] And, of course, the same factors promoting death among the unemployed also promoted death among their dependents.

We have noted deaths incidental to pillory action, and Jews also died from consequences of raids, arrests, and protective custody. A contemporary press report spoke of Jews dying "after heart attacks resulting from grief . . . or from strain and excitement of repeated searches by the police and destruction of their property."[221] Injuries aside, Jews in concentration camps received shorter rations than Aryan inmates.[222] Outside the camps we may be sure deaths occurred from being forced to live in crime-ridden slum neighborhoods, in crowded and blighted buildings. And homeless unemployed Jews fared worse yet.

Nazi policies encouraged Jews to commit suicide. From the regime's earliest days the international press reported such deaths.[223] U.S. diplomats in Berlin forwarded reports to Washington, D.C.[224]

A few examples can illuminate this lethal facet of Nazi policies. A contemporary observer noted the suicide of a Berlin shopkeeper during the April 1, 1933, boycott.[225] Following the Civil Service decree a few days later, a judge "shot himself after he was removed from office for being a Jew. . . . Privy Councilor Hebting of Mannheim, almost seventy years old, jumped into the Neckar River because his lawyer son was forced to resign from the civil service."[226] About the same time a Stuttgart businessman's suicide note said, "Dear Friends! Here is my last farewell! A German Jew could not bring himself to live on in the knowledge of being regarded as a traitor to his country by the movement to which Germany looks for salvation."[227] In 1933 a renowned scholar at Marburg University leaped in front of a train when the civil service law prevented him from further research or teaching.[228] Another dismissed professor whose racial status was unclear in 1933 (in later days he would have been classified as a first-degree *Mischling*) gained reinstatement in 1933, but committed suicide before learning of his reinstatement.[229] In August 1933 a Jewish sportsman killed himself after expulsion by the sports club he founded and promoted for many years.[230] Lawn tennis champion Nelly Neppach left a suicide note in 1933 saying she had taken her life to spare her Aryan husband from ostracism.[231] Five years later a Berlin resident watched Nazis vandalize a Jewish-owned store and bully the owners.

> Next day, when we returned to bring them food and see what else we could do to help them, we found two coffins surrounded by silent neighbors. The faces of the old couple seemed peaceful and serene amid the broken glass and destruction. As we put down our basket and stood there wretchedly, a young woman spoke to me. "It is better for them. They took poison last night."[232]

Diary entry, 1938: "Paul von Schwabach. He was deeply in love with Carmen von Wedell, from Potsdam. They couldn't marry because he was only half-Aryan. For two years, we all tried to pull every possible wire to obtain the necessary special permit from Hitler. Yesterday, the final veto came. He took his life. . . . Carmen tried the same escape. Poison. She is desperately ill in the hospital, but her life may be saved. For what?"[233] During Crystal Night, "sixty-eight-year-old Dr. Sommer in Hilden, a man who lived in a mixed marriage and never bothered about things Jewish, went out into the garden with his wife and their elderly, Aryan, maid, as the house was plundered and he himself was badly mishandled. There they all took poison."[234] Lawyers and doctors who lost their professions took their lives.[235] "The best-known gynecologist in Berlin, a good friend of my mother's, called to ask her to visit him and his wife so they could say good-bye. My mother assumed they had received permission to leave the country. They said their farewells, and two days later the doctor and his wife were found dead. They had committed suicide. That sort of thing was not uncommon."[236]

In 1933 Professor Dr. Gerhard Kittel, at Tübingen University, presented a theologian's perspective on the cost of Nazism: "Whether individual Jews are honest or dishonest Jews, whether individual Jews perish unjustly or whether it serves those individuals right" is irrelevant. "Quite a few nice, noble, educated people *break down mentally and perish* because their avocation is destroyed, the contents of their lives are annihilated, and they do not know where and how they shall rebuild something new. . . . But indeed, *we ought not to become soft!* We ought not out of weakness to permit conditions to continue which have proved a failure both for the German and the Jewish people."[237] To this theologian Nazism had its costs to individuals, yes, but who would reject the blessed benefits it brought to the nation?

Although many Nazi policies had deadly side effects, some policies caused death deliberately. As the regime progressed, more and more crimes were made capital offenses. Judges, however, had no monopoly on decisions to kill victims. Vigilantes, death squads, police, and physicians alike administered death. That aspect of the regime has been so well documented elsewhere that we need only glance at it long enough to see its links with actions described in the present book.

In particular we should note that the Nazi concept of "useless lives" became lethal when combined with the belief that people had no right to control their own bodies, a belief meaning people could be compelled to accept medical measures administered by the state's physician law enforcement officers. Speaking to senior psychiatrists in 1938 an SS officer noted, "the solution of the problem of the mentally ill becomes easy if one eliminates these people."[238] Two years later a local Nazi leader related a typical instance of "euthanasia therapy" being substituted for sterilization:

> A young peasant named Koch was sent to an institution for sterilization, on account of epilepsy.
>
> He wrote to his mother a few weeks ago that all was well with him and that she should send him some tobacco for him to smoke. The mother replied that he should come back soon as his work in the farmyard was very much missed. It is to be noted that the young Koch was a very great help to his mother, the farmer's widow Koch, as he carried out all the agricultural work practically by himself.
>
> The widow was informed one week later that her son had died suddenly and that she should collect the urn with his ashes.[239]

One of the most careful students of these matters emphasized that "doctors were never *ordered* to murder psychiatric patients and handicapped children. They were *empowered* to do so, and fulfilled their task without protest, often on their own initiative. Hitler's original memo of October 1939 was not an order . . . , but an empowerment . . . , granting physicians permission to act. In the abortive euthanasia trial at Limburg in 1964, Hefelmann testified that 'no doctor was ever ordered to participate in the euthanasia program; they came of their own volition.'"[240] The local Nazi leader quoted above noted the care taken in diagnosis: "The doctor also informed me that it was well known that the Commission consisted of one SS Doctor and several subordinate doctors and that the 'patients' were not even examined and that they only pronounced their verdict in accordance with the medical history noted down."[241] Physicians made findings such as the following, justifying "euthanasia" of concentration camp prisoners: "Diagnosis: Fanatical Germanophobe and asocial psychopath. Main symptoms: Hardbitten Communist, unworthy to bear arms, penitentiary sentence for high treason: six years."[242] "Euthanasia," however, was not available on demand; around 1941 a physician declined an elderly Jew's request for a lethal injection.[243] After all, unless a medical need were duly diagnosed and documented, doctors would be murderers rather than therapists.

Once patients can be diagnosed as needing death, no limit exists to the scale on which therapy can be administered—vaccinations can be given to hundreds of patients in a single therapy session; so can gas. Comments from physicians at Auschwitz demonstrated professional pride in their skill and no reflection about consequences of that skill.[244] Operations of mobile killing units and central killing stations are well documented elsewhere. Some personnel hated their work, some relished it, some were numb. Regardless of personal attitude, however, all knew the dogma that they were part of a gigantic public health campaign. Some of their victims were so useless as to need immediate dispatch; others could first perform labor under hygienic supervision and temporarily contribute to the community they had previously threatened. But ultimately all personnel administering death were medical assistants, demonstrating tough love by practicing tough medicine.

BUREAUCRATIC THRUST

An early chronicle of Nazi medicine stated, "For acts of utter horror to prevail, for monstrous thoughts to become the governing policy in everyday life, disaster must first have embarked on its course from many sources."[245] The present book has tried to illuminate those many sources, to show how they interlocked and progressed through a process of destruction culminating in annihilation. The fuel for that process may have been hatred, but the vehicle for the process was bureaucratic thrust.

As more and more persons obtain a stake in a project, a bureaucratic thrust moves it along. The war on Jews made money for Aryan merchants. It provided jobs for Aryan unemployed. It provided good housing. It funded scientists' research grant proposals. It provided construction jobs. It increased railroad revenue. It created new government agencies. It justified budget increases for old agencies. It distracted citizens from problems that Nazi leaders wanted to hide. A continuing need to expand the war effort was obvious to fighters who depended on it. And there was no such thing as a noncombatant; everyone was a soldier in the war on Jews.

Mass killings may forever be the image of the Nazi regime, but although they were an inevitable result of the destruction process, the inevitability was unapparent to participants and observers who focused on shortcomings of current efforts and on proposals to improve inadequate measures. At first the regime called on job applicants to provide genealogical affidavits to demonstrate whether they were Jews. When that requirement proved too cumbersome, Jews had to have their identity documents stamped. When displaying a document proved inadequate for oral interactions, Jews were required to identify themselves as such when speaking to officials. When all those steps still allowed Jews to patronize stores and ride streetcars without detection, in 1941 identifying badges had to be sewn on their clothing. A badge decree seemed so absurd in 1933 that no responsible official even proposed such a thing. Eight subsequent years of bureaucratic thrust created a climate in which a badge decree became reasonable. The meaning of bureaucratic thrust escaped many contemporary observers. Said one in 1933, "The culminating point of the campaign for the annihilation of the Jews was the boycott which the Nazis organized against all Jewish shops."[246] Said another observer as the war on Jews escalated in 1934, "The only alternative left to German Jewry is to remain in Germany and seek to make its peace with the present rulers of the land." He continued, "In spite of the obstructions placed in their path by the government, the great mass of German Jews are determined to adjust themselves to the new scheme of things. They refuse to be legislated out of German life. They decline to accept as final the declaration of the National Socialist state that they are no longer and never can be Germans." The observer concluded, "Barring wholesale expulsion or massacre, which seem rather remote even under the implacable hatred of the National Socialists, what has been called the 'Jewish genius for survival' will manifest itself in Germany."[247] Even victims failed to comprehend the meaning of events. "Who, even as late as 1938, bad as things were, could even in their worst nightmares have dreamed the dream of the gas chamber?"[248] Mused a Crystal Night survivor, "Even up to then, we didn't believe it could happen. We thought the worst was over. They couldn't kill us, we were Germans after all."[249] Perhaps the most chilling illustrations of bureaucratic thrust come from official Nazi declarations and secret records of frank discussions among Nazi officials. These sources document that the Nazis themselves did not realize what they were doing or where they were going. We have already noted Dr. Gercke's 1934 declaration that sterilization was the ultimate means for extinction of an unwanted group. About the same time, however, Dr. Erwin Baur (director of the Kaiser Wilhelm Institute for Genetics) went further:

Every farmer knows that should he slaughter the best specimens of his domestic animals without letting them procreate and should instead continue breeding inferior individuals, his breeds would degenerate hopelessly. This mistake, which no farmer would commit with his animals and cultivated plants, we permit to go on in our midst to a large extent. As a recompense for our humaneness of today, we must see to it that these inferior people do not procreate. A simple operation to be executed in a few minutes makes this possible without further delay. . . . No one approves of the new sterilization laws more than I do, but I must repeat over and over that they *constitute only a beginning.*"[250]

Eight years later Dr. Hellmut Schlamm declared, "For our generation which currently is engaged in the severest struggle with this world pest . . . there is only one possible conclusion: spiritual and physical annihilation of the hereditary Jewish criminality."[251] Yet even after Crystal Night senior Nazi officials did not dream the dream of the gas chamber:

Excerpts from Stenographic Report of
Meeting on "The Jewish Question," November 12, 1938

Goering: Gentlemen! Today's meeting is of a decisive nature. I have received a letter written on the Fuehrer's orders by the Stabsleiter of the Fuehrer's deputy Bormann, requesting that the Jewish question be now, once and for all, coordinated and solved one way or another. And yesterday once again did the Fuehrer request by phone for me to take coordinated action in the matter. Since the problem is mainly an economic one, it is from the economic angle that it shall have to be tackled. . . .

Heydrich: In spite of the elimination of the Jew from the economic life, the main problem, namely to kick the Jew out of Germany, remains. May I make a few proposals to that effect?

Following a suggestion by the Commissioner of the Reich, we have set up a center for the Emigration of Jews in Vienna, and . . . we were so successful because of the cooperation on the part of the competent Ministry for Economic Affairs and of the foreign charitable organizations.

. . . Measures for Emigration ought to be taken in the rest of the Reich for the next 8 to 10 years. The highest number of Jews we can possibly get out during one year is 8,000 to 10,000. . . .

von Krosigk: I'd like to emphasize what Mr. Heydrich has said in the beginning; that we'll have to try everything possible, by way of additional exports, to shove the Jews into foreign countries. . . . The goal must be, like Heydrich said, to move out whatever we can! . . .

Goering: The Fuehrer shall now make an attempt with those foreign powers which have brought the Jewish question up, in order to solve the Madagascar project [to establish a homeland for German Jews there]. He has explained it all to me on 9 November. There is no other way.[252]

In January 1939 the Ministry for Foreign Affairs declared,

The final goal of German Jewish Policy is the emigration of all the Jews living in Reich territory. It is foreseen that already the thorough measures in the economic sphere, which have prevented the Jew from earning and made him live on his dividends, will further the desire to emigrate. Looking back on the last 5 years since the assumption of power, it is, however, obvious that neither the Law for the Reestablishing of the Professional Character of the Civil Service nor the Nurnberg Jewish laws with their executive regulations, which prevented any tendency of Jewry being assimilated, contributed to any extent to the emigration of German Jews.[253]

In February 1939 a decree confirmed, "The emigration of Jews from Germany is the aim of all defensive measures taken by the National-Socialist state against Jewry."[254] Escalation of the war on Jews was so gradual, each additional measure seemed so reasonable in its context, that few persons who accepted the war's premise felt any doubt about wisdom in the next harsher step. Only a small percentage of Nazis were psychopaths. Dr. Baur, quoted above, was a biologist who had won international acclaim. He coauthored an internationally used textbook on genetics and eugenics; his textbook colleagues were Dr. Eugen Fischer (rector of Berlin University and director of the Kaiser Wilhelm Institute of Anthropology, Heredity, and Eugenics which cooperated closely with the Nazi Interior Ministry) and Dr. Fritz Lenz (Berlin University professor of biology and a successor to Fischer as director of the Anthropology Institute). Lenz and Himmler served together on the Committee of Experts for Population and Racial Policy.[255] Another Anthropology Institute director, Dr. Otmar Freiherr von Verschuer (Frankfort University professor of biology) endorsed research conducted by his assistant Dr. Josef Mengele at Auschwitz, who forwarded specimens from Auschwitz to the Anthropology Institute.[256] Two chroniclers of postwar proceedings against Nazi physicians noted,

As for the doctor, he could become a licensed murderer, a publicly appointed torturer, only in the merging of two trends—at the point where his aggressive quest for truth coincided with the ideology of dictatorship. There is not much difference whether a human being is looked on as a "case," or as a number to be tattooed on the arm. These are but two aspects of the faceless approach of an age without mercy. Only the secret kinship between the practices of science and politics can explain why throughout this trial the names of high-ranking men of science were mentioned—men who perhaps themselves committed no culpable act, but who nevertheless took an objective interest in all the things that were to become the cruel destiny of defenseless men.[257]

Most participants in the war on Jews simply saw the necessity of accomplishing a job and were willing to ignore ethics if such ignorance helped get the job done faster. Doubters could find balm for their consciences. Auschwitz doctor Franz Lucas was troubled by orders given to him and asked a bishop for advice. The churchman warned that immoral orders should not be obeyed, but assured Dr. Lucas that he was not obligated to endanger his life over the issue.[258]

Once mass killings were underway, the regime recognized that all the previous regulations and restrictions on Jews had logically led to mass extermination. From the 1943 Nazi book *The Care for Race and Heredity in the Legislation of the Third Reich*: "The aim of the racial legislation may be regarded as already achieved and consequently the racial legislation as essentially closed. It led, as already mentioned above, to a temporary solution of the Jewish problem and at the same time essentially prepared the final solution. Many regulations will lose their practical importance as Germany approaches the achievement of the final goal in the Jewish problem."[259]

The German public was not voiceless. The Roman Catholic church organized opposition to the killing of handicapped Aryans, opposition that vexed the regime and crippled its "euthanasia" program. There is even a claim that a crowd opposing the program once delayed Hitler's railroad train.[260] Whether that incident occurred or not, other crowds did form and did protest. Protestors, whose identities were well known, were not dispatched to concentration camps. Speaking out took bravery, yes, but plenty of ordinary citizens summoned up that bravery on behalf of fellow Aryans. Would consequences have been as benign for anyone participating in mass protests on behalf of Jews? Probably so. In March 1943, deep into savage laws passed during World War II and deep into the final solution, Aryan women staged a vocal demonstration in Berlin against arrest and deportation of their Jewish husbands.

> First tens, then hundreds of the wives assembled on the Rosenstrasse, outside the building in which their husbands were being held. They were soon joined by a crowd of sympathetic bystanders. Attempts to scatter them were unavailing. The women pressed forward, shouting demands that their husbands be released. Each morning for several days the demonstration continued. "We want our men!" the women chorused. Their cries could be heard many blocks away. Finally the Gestapo relented and set the husbands free.[261]

Race-defiling Aryan women and their supporters hardly dealt from a position of strength, yet not only did they suffer no consequences, the Jews scheduled to "go east" were released. This public demonstration was apparently unique, but its consequences suggest the hazard of mass protest was lower than claimed by Germans who later explained away their inaction. Subsequent research suggests a more compelling explanation for the German public's silence. Not fear but indifference caused the silence. In 1942 a German surveyed feelings of associates: 5 percent supported the war on Jews, 5 percent opposed, 21 percent were undecided, and 69 percent did not give a damn—they had no interest in what happened to their Jewish neighbors.[262] A later student of German opinion discovered a public that "generally accepted the government's anti-Jewish measures when these were 'legally' enacted and more or less quietly applied."[263] A student of opinion in Bavaria found the population indifferent,[264] a conclusion supported by a student of Gestapo records.[265] Indifference was nurtured by rhetoric portraying Jews as nonhuman. Said one student of Nazi attitudes, "If one is trained to think that another group is not really made up of 'human beings like us' and what happens to them is really no concern of ours, then we gradually cease to feel for them as human beings." They become "mere shadows."[266] Hate propaganda can then become deadly. "Along Berlin's elegant boulevard, the *Kurfürstendamm*, Jewish shops were plastered with swastikas and obscene cartoons. . . . Illustrations of Jews being beheaded and otherwise maimed were posted on poles and billboards. The effect was cumulative. Increased official activity in the form of laws, decrees, and Aryanization gave birth to increased unofficial and unsanctioned activity by the radicals."[267] A student of German popular opinion concluded,

> The "Final Solution" would not have been possible without the progressive steps excluding the Jews from German society which took place in full public view, in their legal form met with widespread approval, and resulted in the dehumanisation of the figure of the Jew. It would not have been possible without the atmosphere of hostility which was met only by apathy and widespread indifference. And it would not have been possible, finally, without the silence of the church hierarchies, . . . and without the consent ranging to active complicity of other prominent sections of the German élites—the bureaucracy of the Civil Service, leading sectors of industry, and the armed forces. Ultimately, therefore, dynamic hatred of the masses was unnecessary.[268]

The student quoted above summarized the situation thusly: "The road to Auschwitz was built by hate, but paved with indifference."[269] Annihilation did not require public support, merely public indifference.

Coda: THE NEVERENDING STORY

A political movement which placed a land under the rule of madness, which destroyed all moral and political relations, which dismayed people with fire and terror in order to get matters into its own hands in the general confusion, merited only destruction.

—Joseph Goebbels, August 1935, speaking of German Communists[1]

Most accounts of the Holocaust emphasize mass killings. Focusing on them, however, can leave them incomprehensible no matter how many details are provided. I believe they can only be understood in a certain context. That context is the destruction process in which they are but the climax of the last step. Viewed in such a context, mass killings become so sensible that the surprising thing is that anyone feels surprise at their occurrence.

I also believe that focusing on mass murder trivializes the Holocaust, in the same way that vivid photographs trivialize carnage in an automobile wreck. If we only see the carnage of one wreck after another, again and again, they all become not only incomprehensible but meaningless—an unavoidable facet of life. What we need to know about car wrecks is the safety equipment used by vehicle occupants, condition of vehicle and roadway, what speed was traveled and what speed was lawful, the vehicle operator's driving record and sobriety. With such information "accidents" can sometimes be revealed as the most likely outcome of deliberate decisions, rather than unavoidable bad luck.

We must not allow ourselves to be mesmerized by the dream of the gas chamber. If we merely weep at the gates of Auschwitz, if we merely rend our garments and tell younger generations that what happened was incomprehensible, we betray the victims. Our task is to understand why the Holocaust's mass killings happened and to avoid repetition. The latter task cannot be accomplished until the former one is completed. That is why I wrote this book: not to illuminate a historical curiosity, but to help shape the future.

Why the Holocaust happened, and why its particular victims were chosen, are two different questions.

As we have seen, victims were ordinary persons. Nothing differentiated them from their next-door neighbors. Despite pseudoscientific and pseudolegal identifications of victims, standards of identification were so flexible as to include anyone. Speaking as someone who has studied and pondered these matters, one of the two basic messages I bring to readers of this book is, *disregard identifying labels placed on victims; remember them as ordinary persons*. Nazis thought they targeted persons clearly distinguishable from ordinary people, but that belief was delusion. If we accept the validity of Nazis' labels we participate in the Nazi delusion. Hair color tells us no more about someone than hair length, eye color no more than fingernail length. Holocaust victims differed in no way from you and me.

Because victims were ordinary, in a broad sense the manner in which they were chosen was irrelevant. Anybody could be a victim. And that fact was very relevant. It meant the victim pool had limitless depth. Once the destruction process began it would inevitably annihilate millions.

Therein rests the second basic message I bring to readers of this book. *The outcome of the destruction process is lethal.* Annihilation of victims can be avoided only by abandoning the destruction process. In the beginning it looks so limited, every new increment so reasonable. Perpetrators seduce themselves even as they become rapists of others. Once the decision is made to destroy ordinary people, their premature deaths loom ahead, just beyond the pit's edge.

Here we enter a subtle landscape, appreciated only by those who have sensitive eyes. How many times have we seen pictures of the latest "Holocaust," where authorities or brigands snuffed out lives wholesale? Massacres are not Holocausts. Images of victims may look the same; corpses flung casually into piles higher than a photograph can reach. Something differentiated Nazis from corpse manufacturers of later years, however. Nazis did not realize what they were doing.

Yes, yes, members of mobile killing squads knew they were extinguishing life; Auschwitz physicians knew they were administering death. But those crimes did not occur in 1933. The crimes of 1933 were just little ones: filling out a civil service applicant's genealogical chart in Berlin, boycotting a clothing store in Munich, engaging in a thousand other measures directed against a thousand other individuals in a thousand other locales. All these measures were intended to hinder victims from surviving in German society. Each additional measure made survival more difficult and, in the end, impossible. But in 1933 not even the most ardent Nazis comprehended what they were doing. They did not understand they had begun a destruction process. Instead they saw each measure as discrete. They obliviously stacked one block of plutonium against another, unaware of growing intensity in the pile's radiation, unmindful of the growing heat. Nazis simply reacted to one situation after another, but eventually their reaction became self-sustaining, went out of control, and suffered a catastrophic meltdown destroying victims, perpetrators, and bystanders alike.

To prevent another Holocaust our task must be to recognize any destruction process that is underway and to stop it, perhaps before its perpetrators even realize what they are doing. This is no easy task. The hindsight of 1946 revealed the meaning of all that had happened since 1933, but hindsight is not good enough for our task. Unfortunately human wisdom has made no measurable advance since 1933, but we do have one great advantage over people of that time: we can recognize the destruction process. As soon as we see our productive, ordinary next-door neighbors somehow being identified as deviant by our government, we now know enough to leap to their defense before they are ostracized, before their property is seized, before they are concentrated in certain areas, before they are annihilated.

But shall we do these things? Or shall we accept that our neighbors are responsible for unemployment, poverty, crime, disease, or any other societal problem that remains with us no matter who lives next-door? Such acceptance by Germans of the 1930s is why the Holocaust occurred. Such acceptance made the destruction process seem not only reasonable but necessary. The danger that threatens another Holocaust does not march with tyrants. It sleeps within our hearts.

> Let it be written on our epitaphs, "We have been hard; we have been ruthless; but we have been good Germans."
>
> —Adolf Hitler, June 1933[2]

NOTES

Quotations from German language sources are from cited English translations. Citations such as "NMT 1234-PS" are to documents in the Nuremberg Military Tribunal proceedings ("Red" refers to Office of United States Chief Counsel for Prosecution of Axis Criminality, *Nazi Conspiracy and Aggression*; "Green" refers to *Trials of War Criminals Before the Nurenberg Military Tribunal*; "Blue" refers to *Trial of the Major War Criminals Before the International Military Tribunal*). *NYT* refers to *New York Times* and *TT* refers to *The Times* of London.

A manuscript copy of this book with more citations is on deposit at the Western Historical Manuscripts Collection of the University of Missouri.

Apologia: THE SPIRIT OF LAWS

1. Marcus, 6.
2. Quoted in Hilberg, *Destruction* [1967], 647. This is Hilberg's translation of NMT 1919-PS (Red IV, 564).
3. Fay, "Hitler," 230.
4. Quoted in ibid.
5. Hilberg, *Destruction* [1985], 1189.
6. Quoted in *NYT*, Jan. 25, 1939, p. 7.
7. Waln, 351–52.
8. Quoted in ibid., 74.

Chapter 1: IDENTIFICATION

1. Quoted in NMT 2842-PS, date given in Red I, 297.
2. "Corruption of blood" is most familiar to lawyers in the context of proceedings that

strip children of any right to inherit a parent's property. Even after the Nazi era, however, American jurisprudence still used the term in a racial context. In 1955 Virginia's Supreme Court of Appeals considered whether the United States constitution required states to allow interracial marriages. "We find there no requirement that the State shall not legislate to prevent the obliteration of racial pride, but must permit the corruption of blood even though it weaken or destroy the quality of its citizenship." (Naim v. Naim, 87 S.E.2d 749, 756 (1955)).

3. *Volk* was a concept important to Nazis, but the term resists translation into English. It is more than Reich citizenship; it also has connotations of race, tribe, and mystical communion with soil, forests, and mountains.

4. Diary Nov. 13, 1933, Fromm, 137.

5. Helmut Schmoeckel, quoted in Steinhoff, Pechel, and Showalter, 56.

6. *NYT*: April 4, 1933, p. 13; April 13, p. 22. *TT*, April 18, 1933, p. 10.

7. *NYT*, Aug. 21, 1936, p. 4.

8. *NYT*, April 27, 1933, p. 1; *TT*, April 27, 1933, p. 11.

9. *NYT*, April 25, 1933, p. 8.

10. *NYT*, July 26, 1935, p. 8.

11. Büttner, 273; *NYT*, April 18, 1933, p. 10.

12. Showalter, 85.

13. Engelmann, 33.

14. They could, however, be disguised. A genealogist was apprehended for forging Roman Catholic birth certificates for non-Aryan ancestors of clients (*TT*, June 26, 1937, p. 13). Some Jews achieved legal status as Aryans by swearing they were illegitimate Aryans who had been reared by Jews. To be accepted, however, such oaths typically had to be supported by bribery and by perjury of third parties. (See Dodd, *Ambassador*, 250; Beilenberg, 127-29.) Likewise, an infusion of cash refreshed memories of some elderly Aryan females who suddenly recalled that a person was a long-forgotten Aryan grandchild (*NYT*: Oct. 22, 1933, sec. 4, p. 3; Oct. 26, p. 18). We are speaking here of biological genealogy, not adoptions; Nazis traced victims by biological pedigree (for example see supplemental Civil Service decree of August 8, 1933, cited in *Jews*, 133).

15. Hilberg, *Destruction* [1967], 49.

16. Some churchmen went further, such as Roman Catholic priests who served as Gestapo informants (Weyrauch, 579).

17. Lorch, 33 n. 10.

18. Proctor, 87.

19. Even Hitler made a sharp distinction between the "race" and religion of Jews. He said that around 1904 "I believed their only distinguishing mark was a different religion. That they should be persecuted on this account, as I supposed, often brought my aversion to hostile comments about them almost to the boiling-point." (Hitler, *Mein*, 62.) About three years later, "I still saw in the Jew his religious confession alone, and for reasons of human tolerance, therefore, even in this case I maintained my opposition to religious antagonism. . . . I was oppressed by the memory of certain happenings in the Middle Ages which I hoped not to see repeated." (ibid., 63.) Rather than religious bigotry, the awakening of Hitler's "racial conscience" inspired him to measures exceeding medieval ones. Genealogy actually took precedence over religion in the war on Jews. For example, the government required full and three-quarter Jews to be expelled from Christian organizations regardless of personal religious creed. If such Christians wanted to belong to a religious organization, they had to join one affiliated with Judaism (*NYT*, March 22,

1937, p. 8).

20. 1933 RGBl. I, 195, translated in NMT 2012-PS.

21. *NYT*, Sept. 17, 1933, p. 12.

22. Dodd to Hull, Jan. 8, 1934, in Dept. State, *Foreign*, 1934 v. 2, 286.

23. See examples in Proctor, 110–11, 150; and Marcus, 41.

24. Walter Gross, quoted in Weinreich, 172.

25. Fritz Lenz in Erwin Baur, Eugen Fischer, and Fritz Lenz, quoted in Weinreich, 31.

26. Quoted in Weinreich, 209.

27. Proctor, 347 n. 90. Gunther is reliable as a source regarding Hitler's belief, but his credibility as a scientist has declined.

28. An individual's race could not change, but the race of descendants could change. If descendants of a Jew married only Aryans, Nazi doctrine held that the family would become pure Aryan in three or four generations (see chart in *Jews*, 77–78). This belief was based on Mendelian genetics.

29. Quoted in Proctor, 37–38.

30. NMT M-21. The name of the most famous Nazi periodical resists translation into English but can well be called *The Storming Fighter*.

31. Hermann Alhwardt, quoted in Massing, 300.

32. Hitler, *My*, 24.

33. Abbreviation for *Schutzstaffel* ("security unit").

34. Quoted in Weinreich, 174.

35. Quoted in ibid., 212.

36. 1933 RGBl. I, 685, quoted in NMT 1402-PS.

37. Quoted in *NYT*, April 6, 1934, p. 13.

38. *NYT*, Dec. 30, 1935, p. 12.

39. Schleunes, 119; Proctor, 150–51.

40. *NYT*, Oct. 20, 1935, p. 28.

41. "Storm division," i.e., a storm trooper or brownshirt.

42. Proctor, 149.

43. Deuel, 213.

44. Quoted in David Bankier, "Mischlinge," in Gutman, 982.

45. 1935 RGBl. I, 1333, quoted in NMT 1417-PS.

46. 1935 RGBl. I, 1146, quoted in NMT 1416-PS.

47. Lorch, 30.

48. *TT*, Feb. 8, 1938, p. 13.

49. *TT*, July 2, 1938, p. 12.

50. *TT*, Oct. 17, 1936, p. 13.

51. *TT*, Oct. 17, 1936, p. 13; Nov. 12, 1937, p. 12.

52. 1935 RGBl. I, 1333 (Art. 2, par. 2), quoted in NMT 1417-PS.

53. "Because a Catholic priest at Kaumberg, Lower Austria, has Jewish ancestry, the local Storm Troopers have posted on the parish house a huge placard bearing the words, 'Jewish Shop.'" (*NYT*, May 11, 1938, p. 12.)

54. Waln, 99.

55. Quoted in *NYT*, April 2, 1933, p. 1.

56. Hausheer, 341.

57. *Deutsche-Allgemeine Zeitung* quoted in *NYT*, March 21, 1933, p. 10.

58. Garner, 98.

59. *NYT*, July 1, 1933, p. 16. In *NYT*, Nov. 5, 1935, p. 18, the official total is still 1.5

million despite two years of Jews fleeing from Germany.

60. *NYT*, Sept. 21, 1935, p. 3.

61. Ibid. During a meeting of Nazi leaders in November 1938 Economics Minister Walther Funk indicated Germany had three million Jews, but that figure was for Greater Germany, not the Old Reich (NMT 1816-PS [Red IV, 454]).

62. Bernays, 527.

63. *TT*, Oct. 10, 1935, p. 13.

64. *NYT*: Nov. 4, 1933, p. 9; Nov. 6, p. 18. Other authorities are skeptical that definitions of Jew and *Mischling* added appreciably to the victim pool. One authority found fewer than 85,000 *Mischlinge* in the Old Reich's 1939 population and fewer than 20,000 Jews by genealogy (as opposed to religious profession). This authority put all categories of Jew and *Mischling* at about 1 percent of the general population (Noakes, 293), a percentage virtually unchanged from official Nazi figures in 1936 (cited in *Yellow*, 18) despite the huge documented loss of Jewish population during the intervening years. Other authorities put Greater Germany's 1939 *Mischlinge* population under 400,000 (Büttner, 271; Warburg, 46–47). Warburg calls a figure of 1.5 million *Mischlinge* "fantastic."

65. *NYT*, June 20, 1933, p. 4.

66. NMT 069-PS.

67. Müller, 99.

68. Hilberg, *Destruction* [1967], 72.

69. Ibid., 49.

70. Ibid.

71. Bankier, "Mischlinge," in Gutman, 983. The smaller figure of 260 given by Noakes (p. 319) is not necessarily inconsistent with Gutman because the Noakes figure covers only 1936 and 1938 to mid-1941.

72. Quoted in Hilberg, *Destruction* [1967], 218.

73. See *Yellow*, 17.

74. Quoted in Lore, "Nazi," 440-41.

75. Bolitho, 223.

76. Roberts, 16.

77. Ibid., 260.

78. Hitler, *Mein*, 643.

79. Ibid., 317.

80. Ibid., 642.

81. Dodd, *Ambassador*, 89.

82. Quoted in *NYT*, Nov. 18, 1935, p. 9.

83. *NYT*, Jan. 30, 1936, p. 10.

84. Quoted in *Volkischer Beobachter*, Sept. 11, 1936, as given in Zeman, 101.

85. *TT*, Sept. 10, 1937, p. 12.

86. Gordon, 103.

87. Quoted in *TT*, March 16, 1933, p. 14.

88. *TT*, March 27, 1933, p. 11.

89. *TT*, Sept. 4, 1933, p. 9.

90. NMT 3050 A-E-PS.

91. C. Schneider, as given in *Psychological Abstracts* 15 (1941): #410.

92. G. Eggert, as given in *Psychological Abstracts* 13 (1939): #4243.

93. Gordon to Acting Secretary, July 8, 1933, in Dept. State, *Foreign*, 1933 v. 2, 355.

94. Dodd, *Through*, 131.

95. Quoted in Schleunes, 107–8.

96. *NYT*, Sept. 12, 1936, p. 1.

97. Quoted in *Jews*, 60.

98. *TT*, Sept. 6, 1937, p. 12.

99. Quoted in Weinreich, 142.

100. Quoted in ibid., 144.

101. Quoted in ibid., 146.

102. Herzstein, 178.

103. Quoted in ibid.

104. Quoted in Weinreich, 205.

105. Quoted in ibid., 113–14.

106. Bettelheim, "Individual," 447.

107. "Protected," 90.

108. Hilberg, *Destruction* [1967], 298.

109. *NYT*, Sept. 11, 1933, p. 9; *TT*, Sept. 11, 1933, p. 8.

110. The quoted language is found in both articles cited in the previous note.

111. Herzstein, 179.

112. Quoted in Gilbert, *Psychology*, 260.

113. The rhetoric of an extremist Israeli settler, who murdered dozens of Arabs in 1994, is instructive in this regard. His references to "Jews" and "Arabs" can be interchanged with Nazi references to "Aryans" and "Jews." (*Washington Post* section, *Manchester Guardian Weekly*, March 20, 1994, p. 16).

114. Heck, 134.

115. *TT*, May 15, 1933, p. 13.

116. Bolitho, 255.

117. Quoted in ibid.

118. *NYT*, June 20, 1933, p. 4.

119. Cohn, 327–28, 347; 336–337, 337 n. 42; *NYT*, Nov. 4, 1933, p. 9.

120. Quoted in *NYT*, Jan. 30, 1936, p. 10.

121. Dodd, *Ambassador*, 444.

122. High, 26.

123. Quoted in *Yellow*, 147.

124. Quoted in Dodd to Hull, April 1, 1935, in Dept. State, *Foreign*, 1935 v. 2, 392.

125. Quoted in *Yellow*, 63. Nazi statistics for 1936 showed the percentage of Jews convicted as criminals to be the same as the percentage of persons convicted from the general population; Nazi numbers (as opposed to Nazi rhetoric) indicated Jews were not crime prone (Warburg, 32–34).

126. Quoted in *Yellow*, 63.

127. Marcus, 44.

128. Büttner, 281.

129. Proctor, 204.

130. Quoted in *TT*, June 2, 1938, p. 13.

131. *NYT*, April 28, 1938, p. 1.

132. *TT*, July 28, 1938, p. 8.

133. Quoted in *TT*, March 29, 1933, p. 14.

134. Quoted in *Jews*, 58.

135. NMT M-46.

136. Quoted in *NYT*, Aug. 4, 1935, p. 19.

137. Dodd, *Ambassador*, 131.

138. NMT L-205.

139. NMT 1816-PS, p. 452.

140. Criminal Inspector Bracken, quoted in Hilberg, *Destruction* [1967], 150. The *Kripo* (*Kriminalpolizei*) was the ordinary police.

141. Hermann Ahlwardt, quoted in Massing, 302.

142. Nov. 24, 1938, quoted in Heiden, 147–48.

143. Proctor, 204.

144. Hitler, *Mein*, 69.

145. *Der Stürmer*, No. 37, Sept. 1934, quoted in *Yellow*, 53.

146. NMT 1778-PS.

147. *Yellow*, 219, 221. A modern reader might be tempted to dismiss Streicher's rhetoric as so unbelievable that no German could have taken it seriously. Here, however, is what the December 22, 1934, *Deutsches Ärzteblatt* medical journal said: "What no scientist has discovered during the last decade by way of logic and experiment has been intuitively recognised and proclaimed by Julius Streicher" (quoted in *Yellow*, 149).

148. NMT M-20.

149. Schuman, 215-16.

150. Quoted in Hecht, 66-67.

151. *Yellow*, 241-42; NMT M-46; Gisevius, 175.

152. Quoted in *Yellow*, 78.

153. Roberts, 265, 265 n. 1.

154. *TT*, Jan. 24, 1938, p. 12.

155. Zeller, 131.

156. Dickinson, 183.

157. NMT M-45.

158. NMT M-22.

159. Wistrich, 307.

160. *Yellow*, 254–55; Wunderlich, 350; Gordon to Acting Secretary, July 8, 1933, in Dept. State, *Foreign*, 1933 v. 2, 356; Ziemer, 158; *NYT*: March 10, 1937, p. 10; Aug. 5, p. 4.

161. Diary Oct. 20, 1935, Fromm, 208.

162. Diary Oct. 25, 1935, ibid., 209.

163. Meyer to Dept. State, July 30, 1936, in Dept. State, *Foreign*, 1936 v. 2, 181.

164. Albert Bastian, quoted in Steinhoff, Pechel, and Showalter, 14–15.

165. NMT M-32.

166. Weiss, 44.

167. Quoted in Engelmann, 190.

168. NMT M-36.

169. Quoted in Shirer, 250.

170. Quoted in Proctor, 199.

171. Gouvernment General Secretary of State Bühler, quoted in Arad, Gutman, and Margaliot, 260.

172. Hilberg, *Destruction* [1967], 151.

173. Erik Jaensch, quoted in Boder, 28.

174. Proctor, 195.

175. NMT M-36.

176. Quoted in Dicks, 73.

177. Friedrich Uebelhoer, quoted in Hilberg, *Destruction* [1967], 149.
178. *Le Monde* section, *Manchester Guardian Weekly*, Sept. 25, 1994, p. 15.
179. Alfred Thoss, quoted in Weinreich, 131.
180. Quoted in Gordon, 190.
181. Examples in Jäckel, 58–59 and Binion, 18–19.
182. Leiser, 85.
183. Lifton, 48–49.
184. Bein, 36.
185. Quoted in *Yellow*, 199.
186. NMT 3358-PS.
187. NMT 3430-PS.
188. NMT 3461-PS.
189. Quoted in *Yellow*, 105.
190. Quoted in Burleigh and Wippermann, 82.
191. NMT 3358-PS.
192. *Der Stürmer*, May 6, 1943, quoted in NMT M-139.
193. *NYT*, Sept. 11, 1933, p. 9.
194. Hull, 168.
195. Gordon, 187.
196. Quoted in Herzstein, 183.
197. Hull, 169.
198. Ibid., 170, 274 n. 5.
199. Ibid., 173.
200. Hull, 173–74.
201. Ibid., 61, 157; Leiser, 75.
202. Grunberger, 379.
203. Leiser, 17–18, 75–76.
204. Herzstein, 179.
205. Ibid.
206. Dodd to Hull, July 17, 1935, in Dept. State, *Foreign*, 1935 v. 2, 402.
207. *Yellow*, 88, quoting special May 1934 "Ritual Murder" number of *Der Stürmer*.
208. *Yellow*, 85.
209. Quoted in *TT*, March 29, 1933, p. 14.
210. July 1935 issue, quoted in *Yellow*, 201.
211. *NYT*, Sept. 16, 1936, p. 14.
212. Weiss, 44–45.
213. NMT M-140.
214. *Der Stürmer*, June 10, 1943, translated in NMT M-141.
215. NMT 2233-C-PS.
216. Walter Buch, quoted in Weinreich, 89 n. 204.
217. NMT M-36.
218. Burleigh and Wippermann, 42.
219. Hitler, *Mein*, 636.
220. Ibid., 296.
221. Quoted in Burleigh and Wippermann, 33.
222. Quoted in ibid., 35 n. 91.
223. NMT D-736.
224. Dodd, *Through*, 212.

225. Quoted in Waln, 173.

226. Quoted in Bein, 35.

227. Quoted in Haffner, 82.

228. Sarah Gordon made this insightful observation about Hitler's rhetoric on p. 97. Further examples of "nonhuman" rhetoric by Hitler and other Nazis can be found in Blumenthal, 55–56, and Bein, 19–20.

229. Quoted in Bein, 36 n. 94.

230. Quoted in ibid., 27–28.

231. Ibid., 27.

232. Ibid., 26–27.

233. Ernst Krieck, quoted in Weinryb, 380.

234. Eduard Hermann, quoted in Weinreich, 68.

235. E. R. Jaensch, as given in *Psychological Abstracts* 13 (1939): #5290.

236. O. Kutzner, as given in ibid. #4260.

237. O. Kroh, as given in *Psychological Abstracts* 14 (1940): #2719.

238. Schleunes, 171.

239. Proctor, 327–29.

240. Ibid., 6.

241. Ibid., 42.

242. Quoted in ibid., 44.

243. Alexander, 309.

244. Quoted in Burleigh, 14.

245. Ibid., 14.

246. Ibid., 15–16.

247. *NYT*, Nov. 20, 1936, p. 48; Weinreich, 53, 97.

248. Weinryb, 388; *NYT*, Nov. 22, 1936, p. 35.

249. Quoted in Weinreich, 47.

250. Quoted in ibid., 54.

251. Ibid.

252. Gerhard Kittel, quoted in ibid., 56.

253. Hammen, 188.

254. Weinreich, 15; Müller, 11; Ebenstein, 8; Neumann, 45, 125. Such a professor found kindred spirits in high places. The first Gestapo head, Rudolf Diels, stated that Nazis believed "one had to annihilate or render harmless all adversaries or suspected adversaries" (NMT 2544-PS). Kirchheimer (444–45) traced Schmitt's ideas to Nietzsche "who characterized penal law as war measures used to rid oneself of the enemy."

255. Quoted in Weinreich, 40.

256. *TT*, Jan. 12, 1939, p. 9.

257. NMT 171-PS.

258. Quoted in Weinreich, 106.

259. Ibid.

260. Quoted in ibid., 23.

261. Hans Praesent, quoted in ibid., 215.

262. Ibid.

263. Karl Metzger quoted in ibid., 173.

264. Preuss, 107.

265. Ernst Krieck, quoted in ibid.

266. Ibid., 104.

267. Quoted in Weinreich, 173.

268. Boder, 25.

269. Quoted in ibid., 27.

270. Ibid., 29.

271. Quoted in Weinreich, 82.

272. Speech to Old Guard, Nov. 11, 1941, quoted in ibid., 5.

273. Quoted in ibid., 12.

274. Quoted in Boder, 24.

275. Quoted in ibid.

276. Quoted in Weinreich, 129 n. 289.

277. *TT*, Sept. 8, 1937, p. 14.

278. Quoted in Weinreich, 118.

279. Quoted in ibid., 119.

280. Wolfgang Meyer-Christian, quoted in ibid., 236.

281. Quoted in Red I, 136.

282. Adolf Hitler, quoted in Weinreich, 162.

283. Hermann Alhwardt, quoted in Massing, 301. This quotation predates the Nazi era, but is all the more important because of that.

284. One trustworthy authority denies the existence of *pro forma* members: "It is an error to believe that membership in the party was a mere formality. It carried with it definite privileges and duties" (Loewenstein, 443). Anti-Defamation League official Eliott Welles agrees, "There's no such thing as a little Nazi" (quoted in Posner, 46).

285. Red I, 984.

286. Shuster, 143.

287. From *Der Angriff*, July 23, 1935, quoted in *NYT*, July 24, 1935, p. 9.

288. Quoted in Bein, 4 n. 2.

289. Lorch, 32-33.

290. Bach Zelewski, quoted in Red Supp. A, 65; Alexander, 312.

291. Green III, 94.

292. Red II, 709.

293. Quoted in Bein, 4.

294. Dodd, "Closing Statement for the United States of America on the Indicted Organizations," Red Supp. A, 280.

295. Yolande Zauberman quoted in *Le Monde* section of *Manchester Guardian Weekly*, July 11, 1993, p. 14.

296. *Kansas City Star*, Nov. 7, 1991, p. A-2.

Chapter 2: OSTRACISM

1. Roberts, 14; Gisevius, 27.

2. Quoted in Kersten, 104–5.

3. Rusche and Kirchheimer, 185.

4. Taylor, "Legal," in Friedlander and Milton, 137, 140. I am indebted to Taylor's account for my one-paragraph summary of Germany's legal atmosphere before Hitler. Wolff agreed that traditionally "judge and prosecutor are on a par, only representing different sides of the same function of the state, and both meet the accused from a standpoint superior to his own" (1076).

5. Quoted in NMT 3593-PS.

6. Zeman, 94.

7. 1933 RGBl. I, 83, quoted in NMT 1390-PS.

8. Constitution quoted in NMT 2050-PS.

9. More precisely, Diels was chief of the Prussian police political department, which was not called Secret State Police (*Geheime Staatspolizei* or "Gestapo" for short) until 1934. The more familiar name "Gestapo" is used in the text so that readers may better appreciate the power wielded by Diels.

10. NMT 2544-PS. In practice neither courts nor executive agencies intervened against Gestapo decisions. For examples see NMT 3601-PS; Fraenkel, 28; Hilberg, *Destruction* [1985], 995-96; Müller, 47. Reich legal principles prohibiting court intervention in Gestapo matters are explained by a Nazi legal scholar in NMT 2232-PS. By a 1936 court ruling regular police in Prussia gained immunity from judicial review of conduct related to political matters, i.e., investigation and thwarting of citizen activity deemed subversive. That immunity spread to police in other areas of Germany and was confirmed by statute in 1938 (Ebenstein, 77; Herz, 699). The SA received the same immunity from civil law under a decree of April 28, 1933 (*TT*, May 1, 1933, p. 13). Dr. Hans Frank, president of the Germany Academy of Law, declared in 1936 that judges must not "apply a legal order that is higher than the racial community, or [try] to enforce some system of universal values. . . . A judge has no right to examine a decision of the Führer which has been issued in the form of a law or decree" (quoted in Tal, 388).

11. NMT 2371-PS.

12. Quoted in *TT*, March 2, 1933, p. 12.

13. Fay, "Nazi 'Totalitarian,'" 615.

14. 1933 RGBl. I, 141, quoted in NMT 2001-PS.

15. Koch, "1933," in Koch, *Aspects*, 57.

16. Ibid., 58; NMT 2962-PS.

17. Frick interrogation, Red A, 1416-18.

18. Ibid., 1416–17; Green III, 110–11.

19. Roberts, 14.

20. 1933 RGBl. I, 1016, quoted in NMT 1395-PS.

21. NMT 1669-PS. See NMT 2315-PS for Goebbels comments on same theme.

22. Marx, *Government*, 75.

23. *NYT*, Jan. 7, 1934, p. 28.

24. 1935 RGBl. I, 844, quoted in NMT NG-715 (Green III, 179).

25. 1934 RGBl. I, 747, quoted in NMT 2003-PS.

26. NMT D-902 (Red Supp. A, 1042–43); *TT*: Nov. 4, 1933, p. 9; Oct. 1, 1934, p. 11.

27. Goebbels stated that purpose explicitly to the German Jurists' Congress (*TT*, May 21, 1936, p. 18).

28. Quoted in Fraenkel, 218 n. 113.

29. *TT*, Oct. 1, 1934, p. 11.

30. Dodd to Hull, Nov. 4, 1933, in Dept. State, *Foreign*, 1933 v. 2, 263. Jews who voted were punished for defiling the *Volk*, but Jews who failed to vote were punished for lack of civic duty (*NYT*, March 10, 1936, p. 15).

31. Quoted in Müller, 66.

32. *NYT*, April 6, 1936, p. 1. A vote against the regime's stance on an issue was also a firing offense (NMT D-901 [Red Supp. A, 1042–43]). Discouraging citizens from voting

resulted in protective custody (*TT*, Oct. 28, 1933, p. 11).

33. *NYT*, July 31, 1938, p. 29.

34. *TT*, Nov. 17, 1933, p. 13.

35. *TT*, Nov. 4, 1933, p. 9.

36. Ruling quoted in Fraenkel, 47.

37. Deuel, 309–10.

38. Quoted in Müller, 48.

39. *Reichsgericht* decision of Sept. 24, 1935, quoted in Fraenkel, 15.

40. Carl Schmitt, quoted in Müller, 75.

41. *TT*, June 24, 1935, p. 13.

42. Quoted in NMT NG-417 (Green III, 453).

43. Quoted in NMT 2904-PS.

44. Quoted in Schleunes, 149.

45. 1933 RGBl. I, 175, quoted in NMT 1397-PS.

46. Rector's decree, Nov. 3, 1933, in Hilberg, *Documents*, 17–18.

47. *NYT*, July 2, 1935, p. 6.

48. 1935 RGBl. I, 839, quoted in NMT NG-715 (Green III, 177).

49. 1935 RGBl. I, 844, quoted in NMT NG-715 (Green III, 178).

50. Ibid.

51. "No punishment without law." The phrase means that state action cannot be arbitrary and is restrained by rules that even the state must obey. *Nulla poena sine lege* requires criminal offenses to be defined precisely and to be published so that citizens can know exactly what is forbidden (see Müller, 73–74). *Nulla poena sine lege* thereby prohibits ex post facto laws and the educational nature of law.

52. NMT 2549-PS, author identified in Red I, 243.

53. Fearnside, 152; Kirchheimer, 449–50.

54. Quoted in *NYT*, Aug. 30, 1942, p. 14.

55. Kirchheimer, 463.

56. NMT 1919-PS (Red IV, 563-64).

57. NMT 1816-PS (Red IV, 427).

58. *TT*: July 4, 1938, p. 14; July 5, p. 13. Grunberger, 103, citing *Frankfurter Zeitung*, July 4, 1938.

59. *TT*, July 6, 1938, p. 15.

60. Quoted in NMT 1757-PS (Red IV, 286).

61. *NYT*, Aug. 8, 1935, p. 8; *TT*, Aug. 8, 1935, p. 11.

62. *NYT*, Aug. 18, 1935, p. 2.

63. Quoted in NMT NG-715 (Green III, 177 n.).

64. 1935 RGBl. I, 839, quoted in NMT NG-715 (Green III, 176).

65. Ebenstein, 73.

66. Grunberger, 122. Examples of decrees enhancing penalties retroactively can also be found in Fearnside, 148.

67. 1935 RGBl. I, 844, quoted in NMT NG-715 (Green III, 178).

68. Ibid.

69. Ibid.

70. Green III, 55. Examples can be found in NMT D-229 (Red) and NG-298 (Green III). Such exhortation was noticed and commented upon before World War II (*NYT*, Oct. 31, 1936, p. 8).

71. Quoted in *TT*, Aug. 19, 1935, p. 9.

72. 1939 RGBl. I, 1841, quoted in NMT 2550-PS.

73. Neumann, 456.

74. Hans Anschuetz, NMT 2967-PS. This concern extended to civil proceedings. In 1933 two judges were suspended for failing to impose penalties harsher than warnings and job transfers against two schoolmasters who did not follow the regime's lesson plan for teaching the Treaty of Versailles (*TT*, July 6, 1933, p. 13).

75. Hans Anschuetz, NMT 2967-PS; Koch, *In*, 113–14.

76. 1933 RGBl. I, 175, quoted in NMT 1397-PS; Müller, 72; Neumann, 454. A contemporary report said the civil service law provided for resumption of judicial tenure in autumn 1933 (*TT*, July 5, 1933, p. 13), but surely judges could expect no more protection than any other citizen when insisting on legal rights in a dispute with the regime.

77. NMT 654-PS.

78. "Protected," 86–87.

79. Mendelsohn, 136–37.

80. Beilenberg, 34.

81. NMT L-179.

82. NMT 701-PS.

83. 1943 RGBl. I, 372, quoted in NMT 1422-PS.

84. Quoted in NMT 2552-PS.

85. NMT 1852-PS.

86. Ibid.

87. Rheinstein, 253.

88. Ibid., 261.

89. Loewenstein, 432.

90. Quoted in Fearnside, 147. Preuss (269–80) presents other Nazi arguments for natural law.

91. 1940 RGBl. I, 754, quoted in NMT NG-715 (Green III, 196). Even the Nazi regime found the illegal drug trade difficult to suppress. Members of one cocaine ring smashed in the Lower Palatinate included Berg's mayor (*TT*, Feb. 22, 1934, p. 13).

92. Green III, 20, 24, 48. Although prosecutors cited the 1940 measure, extension began with the 1935 Nuremberg blood and honor act. We are talking here of acts committed abroad by foreigners, not by German citizens.

93. Neumann, 114, 457; Ebenstein, 73–74.

94. May 20, 1940, quoted in Ebenstein, 73–74.

95. Fromm, 290–98.

96. NMT 775-PS.

97. *TT*: March 27, 1935, p. 13; March 29, p. 15; March 30, p. 13.

98. Dodd, *Ambassador*, 230.

99. For this insight I am indebted to Kershaw, "Persecution," 287.

100. Quoted in *TT*, Oct. 17, 1936, p. 13.

101. Quoted in Red II, 725.

102. Marcus, 268.

103. *NYT*: March 31, 1933, p. 15; March 10, p. 13; March 25, p. 10. *TT*: March 9, 1933, p. 11; March 10, p. 13; March 25, p. 11; March 29, p. 14. NMT L-198 (Red VII, 1031); *Yellow*, 37; Huttenbach, 14.

104. NMT 2431-PS.

105. Quoted in diary April 3, 1933, Fromm, 104.

106. NMT L-198 (Red VII, 1031).

107. *Yellow*, 111.

108. *NYT*: June 27, 1938, p. 7; July 2, p. 5; July 26, p. 10. Probably such signs had to be erected at the owners' expense; they were billed even for paint used to daub *"Jude"* on their shops (*TT*, June 18, 1938, p. 15).

109. NMT 3050 A-E-PS.

110. *NYT*: Aug. 12, 1935, p. 1; Aug. 18, p. 2; Aug. 25, p. 1. *TT*: July 12, 1935, p. 13; Aug. 8, p. 11; March 6, 1937, p. 13. "Jews," 13.

111. Dodd, "Germany," 177.

112. Diary March 20, 1935, Fromm, 191.

113. Marcus, 269.

114. Gordon to Acting Secretary, July 8, 1933, in Dept. State, *Foreign*, 1933 v. 2, 355; *NYT*, March 30, 1933, p. 12; *TT*, April 5, 1935, p. 15; Marcus, 269; Allen, 212; "Jews," 13.

115. Deutsch, "Disfranchisement," in Van Paassen and Wise, 55; Burleigh and Wippermann, 327 n. 53.

116. Wilson to Hull, June 22, 1938, in Dept. State, *Foreign*, 1938 v. 2, 382; *NYT*, June 22, 1938, p. 14; *TT*, June 22, 1938, p. 16.

117. Fay, "Nazi Rally," 207; *NYT*, Sept. 10, 1935, p. 11.

118. NMT 3050 A-E-PS.

119. Deutsch, "Disfranchisement," in Van Paassen and Wise, 56-57.

120. *TT*, Aug. 23, 1933, p. 9.

121. *NYT*, April 28, 1938, p. 8. These were Austrian villages after the *Anschluss*.

122. Quoted in *NYT*, July 22, 1935, p. 4.

123. *TT*, Oct. 10, 1935, p. 13; Marx, *Government*, 85–86.

124. *NYT*, May 28, 1934, p. 7; *TT*, May 28, 1934, p. 14.

125. Waln, 97–98. See also Dodd, *Ambassador*, 182; diary Sept. 20, 1934, Fromm, 183.

126. *Yellow*, 122.

127. Ludwig Landau, quoted in Boas, 250.

128. Quoted in *Yellow*, 110.

129. Loewenstein, 799–800; Dell, *Germany*, 92. This law applied to certain farmers, but not all farmers.

130. *Yellow*, 177; Burleigh and Wippermann, 80; Marcus, 18; *TT*, July 11, 1933, p. 13.

131. Ibid., Dec. 15, 1934, p. 11.

132. Quoted in *Yellow*, 106-7.

133. *TT*, Jan. 4, 1937, p. 11; *NYT*, Jan. 5, 1937, p. 8.

134. *Yellow*, 177.

135. *NYT*, Sept. 24, 1936, p. 17.

136. Quoted in Dickinson, *German*, 187.

137. *TT*, April 15, 1933, p. 9.

138. Quoted in Zeller, 141.

139. Diary June 28, 1938, Fromm, 274–75.

140. Heiden, 63–64.

141. Dickinson, 217.

142. NMT 374-PS.

143. Dickinson, 174–75.

144. Ibid., 154.

145. Deuel, 211.

146. Quoted in Waln, 280.

147. *Yellow*, 122.

148. NMT 374-PS.

149. Dodd, *Through*, 276.

150. *NYT*, Aug. 23, 1935, p. 9.

151. *NYT*, Feb. 5, 1935, p. 7.

152. Müller, 61.

153. *TT*, Aug. 24, 1935, p. 9.

154. *Frankfurter Zeitung*, Oct. 18, 1935, cited in *TT*, Nov. 8, 1935, p. 16.

155. *NYT*, March 15, 1935, p. 9.

156. *TT*, Feb. 27, 1934, p. 13.

157. Barkai, 35. See also Marcus, 13; Deutsch, "Disfranchisement," in Van Paassen and Wise, 53; *Jews*, 89, 175.

158. Berlin, notice of Welfare Bureau of NSDAP, district Prenzlauer Berg, July 31, 1935, quoted in *Yellow*, 281.

159. Grunberger, 313.

160. *TT*, June 13, 1935, p. ll; Gellately, 131.

161. Quoted in Gellately, 72.

162. Ibid., 140; *NYT*, April 16, 1933, sec. 4, p. 3

163. Quoted in Fay, "Is," 745.

164. Quoted in Gellately, 139.

165. Ibid., 149.

166. *TT*, May 22, 1933, p. 13. The regime offered a RM 50 reward to anyone who denounced a false denouncer (ibid., July 4, 1938, p. 14).

167. *TT*, May 9, 1938, p. 16.

168. Gellately, 167.

169. Ibid., 167–68.

170. Ibid., 144, 146, 163 (quotation), 174.

171. *Yellow*, 283.

172. *NYT*, March 31, 1933, p. 15; *TT*, April 1, 1933, p. 10.

173. *Yellow*, 280–81.

174. *NYT*, Aug. 27, 1933, p. 13.

175. Marx, *Government*, 85–86.

176. *TT*, Aug. 28, 1933, p. 10.

177. *TT*, April 18, 1934, p. 17.

178. *NYT*, March 21, 1934, p. 10.

179. NMT 374-PS.

180. *NYT*, Aug. 1, 1935, p. 6.

181. *NYT*, Nov. 14, 1935, pp. 1, 10.

182. *Yellow*, 267.

183. *Der Stürmer*, No. 11, March 1936, NMT M-27.

184. *Der Stürmer*, No. 11, March 1936, NMT M-28. *Stahlhelm* ("Steel Helmet") was a right-wing World War I veterans association that supported the Nazis in their rise to power and functioned as a Nazi auxilliary police force.

185. School essay, ca. 1935, quoted in *Yellow*, 246.

186. Bukert in *Der Stürmer*, No. 35, 1935, quoted in *Yellow*, 242.

187. *Der Stürmer*, Nos. 25 and 33, ca. Aug. 1935, quoted in *Yellow*, 76-77.

188. *Frankfurter Zeitung*, Sept. 7, 1935, quoted in *Yellow*, 231; *NYT*, Sept. 6, 1935, p. 2; *TT*, Sept. 6, 1935, p. 12.

189. *TT*, April 9, 1935, p. 15.

190. Ibid.

191. *NYT*, Aug. 21, 1933, p. 2.

192. Gellately, 192.

193. Ibid, 193.

194. Court decision quoted in *Yellow*, 22.

195. *Yellow*, 135-36.

196. *NYT*, May 25, 1938, p. 16.

197. Marx, "Germany's," 879; *NYT*, Aug. 27, 1933, p. 13.

198. Müller, 117.

199. Quoted in Engelmann, 28.

200. Kulka, 131.

201. *Yellow*, 111-12.

202. *Yellow*, 136; *NYT*: Nov. 14, 1935, pp. 1, 10; Nov. 26, p. 20; Dec. 5, p. 20; Dec. 10, p. 14. *TT*: Nov. 26, 1935, p. 13; Dec. 5, p. 15. Dr. Sahm was not the only mayor to lose office for such an offense (*NYT*: July 6, 1937, p. 30; Aug. 20, p. 4).

203. NMT NG-901 (Green III, 364–65). Unlike American notaries, German notaries pursue a professional occupation. They have law degrees and conduct business that would be limited to attorneys in the United States. In the Nazi era most German notaries were lawyers.

204. NMT L-198 (Red VI, 1031).

205. Quoted in *Yellow*, 70.

206. *NYT*, May 17, 1935, p. 14.

207. *NYT*, July 20, 1935, p. 1.

208. *Yellow*, 62.

209. *NYT*: July 19, 1935, p. 2; July 16, p. 1 (quotation).

210. *Yellow*, 62; *NYT*, July 21, 1935, p. 1.

211. *NYT*: April 25, 1938, p. 4; April 24, p. 36.

212. *NYT*, June 22, 1938, p. 14.

213. *NYT*, Sept. 1, 1933, p. 12.

214. *TT*, Aug. 31, 1933, p. 9.

215. *TT*, Aug. 18, 1933, p. 9.

216. Dodd, *Through*, 28–29, 32; *TT*: Aug. 18, 1933, p. 9; Aug. 19, p. 7; Aug. 23, p. 10; Sept. 4, p. 9. *NYT*: Aug. 19, 1933, p. 5; Sept. 4, p. 2.

217. *Der Stürmer*, No. 37, 1935, quoted in *Yellow*, 267–68.

218. Letter of October 1935, quoted in *Yellow*, 267.

219. Roberts, 247–48.

220. I am indebted to *Yellow* 56 and 63, for pointing out the typical sequence.

221. Ibid., 58.

222. *NYT*: March 31, 1933, p. 15; April 4, p. 12. *TT*, March 31, 1933, p. 13. Nazis long claimed that Jewish businessmen were bad credit risks while they had a passport, because they might emigrate without paying debts owed to Aryans. Passport restrictions supposedly protected Aryan creditors. (*TT*, April 18, 1936, p. 11.)

223. *TT*, Aug. 1, 1936, p. 14.

224. *NYT*, Aug. 7, 1935, p. 2; *TT*, Aug. 8, 1935, p. 11.

225. *TT*, Aug. 30, 1933, p. 9.

226. *NYT*: Aug. 5, 1935, p. 1; Nov. 21, p. 15; Nov. 26, p. 20. Marx, *Government*, 85–86; Mayer to Hull, Sept. 12, 1936, in Dept. State, *Foreign*, 1936 v. 2, 203. Those administrative refusals soon received court endorsement (*TT*, Nov. 26, 1935, p. 13), and in December 1938 Jews were outright banned from purchasing or leasing real estate (*NYT*, Dec. 6, 1938, p. 13; *TT*, Dec. 13, 1938, p. 16).

227. *TT*, Oct. 12, 1935, p. 11; *Yellow*, 192.

228. *NYT*, Aug. 13, 1937, p. 8; Fraenkel, 41, 43–44.

229. Diary June 28, 1938, Fromm, 275.

230. Diary Aug. 23, 1938, ibid., 279.

231. Wilson to Hull, Aug. 30, 1938, in Dept. State, *Foreign*, 1938 v. 2, 389–90.

232. NMT 2682-PS.

233. Geist to Hull, July 28, 1934, in Dept. State, *Foreign*, 1934 v. 2, 299. Jews later even lost their bicycles (Ball-Kaduri, 272).

234. "Jews," 13.

235. Marx, *Government*, 85-86; *NYT*: Aug. 25, 1935, p. 7; Aug. 26, p. 5.

236. *TT*, Dec. 7, 1938, p. 13.

237. Victor Klemperer quoted in Burleigh and Wippermann, 94.

238. NMT L-167.

239. Quoted in Fraenkel, 39–40.

240. *Yellow*, 182; *TT*: April 22, 1933, p. 9; July 31, p. 12; Aug. 10, p. 9. *NYT*: July 30, 1933, p. 16; Aug. 10, p. 12; Jan. 18, 1934, sec. 4, p. 3; June 2, p. 9.

241. Dodd, *Through*, 309.

242. *Yellow*, 62.

243. Burleigh and Wippermann, 83.

244. *NYT*, Aug. 5, 1933; March 21, 1934, p. 10; July 23, 1935, p. 1; July 25, p. 9; July 26, p. 8; July 27, p. 2; Aug. 22, p. 11; Feb. 11, 1936, p. 4. *TT*: Aug. 5, 1933, p. 9; Aug. 7, p. 10; Aug. 19, p. 7; July 22, 1935, p. 11; Jan. 7, 1938, p. 11. "Public morality" quotation from *TT*, Aug. 28, 1933, p. 10.

245. *Das Schwarze Korps* quoted in *TT*, Aug. 8, 1935, p. 11.

246. *NYT*, March 21, 1934, p. 10.

247. *NYT*, July 12, 1935, p. 11; *TT*, July 12, 1935, p. 13.

248. *NYT*, June 21, 1936, p. 30.

249. *NYT*, July 26, 1935, p. 8.

250. *TT*, July 26, 1935, p. 13.

251. *TT*, July 17, 1934, p. 13.

252. Hilberg, *Documents*, 35–36.

253. *NYT*, March 9, 1937, p. 5.

254. *TT*: May 7, 1938, p. 11; July 11, p. 13.

255. The following examples are from *Yellow*, 204-7; Marcus, 18; *TT*: April 18, 1933, p. 10; April 25, p. 14; May 20, p. 11; July 11, p. 13. *NYT*: April 24, 1933, p. 19; April 26, p. 20; July 10, p. 7; Nov. 24, p. 26.

256. Quoted in *Yellow*, 204.

257. *NYT*, July 28, 1933, p. 7.

258. *NYT*, June 30, 1934, p. 6.

259. *NYT*, Aug. 18, 1935, p. 2.

260. *TT*, Nov. 8, 1935, p. 16.

261. *NYT*, Aug. 17, 1935, p. 2; *TT*, Aug. 17, 1935, p. 10.

262. *TT*, Sept. 16, 1933, p. 9; 1937 RGBl. I, 179, cited in Burleigh and Wippermann, 84.

263. Smith, 42.

264. *TT*, June 27, 1938, p. 13.

265. Wertheimer, 176; *NYT*, April 2, 1933, p. 28; *TT*, April 3, 1933, p. 10.

266. *Yellow*, 191.

267. Kamenetsky, 212.

268. Quoted in *TT*, Dec. 31, 1938, p. 9.

269. Kamenetsky, 166–67.

270. NMT L-199.

271. 1933 RGBl. I, 225, quoted in NMT 2022-PS.

272. *NYT*, April 9, 1933, p. 12; Proctor, 147–48; *Jews*, 85, 159–60.

273. *TT*, April 15, 1933, p. 9.

274. *Jews*, 100.

275. *TT*, May 4, 1933, p. 11.

276. Deutsch, "Disfranchisement," in Van Paassen and Wise, 56; *TT*, Feb. 21, 1933, p. 11.

277. Burleigh and Wippermann, 80.

278. High, 27; Marcus, 11.

279. Deutsch, "Disfranchisement," in Van Paassen and Wise, 56.

280. Hartshorne, 84; Proctor, 152.

281. *Yellow*, 164; Fuchs, 9.

282. Fuchs, 9; Proctor, 152.

283. Proctor, 152.

284. *NYT*, Nov. 26, 1938, p. 2.

285. Ibid.

286. Zeller, 28.

287. Henry, 61.

288. Zeller, 33.

289. Wunderlich, 355.

290. *NYT*, March 21, 1934, p. 10.

291. *NYT*, March 5, 1934, p. 10.

292. Quoted in *Yellow*, 247.

293. Quoted in Schleunes, 107–8.

294. Quoted in *Jews*, 101-2.

295. *Manchester Guardian*, Oct. 9, 1933, quoted in *Jews*, 103.

296. Hedy, in Heifetz, 63.

297. Quoted in *Yellow*, 240.

298. After the *Mischlinge* classification was created, however, teachers might defend them. A *Mischling* girl recalled schoolmates: "One or two of them started making remarks about my 'non-Aryan' ancestry. When Fräulein Riecke heard this, she asked me to leave the classroom a moment. Then she impressed on the others that I didn't belong to one 'side' or the other—that I'd fallen between two stools, so they must treat me fairly and decently." (Quoted in Hecht, 32.)

299. Büttner, 274–75.

300. Quoted in Burleigh and Wippermann, 214.

301. 1933 RGBl. I, 661, quoted in NMT 2082-PS; 1933 RGBl. I, 797, quoted in NMT 2415-PS.

302. *NYT*, Oct. 8, 1937, p. 6.

303. *Yellow*, 161–62.

304. Dodd, *Ambassador*, 217.

305. Quoted in Meyer, 654.

306. Quoted in ibid. Note dovetailing with psychological findings of Erik Jaensch discussed in the previous chapter.

307. Quoted in ibid.

308. Quoted in Hirschmann, "Degradation," in Van Paassen and Wise, 103.

309. Quoted in *NYT*, Jan. 8, 1939, p. 26.

310. Quoted in *NYT*, Aug. 8, 1935, p. 11.

311. *NYT*, July 4, 1939, p. 13. Dance restrictions may seem less curious if one realizes that Nazis believed physical stance of the body expressed a person's race. Dr. Hans F. K. Günther, for example, maintained that a woman's race could be inferred from whether she held her legs together or spread them apart while sitting in a streetcar (Deuel, 183).

312. *NYT*, April 6, 1936, p. 11.

313. *NYT*, May 5, 1933, p. 9.

314. 1936 RGBl. I, 133, quoted in MMT 2871-PS.

315. 1935 RGBl. I, 1146, quoted in NMT 1416-PS.

316. Adam, "Anti," in Gutman, 53.

317. *TT*, Feb. 24, 1937, p. 13.

318. *TT*, Dec. 19, 1936, p. 13.

319. *TT*, Nov. 26, 1935, p. 13.

320. Proctor, 155.

321. *TT*, Aug. 8, 1938, p. 9.

322. *TT*, Aug. 20, 1938, p. 10.

323. 1938 RGBl. I, 1044, quoted in NMT 1674-PS.

324. Quoted in Büttner, 281.

325. Mayer, 38.

326. NMT D-229 (Red VI, 1091).

327. *NYT*: Oct. 9, 1934, p. 6; Oct. 14, p. 29.

328. 1941 RGBl. I, 547, quoted in NMT 2877-PS. See also NMT 2673-PS. Two years earlier an SS colonel in Poland ordered local Jews to wear yellow triangles on their backs (Friedman, 12). By Reich order, Jews throughout Poland thereafter began wearing a white armband bearing a Star of David (NMT 2672-PS; *TT*, Nov. 25, 1939, p. 5). As early as 1938 Heydrich told a meeting of top Nazis that he wanted German Jews to wear an insignia (NMT 1816-PS [Red IV, 452]). Soon after his private remarks a newspaper said, "It is reported that an order will be issued within the next few days requiring all Jews to wear prominently a rosette of yellow ribbon" (*TT*, Dec. 5, 1938, p. 11), but the idea was dropped (*TT*, Dec. 12, 1938, p. 13). In December that year, however, Austrian Jews press ganged into construction work wore yellow insignia on their right arms (*NYT*, Dec. 8, 1938, p. 17). Even earlier, in 1934, Agriculture Minister Richard-Walther Darré suggested that badges be issued to identify Jewish women (Marcus, 21).

329. Quoted in Friedman, 16.

330. Victor Klemperer quoted in Burleigh and Wippermann, 94.

331. Lilo Clemens, quoted in Steinhoff, Pechel, and Showalter, 290.

332. Quoted in Friedman, 24. Such fear was nothing new. In the 1930s a former American resident in Germany wrote, "One Jewish friend of mine told me that he prays for drenching rains so that he can go unannoyed on outside errands" (Dodd, "Germany," 177).

333. 1938 RGBl. I, 1342, quoted in NMT 2120-PS; Burleigh and Wippermann, 87.

334. Diary Sept. 6, 1938, Fromm, 283.

335. Tenenbaum, 53–54; *Le Monde* section of *Manchester Guardian Weekly*, Jan. 16, 1994, p. 16. Switzerland had a long-standing policy of unfriendliness toward refugees from the Nazis (*NYT*, March 6, 1933, p. 7; *TT*, Aug. 19, 1938, p. 11).

336. Tenenbaum, 56.

337. *TT*, April 29, 1935, p. 13.

338. 1935 RGBl. I, 1146, quoted in NMT 2000-PS.

339. Grunberger, 24.

340. Müller, 83.

341. *TT*, May 15, 1935, p. 13.

342. *NYT*, Feb. 27, 1935, p. 12.

343. Büttner, 280; Burleigh and Wippermann, 84.

344. Burleigh and Wippermann, 84.

345. Müller, 66.

346. Ibid., 83.

347. *NYT*, Dec. 14, 1935, p. 10.

348. *Yellow*, 190.

349. Marx, *Government*, 133.

350. Proctor, 252.

351. *NYT*, Sept. 28, 1934, p. 32.

352. Quoted in *Yellow*, 194.

353. Quoted in Marx, *Government*, 85–86.

354. Quoted in *NYT*, July 27, 1935, p. 2.

355. Marx, *Government*, 85–86; *NYT*, Aug 17, 1935, p. 2.

356. 1935 RGBl. I, 609, quoted in NMT 2984-PS; Schleunes, 116–17; Marx, *Government*, 120; *NYT*, June 28, 1935, p. 1.

357. *NYT*, July 24, 1937, p. 5.

358. 1933 RGBl. I, 480, cited on Red I, 980; 1933 RGBl. I, 538, quoted in NMT 2870-PS.

359. 1935 RGBl. I, 1146, quoted in NMT 1416-PS.

360. 1935 RGBl. I, 1333, quoted in NMT 1417-PS.

361. 1941 RGBl. I, 722, quoted in Green III, 200.

362. NMT NG-629 (Green III, 597).

363. Heneman, 742.

364. NMT 1816-PS (Red IV, 432-33).

365. NMT 1816-PS (Red IV, 454). The Nuremberg Military Tribunal here misspelled and only partially translated *Volksgenossen*, which means "fellow Germans" or "racial comrades."

366. Burleigh and Wippermann, 87.

367. 1938 RGBl. I, 1676, quoted in NMT 1415-PS.

368. NMT 2682-PS.

369. *Volkischer Beobachter*, Dec. 5, 1938, p. 5 in NMT 2682-PS.

370. "Jews," 13; Ball-Kaduri, 272; Hecht, 88. Ownership of carrier pigeons had already been banned on November 29 (RGBl. I, 1938. p. 1749, cited by Burleigh and Wippermann, 93; *TT*, Dec. 15, 1938, p. 15).

371. Engelmann, 264.

372. *NYT*, Nov. 27, 1938, p. 46. Hunting permits had also been withdrawn in 1937; the Crystal Night measure was a typical Nazi redundancy designed to focus public attention on an issue.

373. *NYT*, Dec. 16, 1398, p. 19.

374. *NYT*, Dec. 18, 1938, p. 41.

375. *NYT*, Dec. 25, 1938, p. 10.

376. *NYT*, Nov. 30, 1938, p. 14; *TT*, Nov. 30, 1938, p. 13.

377. *TT*, Dec. 1, 1938, p. 13.

378. Ball-Kaduri, 272; Burleigh and Wippermann, 93; NMT NG-629 (Feb. 1, 1939) in Green III, 597.

379. Ball-Kaduri, 272; Hecht, 90; Huttenbach, 31.

380. *Frankfurter Zeitung*, Aug. 13, 1933, cited in Wertheimer, 183.

381. Ball-Kaduri, 272.

382. NMT 069-PS.

383. *NYT*, Dec. 4, 1938, p. 1; *TT*, Dec. 5, 1938, p. 11.

384. Quoted in Burleigh and Wippermann, 83.

385. NMT 1816-PS (Red IV, 432–33).

386. See decree of Sept. 10, 1935, by Reich Minister of Education Rust noting that segregation by religion was insufficient, that segregation had to be by genealogy (NMT 2894-PS). Under this decree Jews and first-class *Mischlinge* had to attend Jewish schools, although second-class *Mischlinge* could continue in Aryan ones (Dodd to Hull, Sept. 16, 1935, in Dept. State, *Foreign*, 1935 v. 2, 382–83).

387. *NYT*, April 8, 1936, p. 18.

388. Gaertner, 128.

389. Quoted in Burleigh and Wipperman, 232.

390. Fuchs, 9.

391. NMT L-152; Gordon, 191.

392. Fay, "Nazi Treatment," 299; Gordon to Hull, May 1, 1933, in Dept. State, *Foreign*, 1933 v. 2, 314–15; NMT L-201 (Red VII, 1036); *TT*: Jan. 26, 1933, p. 11; April 26, p. 15; April 29, p. 13; May 6, p. 11. Examples in the NMT document are political rather than racial, but the same process was used with Jewish professors.

393. Quoted in Hamilton, 164.

394. Dominion to Hull, Feb. 21, 1933, in Dept. State, *Foreign*, 1933 v. 2, 196; *TT*: May 1, 1933, p. 14; May 4, p. 11. Violent incidents occurred even before Hitler was chancellor (*NYT*, Jan. 15, 1933, p. 15).

395. Dodd, *Ambassador*, 273. Dodd does not say the professor is Jewish, but the same procedure was used for Jews and political opponents of the regime.

396. Geist to Hull, Jan. 3, 1934, in Dept. State, *Foreign*, 1934 v. 2, 528.

397. Burleigh and Wippermann, 214.

398. *NYT*, May 27, 1933, p. 4; Gordon to Acting Secretary, July 8, 1933, in Dept. State, *Foreign*, 1933 v. 2, 356.

399. Burleigh and Wippermann, 80.

400. Müller, 63.

401. *NYT*, July 22, 1935, p. 4.

402. *NYT*, Feb. 6, 1936, p. 14.

403. *Internationales Ärztliches Bulletin*, cited in Proctor, 148.

404. Hartshorne, 90.

405. Proctor, 69.

406. Quoted in Engelmann, 13.

407. Wertheimer, 181; High, 26; *Yellow*, 141; *Jews*, 94–96; Warburg, 80–81.

408. *NYT*, March 31, 1933, p. 15.

409. Deutsch, "Disfranchisement," in Van Paassen and Wise, 53; Proctor, 91; *Jews*, 137–38, 151–52.

410. 1933 RGBl. I, 222, cited in Schleunes, 106.

411. Quoted in *Yellow*, 141.

412. Quoted in Bernstein, 729–30.

413. *Jews*, 107.

414. *TT*, Jan. 5, 1938, p. 9.

415. *Jews*, 95.

416. *NYT*, March 13, 1935, p. 10.

417. *Jews*, 107.

418. Messersmith to Hull, March 31, 1933, in Dept. State, *Foreign*, 1933 v. 2, 340; *NYT*: July 9, 1933, p. 3; July 16, sec. 4, p. 2. A December 1937 decree withdrew private insurance panel membership by doctors who had been relying on the Hindenburg Exception; by then they had already been banned from government panels (*NYT*, Dec. 30, 1937, p. 4; Jan. 4, 1938, p. 4).

419. Gordon to Acting Secretary, July 8, 1933, in Dept. State, *Foreign*, 1933 v. 2, 356.

420. *TT*, April 18, 1933, p. 9; April 22, p. 9. Proctor, 91.

421. Proctor, 91.

422. Ibid., 148.

423. High, 26.

424. Burleigh and Wipperman, 78.

425. 1933 RGBl. I, 350, cited in ibid., 80; *Jews*, 83, 152–53; Deutsch, "Disfranchisement," in Van Paassen and Wise, 53; *NYT*, July 30, 1933, p. 16.

426. Deutsch, "Disfranchisement," in Van Paassen and Wise, 53; High, 26; *NYT*, Aug. 20, 1933, p. 5.

427. *TT*, Aug. 2, 1933, p. 10.

428. Messersmith to Hull, March 31, 1933, in Dept. State, *Foreign*, 1933 v. 2, 340; *NYT*: March 21, 1933, p. 10; March 30, p. 12.

429. *NYT*, March 18, 1933, p. 6.

430. Quoted in *TT*, March 29, 1933, p. 13.

431. *TT*, Nov. 24, 1933, p. 14.

432. *TT*, Feb. 15, 1936, p. 11.

433. Deutsch, "Disfranchisement," in Van Paassen and Wise, 55; *Yellow*, 141; *Jews*, 84–85, 156; *NYT*, Nov. 24, 1933, p. 14.

434. 1934 RGBl. I, 399, cited in Burleigh and Wippermann, 80; Proctor, 148.

435. *Frankfurter Zeitung*, July 9, 1933, cited in Wertheimer, 181.

436. *NYT*, Dec. 19, 1935, p. 22.

437. Heymann, 41.

438. High, 26.

439. *TT*, Nov. 7, 1933, p. 13.

440. Proctor, 152.

441. Quoted in *Yellow*, 56.

442. Ibid.

443. *NYT*, Dec. 19, 1935, p. 22; *TT*, April 8, 1936, p. 13.

444. 1936 RGBl. I, 317, cited in Burleigh and Wippermann, 84.

445. Warburg, 84.

446. 1938 RGBl. I, 1309, cited in Burleigh and Wippermann, 96.

447. Proctor, 154.

448. Quoted in *NYT*, May 23, 1933, p. 3.

449. Quoted in *TT*, March 27, 1933, p. 11.

450. *Yellow*, 58.

451. Burleigh and Wippermann, 78.

452. Quoted in *TT*, Nov. 8, 1935, p. 16.

453. *NYT*, Aug. 15, 1935, p. 3.

454. *NYT*, Oct. 20, 1935, p. 28.

455. Diary Aug. 20, 1937, Fromm, 250.

456. Messersmith to Hull, March 31, 1933, in Dept. State, *Foreign*, 1933 v. 2, 340. For example, see *NYT*, March 31, 1933, p. 15.

457. *NYT*, March 22, 1933, p. 7.

458. Lifton, 36.

459. *NYT*: July 8, 1933, p. 5; July 9, p. 3; July 16, sec. 4, p. 2. *TT*: July 8, 1933, p. 11; July 10, p. 13; July 15, p. 11.

460. Brieger, "Medical," in Friedlander and Milton, 145.

461. 1938 RGBl. I, 969, quoted in NMT 2872-PS; Esh, 89; *TT*, Aug. 10, 1938, p. 11.

462. Proctor, 154.

463. *TT*, Aug. 4, 1938, p. 9.

464. *TT*, Aug. 10, 1938, p. 11.

465. Proctor, 161.

466. Ibid., 93.

467. Rudolf Ramm, quoted in ibid., 90.

468. Dickinson, 142–43, 209–10.

469. *Frankfurter Zeitung*, March 10, 1933, quoted in *Yellow*, 36.

470. *NYT*: March 30, 1933, p. 12; March 31, p. 15; July 7, p. 3.

471. *NYT*, March 18, 1933, p. 6.

472. Messersmith to Hull, March 31, 1933, in Dept. State, *Foreign*, 1933 v. 2, 339.

473. 1933 RGBl. I, 188, quoted in NMT 1401-PS.

474. Deutsch, "Disfranchisement," in Van Paassen and Wise, 48.

475. Burleigh and Wippermann, 80; Dodd to Hull, Sept. 8, 1934, in Dept. State, *Foreign*, 1934 v. 2, 300.

476. *NYT*, April 26, 1933, p. 20; *TT*, April 5, 1933, p. 13.

477. *NYT*, Aug. 29, 1933, p. 4; *TT*, Aug. 30, 1933, p. 9; Müller, 61.

478. Dickinson, 209; *NYT*, Sept. 14, 1935, p. 5.

479. *NYT*, April 25, 1938, p. 4; *TT*, April 26, 1938, p. 15.

480. *TT*, Dec. 6, 1934, p. 10.

481. Quoted in *Yellow*, 139.

482. Quoted in Müller, 61.

483. Quoted in Deutsch, "Disfranchisement," in Van Paassen and Wise, 45. Kerrl later

became Minister of Ecclesiastical Affairs, coordinating church policies with state policies.

484. *NYT*, April 12, 1933, p. 6.

485. *NYT*: Dec. 25, 1935, p. 6; March 2, 1936, p. 10. 1937 RGBl. I, 191, cited by Burleigh and Wippermann, 84.

486. *NYT*, March 31, 1933, p. 15; *TT*, April 1, 1933, p. 10.

487. Fay, "Nazi Treatment," 298.

488. *Frankfurter Zeitung*, July 8, 1933, quoted in *Yellow*, 134–35. This type of assessor held a university law degree and was employed in the court system as an assistant judge with the understanding that the person would eventually become a full judge. An apprenticeship as an assessor was also required before someone could become an attorney.

489. *NYT*, Jan. 17, 1936, p. 3.

490. NMT 2536-PS.

491. *NYT*, Feb. 11, 1936, p. 4.

492. 1938 RGBl. I, 1403, quoted in NMT 2874-PS.

493. *TT*, Oct. 22, 1938, p. 11; *NYT*, Nov. 4, 1938, p. 4.

494. *NYT*, Dec. 18, 1938, p. 41.

495. *TT*, Oct. 22, 1938, p. 11; Barkai, 122.

496. 1933 RGBl. I, 175, quoted in NMT 1397-PS.

497. For Hitler's view see NMT 2881-PS. Even Nazis were unable to support his claim: "In one state jurisdiction . . . out of a total of more than 1,600 civil servants removed under the Restoration Act only 19 were actually dismissed as 'party-made' officials" (Marx, *Government*, 130-31). As of October 1936 Nazi Party members received hiring preference over other civil service applicants (1936 RGBl. I, 893, quoted in NMT 3183-PS).

498. See explicit regulations 1933 RGBl. I, 195 and 433, quoted in NMT 2012-PS and 1398-PS respectively.

499. *NYT*: March 21, 1933, p. 10; March 31, p. 15; March 30, p. 12.

500. Messersmith to Hull, March 31, 1933, in Dept. State, *Foreign*, 1933 v. 2, 338.

501. Wertheimer, 178.

502. Marcus, 9.

503. Supplemental decree quoted in Deutsch, "Disfranchisement," in Van Paassen and Wise, 47; Dodd to Dept. State, Jan. 15, 1936, in Dept. State, *Foreign*, 1936 v. 2, 192.

504. Preuss, 113 n. 43.

505. Wilhelm Stuckart, quoted in Dodd to Dept. State, Jan. 15, 1936, in Dept. State, *Foreign*, 1936 v. 2, 193.

506. Marx, "German," 479.

507. *Yellow*, 130–31.

508. Quoted in *Yellow*, 138.

509. Hilberg, *Destruction* [1967], 56-57.

510. 1935 RGBl. I, 1333, quoted in NMT 1417-PS; Marx, *Government*, 130-31; Burleigh and Wippermann, 82; Dodd to Dept. State, Jan. 15, 1936, in Dept. State, *Foreign*, 1936 v. 2, 192. Such eliminations were already underway before September, however (*NYT*, March 29, 1935, p. 3).

511. *Yellow*, 126.

512. 1933 RGBl. I, 713, quoted in NMT 2083-PS.

513. Roberts, 247–48; Deutsch, "Disfranchisement," in Van Paassen and Wise, 54–55; Dodd to Hull, May 2, 1935, in Dept. State, *Foreign*, 1935 v. 2, 262–63.

514. Diary June 15, 1933, Fromm, 115.

515. Diary Jan. 4, 1934, ibid., 147. The regulation can be found in 1933 RGBl. I, 713, quoted in NMT 2083-PS (Red IV, 713).

516. Diary Jan. 15, 1938, Fromm, 264.

517. Deutsch, "Disfranchisement," in Van Paassen and Wise, 52.

518. Ebenstein, 102–3; Deutsch, "Disfranchisement," in Van Paassen and Wise, 52, 56.

519. *NYT*, July 14, 1933, p. 6.

520. Deutsch, "Disfranchisement," in Van Paassen and Wise, 52.

521. 1933 RGBl. I, 217, quoted in NMT 2868-PS.

522. 1938 RGBl. I, 1545, cited in Burleigh and Wippermann, 96; *NYT*, Nov. 4, 1938, p. 4.

523. 1933 RGBl. I, 257, quoted in NMT 2869-PS.

524. Deutsch, "Disfranchisement," in Van Paassen and Wise, 53.

525. Ibid., 205.

526. Ibid., 206. Such restriction was announced earlier in Prussia (*NYT*, Oct. 7, 1933, p. 3).

527. Deutsch, "Disfranchisement," in Van Paassen and Wise, 53; Fay, "Is," 744; Hull, 26.

528. Fay, "Nazis' Birthday," 103; *Jews*, 166.

529. *Yellow*, 126; *NYT*, Aug. 8. 1933, p. 2.

530. *NYT*, Sept. 30, 1933, p. 7; Messersmith to Hull, Nov. 1, 1933, in Dept. State, *Foreign*, 1933 v. 2, 363.

531. Fay, "Nazi Rally," 207; *TT*, Sept. 2, 1935, p. 9.

532. *NYT*, March 14, 1935, p. 13.

533. *NYT*, May 17, 1935, p. 14.

534. *NYT*, June 9, 1935, p. 30.

535. *NYT*, Sept. 2, 1935, p. 7; Sept. 3, p. 15. *TT*: Sept. 2, 1935, p. 9; Jan. 2, 1936, p. 9.

536. *NYT*, March 13, 1935, p. 10.

537. *NYT*, Oct. 8, 1935, p. 13.

538. Hathaway to Hull, Feb. 13, 1936, in Dept. State, *Foreign*, 1936 v. 2, 285–86.

539. 1936 RGBl. I, 524, cited by Burleigh and Wippermann, 84.

540. 1936 RGBl. I, 563, cited in ibid.

541. *NYT*, Dec. 28, 1937, p. 16; Heymann, 43.

542. Heymann, 43; *NYT*, Dec. 30, 1937, p. 4.

543. *NYT*, Aug. 21, 1938, p. 30.

544. *NYT*, Feb. 21, 1935, p. 8.

545. *TT*, Feb. 8, 1938, p. 13.

546. *TT*, Feb. 15, 1938, p. 13.

547. 1938 RGBl. I, 265, cited in Burleigh and Wippermann, 96. After November, Jews could not even own guns (*NYT*, Nov. 11, 1938, p. 4).

548. 1938 RGBl. I, 823, cited in Burleigh and Wippermann, 96, and Schleunes, 221–22, and in Hilberg, *Destruction* [1967], 84; 1938 RGBl. I, 107, cited in Wilson to Dept. State, July 16, 1938, in Dept. State, *Foreign*, 1938 v. 2, 387; *NYT*, July 10, 1938, p. 20; *TT*, July 11, 1938, p. 13. In 1936 local police chiefs already had the power to deny licenses to Jewish traveling salesmen, but exercise of that power was not mandatory (*NYT*, Jan. 1, 1936, p. 23). Berlin police found a way to strike at Jewish salesmen even if license renewal was granted; the word "Jew" was written across the document in bold letters, as

a warning for Aryans to boycott the salesman (*NYT*, Jan 12, 1936, p. 7).

549. Strauss, 345.

550. Schleunes, 221–22.

551. *NYT*, Sept. 21, 1938, p. 3.

552. Ibid.

553. Red II, 721-22; 1938 RGBl. I, 823, cited in Hilberg, *Destruction* [1967], 84; 1938 RGBl. I, 107, cited in Wilson to Dept. State, July 16, 1938, in Dept. State, *Foreign*, 1938 v. 2, 387; Gilbert to Hull, Dec. 29, 1938, in ibid., 418; *NYT*, July 10, 1938, p. 20; *TT*, July 11, 1938, p. 13. Some of these bans were proclaimed in 1938 but took effect the next year.

554. *NYT*, March 13, 1935. p. 10.

555. NMT 3577-PS; Deutsch, "Disfranchisement," in Van Paassen and Wise, 57.

556. Marcus, 284–85, 296; Strauss, 324.

557. Marx, *Government*, 85–86.

558. *NYT*, Aug. 10, 1935, p. 6.

559. Quoted in Roberts, 266.

560. *TT*, March 6, 1937, p. 13.

561. *NYT*, March 24, 1934, p. 7.

562. Dickinson, 169; *NYT*, Aug. 23, 1933, p. 13.

563. *C. V.-Zeitung*, Sept. 7, 1934, cited in Boas, 249.

564. *NYT*, Aug. 5, 1935, p. 1.

565. Kershaw, *Popular*, 241–43.

566. *NYT*, July 6, 1937, p. 30.

567. Deutsch, "Disfranchisement," in Van Paassen and Wise, 53.

568. Ibid.; *NYT*, April 5, 1933, p. 10.

569. *Jews*, 177.

570. Boas, 249.

571. *TT*, May 28, 1934, p. 14.

572. Gellately, 105.

573. "Jews," 13; *Yellow*, 120–21.

574. *Yellow*, 106–7.

575. 1933 RGBl. I, 685, quoted in NMT 1402-PS; Red I, 981; *NYT*, Aug. 11, 1935, p. 19; Schleunes, 112.

576. Proctor, 88.

577. *Yellow*, 192.

578. *NYT*, Aug. 12, 1935, p. 1.

579. Gordon to Hull, March 23 and March 25, 1933, in Dept. State, *Foreign*, 1933 v. 2, 328–29, 332; Messersmith to Hull, Nov. 1, 1933, in ibid., 364; *TT*: April 1, 1933, p. 10; April 4, p. 15; April 6, p. 13; April 10, p. 11. Dismissals followed the flag; German companies were expected to fire Jewish employees and contractors from their foreign branches (*NYT*: Jan. 16, 1934, p. 12; Aug. 25, 1935, p. 7; Sept. 4, p. 14; Oct. 26, 1936, p. 12; June 11, 1937, p. 12. *TT*: Sept. 3, 1937, p. 12; Dec. 16, 1938, p. 7; Dec. 23, p. 4). Nazis warned South American companies to fire Jewish employees if continued business with the Reich were desired (*NYT*, Jan. 3, 1939, p. 1). Facing lack of cooperation from German branches of U.S. companies, the regime ordered them to fire Jews (*NYT*, April 2, 1933, p. 1). Nonetheless German units of U.S. companies long resisted Nazi urgings to fire Jewish employees and remained in business (Wiley to Hull,

March 25, 1938, in Dept. State, *Foreign*, 1938 v. 2, 359). Those companies faced the same laws and pressures as any other commercial enterprise in Germany, and their experience suggests that other employers cooperated with the Nazi program willingly rather than from fear of legal or mercantile consequences. Swedish companies, too, resisted Nazi demands to fire Jewish employees (*TT*, Dec. 9, 1938, p. 15; *NYT*, Dec. 9, 1938, p. 18).

580. Barkai, 33.

581. Ibid.

582. Müller, 118.

583. Karstadt statement quoted in *Yellow*, 124.

584. *Der Angriff*, Aug. 30, 1933, quoted in *Yellow*, 124.

585. *Frankfurter Zeitung* of July 1, 1933, cited in *Yellow*, 124-25.

586. Deutsch, "Disfranchisement," in Van Paassen and Wise, 55.

587. Marcus, 9.

588. Messersmith to Hull, April 11 and April 18, 1933, in Dept. State, *Foreign*, 1933 v. 2, 420, 422.

589. Dodd to Hull, June 18, 1934, in ibid., 1934 v. 2, 296.

590. Fraenkel, 92.

591. Arnold Biegeleisen, quoted in Steinhoff, Pechel, and Showalter, 44.

592. "Jews," 22; Dodd to Hull, May 17, 1935, in Dept. State, *Foreign*, 1935 v. 2, 399.

593. Bernstein, 729.

594. Quoted in *Yellow*, 56–57.

595. Fraenkel, 95–96.

596. Müller, 116.

597. *NYT*, May 12, 1933, p. 12.

598. *NYT*, May 13, 1933, p. 7.

599. Ibid.

600. *NYT*, June 19, 1933, p. 23.

601. 1935 RGBl. I, 1146, quoted in NMT 3179-PS.

602. *NYT*, Sept. 17, 1935, p. 14.

603. *NYT*, Nov. 14, 1935, p. 10; *TT*, Nov. 15, 1935, p. 15.

604. Warburg, 225.

605. Ibid., 223–24.

606. *NYT*, Jan. 26, 1938, p. 10.

607. *NYT*, March 1, 1938, p. 6.

608. Huttenbach, 44.

609. Section 3 of Paragraph 12 in the First Schedule in Amplification of the Law for Protection of German Blood and German Honor, Nov. 14, 1935, cited in *Yellow*, 272; Dodd to Hull, Nov. 15, 1935, in Dept. State, *Foreign*, 1935 v. 2, 408; *NYT*, Nov. 16, 1935, p. 6; *TT*, Nov. 16, 1935, p. 11; Warburg, 223. The compromise, however, was not always observed.

610. *News Chronicle*, Dec. 31, 1935, quoted in *Yellow*, 128.

611. *NYT*, Dec. 31, 1935, p. 7.

612. *NYT*, Jan. 2, 1936, p. 11; *TT*, Jan. 2, 1936, p. 11.

613. *NYT*, Jan. 2, 1936, p. 11; *TT*, Jan. 1, 1936, p. 11.

614. 1938 RGBl. I, 1580, quoted in 1662-PS. Compare different translation in NMT 2875-PS. The decree is discussed by top Nazi officials in NMT 1816-PS (Red IV, 445-

46).

615. *NYT*, Nov. 26, 1938, p. 2; *TT*: Nov. 14, 1938, p. 12; Nov. 17, p. 14.

616. *NYT*, Dec. 1, 1938, p. 10.

617. *TT*, Nov. 14, 1938, p. 12.

618. 1938 RGBl. I, 1902, cited in Red II, 724.

619. *NYT*, Dec. 8, 1938, p. 17.

620. *NYT*, Dec. 6, 1938, p. 13.

621. 1938 RGBl. I, 1893, cited in Burleigh and Wippermann, 86.

622. 1939 RGBl. I, 47, cited in Red I, 981.

623. 1939 RGBl. I, 895, cited in Red II, 724–25.

624. Gordon to Acting Secretary, July 8, 1933, in Dept. State, *Foreign*, 1933 v. 2, 354.

625. *Yellow*, 123–24, 127; *NYT*, Dec. 14, 1935, p. 10.

626. Dell, "German," 434.

627. NMT 1816-PS (Red IV, 451–52).

628. Bernays, 525.

629. Zeller, 101–2.

630. *NYT*, Nov. 16, 1935, p. 6.

631. Hans Radziewski, quoted in Steinhoff, Pechel, and Showalter, 61.

632. Dickinson, 255, 258.

633. *TT*, June 3, 1938, p. 13.

634. *NYT*, March 6, 1939, p. 1; *TT*: March 7, 1939, p. 14; March 8, p. 15; Huttenbach, 5, 33 n. 5.

635. Kwiet, 392.

636. *NYT*, March 7, 1939, p. 13.

637. Callender, 23.

638. *TT*, Nov. 8, 1935, p. 16.

639. Henry, 99.

640. Heymann, 43; *NYT*, Aug. 15, 1935, p. 3.

641. "Jews," 25.

642. Dodd, *Ambassador*, 14.

643. Dodd, *Through*, 307.

644. Bolitho, 31.

645. *Yellow*, 164.

646. Burleigh and Wipperman, 271. See also a contemporary observation about the joy of attorneys no longer burdened by competition from former Jewish colleagues, in Marx, *Government*, 145.

647. For example, see *NYT*, May 25, 1938, p. 16.

648. *NYT*, July 1, 1938, p. 13.

Chapter 3: CONFISCATION

1. *NYT*, Oct. 17, 1935, p. 20.

2. *NYT*, Feb. 8, 1939, p. 17.

3. 1933 RGBl. I, 83, quoted in NMT 1390-PS.

4. Ebenstein, 215–16.

5. *TT*, April 5, 1934, p. 4.

6. 1933 RGBl. I, 293, quoted in NMT 1396-PS.

7. *TT*: March 9, 1933, p. 11; March 16, p. 14; April 3, p. 10. *NYT*, April 2, 1933, p. 1.

8. *NYT*, Nov. 10, 1935, p. 42.

9. Hilberg, *Destruction* [1967], 301.

10. 1933 RGBl. I, 479, quoted in NMT 1388-PS.

11. *TT*: Jan 18, 1938, p. 11 [six-year-old children]; Oct. 29, 1937, p. 15 [four-year-old boy]; Jan. 22, 1938, p. 9, [infant loses any property owned].

12. *NYT*, Dec. 12, 1935, p. 15.

13. *NYT*, Nov. 18, 1938, p. 16.

14. *NYT*, Sept. 25, 1933, p. 11.

15. *NYT*, May 22, 1933, p. 13.

16. 1933 RGBl. I, 285, quoted in NMT 2759-PS.

17. Dodd to Hull, June 11, 1935, in Dept. State, *Foreign*, 1935 v. 2, 275–76.

18. Ibid., Aug. 11, 1933, p. 11.

19. Dodd, *Ambassador*, 9.

20. Quoted in Engelmann, 49.

21. Thyssen, 19, 20, 22. Although grave question exists about authenticity of the "Thyssen memoirs," the cited passage is accepted here because it refers to public documents.

22. *TT*: May 11, 1933, p. 14; May 12, p. 13; May 13, p. 11.

23. 1936 RGBl. I, 999, quoted in NMT NG-715 (Green III, 182).

24. Zeller, 153.

25. Waln, 266–67.

26. Ibid., 369.

27. *NYT*, July 26, 1935, p. 8.

28. *TT*, Aug. 12, 1939, p. 9.

29. Gellately, 204.

30. Proctor, 149.

31. Dodd, *Ambassador*, 169–70.

32. *Jews*, 176.

33. That retreated from an earlier policy holding that if one stockholder was Jewish, so was the business (Messersmith to Hull, April 18, 1933, in Dept. State, *Foreign*, 1933 v. 2, 423).

34. 1938 RGBl. I, 627, quoted in NMT 1404-PS (Green VI, 477–79); NMT 1816-PS (Red IV, 430). Implementing regulations can be found in 1938 RGBl. I, 628 and 1711.

35. Such action was already underway in 1933 (Sommer v. Mathews, 49 Lloyd's List L. Rep. 154, 159 (1934); Messersmith to Hull, Nov. 1, 1933, in Dept. State, *Foreign*, 1933 v. 2, 363; *TT*, May 10, 1934, p. 4).

36. 1938 RGBl. I, 627, quoted in NMT 1404-PS (Green VI, 479).

37. *NYT*, Oct. 10, 1935, p. 13.

38. Roberts, 247–48.

39. 1937 RGBl. I, 1333, Art. 1, quoted in NMT 1403-PS.

40. 1937 RGBl. I, 1333, Art. 2.

41. 1937 RGBl. I, 1333, Art. 4.

42. 1937 RGBl. I, 1333, Art. 5.

43. 1937 RGBl. I, 1333, Arts. 6, 12–14, 20, 36, 39.

44. NMT 1759-PS (Red IV, 302).

45. 1938 RGBl. I, 414, quoted in NMT 1406-PS.

46. Hans Quecke, quoted in Red II, 726.

47. *NYT*, Feb. 24, 1939, p. 3.

48. Quoted in *TT*, April 28, 1938, p. 13.

49. *NYT*, April 28, 1938, p. 1.

50. Wilson to Roosevelt, June 2, 1938, in Dept. State, *Foreign*, 1938 v. 2, 375.

51. *NYT*, May 13, 1938, p. 7.

52. *NYT*, June 12, 1938, p. 26.

53. Burleigh and Wippermann, 86.

54. Ebenstein, 103.

55. *NYT*, June 12, 1938, p. 26.

56. See NMT 1816-PS (Red IV, 449–50) for a Nazi leadership discussion of intentions to seize objects of value owned by Jews, and of Jews engaging in panic selling of assets in hopes of thwarting seizures.

57. NMT 841-PS (direct quotation "for the time being" from alternate translation in NMT 069-PS). For a childless couple the ban on property transfers from a Jewish husband to an Aryan wife was explicit. If the couple had children the ban was only implicit, but we may be serene that the educational nature of law did not require explicit language.

58. Dickinson, 154.

59. *TT*, Aug. 20, 1938, p. 10; *NYT*, Aug. 24, 1938, p. 1.

60. *TT*, July 25, 1939, p. 11.

61. Gürtner, "Administration," in *Germany Speaks*, 89.

62. Quoted in NMT Red I, 1101.

63. NMT 001-PS.

64. NMT L-188.

65. 1941 RGBl. I, 722, quoted in NMT NG-715 (Green III, 200).

66. Dodd to Hull, Aug. 28, 1933, in Dept. State, *Foreign*, 1933 v. 2, 259; Schleunes, 230.

67. Hilberg, *Destruction* [1967], 302–3.

68. *TT*: Oct. 19, 1936, p. 13; Aug. 4, 1938, p. 10. *NYT*, Aug. 4, 1938, p. 9.

69. 1943 RGBl. I, 372, quoted in NMT 1422-PS.

70. Quoted in Bach, 318.

71. Hilberg, *Destruction* [1985], 474.

72. NMT 3951-PS (Red A, 682).

73. Blumenthal, 53.

74. NMT NI-898 (Green VI, 481).

75. NMT 1816-PS (Red IV, 425–26).

76. NMT 3051-PS.

77. Zeller, 141.

78. NMT 1816-PS (Red IV, 436-37, 440). Not all Nazi leaders shared the sentiments of Goering and the police. After Crystal Night, Goebbels confided to his diary: "Berlin's man in the street, at long last, had an opportunity of filling himself out again. Fur coats, carpets, valuable textiles, were all to be had for nothing. The people were enraptured." (Quoted in Grunberger, 259n.) An eyewitness watched children "with their mouths smeared with candy from wrecked candy shops or flaunting toys from wrecked toy shops." (*NYT*, Nov. 11, 1938, p. 4.) Nazi squads threw loot into streets with the cry, "Here are some cheap Christmas presents." (Quoted in ibid.) Officially, however, the attitude of Goebbels did not prevail. Even in areas of the Soviet Union where Nazi death

squads hunted Jews, orders declared "strict measures are to be taken against street mobs and other evil elements for whom it concerns only plunder of Jewish stores and stealing Jewish property for their own personal gain." (NMT 212-PS.)

79. NMT 1816-PS (Red IV, 425).

80. Quoted in Heiden, 137-38.

81. 1933 RGBl. I, 685, translated in NMT 1402-PS.

82. Proctor, 88.

83. NMT 1816-PS (Red IV, 427).

84. *NYT*, Feb. 16, 1939, p. 11.

85. Neumann, 119.

86. Quoted in Grunberger, 102.

87. NMT 1816-PS (Red IV, 427).

88. NMT 1816-PS (Red IV, 426, 430).

89. NMT 1208-PS.

90. *NYT*, Feb. 16, 1939, p. 11; *TT*, Feb. 16, 1939, p. 13.

91. Esh, "Entjudung," in Gutman, 446.

92. 1938 RGBl. I, 1709, quoted in NMT 1409-PS.

93. Gilbert to Hull, Dec. 6, 1938, in Dept. State, *Foreign*, 1938 v. 2, 409; Geist to Gilbert, Dec. 14, 1938 in ibid., 417.

94. Esh, "Entjudung," in Gutman, 446.

95. Hilberg, *Destruction* [1967], 85, 85 n. 115.

96. Ibid., 81; *TT*, Dec. 6, 1938, p. 13.

97. *TT*, July 4, 1938, p. 14.

98. Dickinson, 202.

99. See concerns expressed by *Kölnische Zeitung*, Oct. 13, 1935, quoted in *Yellow*, 116.

100. *NYT*, Dec. 6, 1938, p. 13.

101. *Yellow*, 119.

102. *NYT*, Oct. 25, 1938, p. 16.

103. *TT*, March 25, 1933, p. 11.

104. *TT*, Aug. 4, 1938, p. 9.

105. *TT*, Nov. 15, 1938, p. 14.

106. *NYT*, Dec. 1, 1938, p. 10.

107. The previous year everyone, Aryan and Jew alike, was forbidden to export old silver coinage (*TT*, May 25, 1937, p. 15).

108. Protection of Aryan creditors was controversial in senior Nazi circles. In June 1938 Interior Minister Wilhelm Frick maintained that Aryans who were insensitive and foolish enough to extend credit to Jews merited loss of their investment. In contrast, Finance Minister Lutz Schwerin von Krosigk felt that Aryans who bought a Jewish firm acquired not only its assets but its debts to Aryans as well. (Hilberg, *Destruction* [1967], 82–83).

109. 1938 RGBl. I, 1709, quoted in NMT 1409-PS.

110. Geist to Hull, March 6, 1939, in Dept. State, *Foreign*, 1939 v. 2, 583–89; *NYT*, Feb. 24, 1939, p. 3; Neumann, 119–20; Burleigh and Wippermann, 93. A contemporary report noted that such valuables were exactly the sort of assets that could be converted easily into foreign currency, so confiscation hindered Jews' ability to emigrate while adding to the Reich's foreign currency reserves (*TT*, Feb. 24, 1939, p. 15). A more subtle control over property involved measures such as the 1936 order to turn over all foreign

securities (government and private) to the Reichsbank or its agents. Ownership did not change, but owners were only entitled to receive cash value of their securities back from the bank. The Reichsbank could thereby use the securities as collateral for foreign loans to bring in foreign exchange. This policy encouraged German investors to sell foreign securities and buy German government bonds. (*NYT*, Nov. 20, 1936, p. 7).

111. Schleunes, 158.

112. *TT*, April 28, 1938, p. 13.

113. Quoted in *TT*, Dec. 8 1938, p. 15.

114. NMT 3358-PS.

115. *NYT*, Nov. 21, 1935, p. 15; NMT 1816-PS (Red IV, 426, 447, 449). One goal of the Aryanization program was to assure that by 1943 the only means of personal support available to Jews would be money received from Aryanization of businesses (*TT*, Aug. 20, 1938, p. 10), a goal leading to utter destitution for most Jews (who had not owned businesses) and virtual destitution for the remainder (who had limited access to their blocked bank accounts). At least twenty varieties of blocked marks existed, not all of them connected to Jews. Their basic purpose was to bring in foreign exchange. Blocked marks could be sold at a discount to foreigners, who could then use them at full face value to pay bills in Germany. In the delicate phraseology of one financial writer, "Traffic with these marks is subject to complicated and changing regulations. But the variety of rules has the great advantage of providing for many special situations in which allowance can be made for particular cases or in favor of particular parties. Furthermore, rigid as the rules are written in the books, their administration is flexible" (*NYT*, Nov. 20, 1938, sec. 3, p. 6). A Jew emigrating in early 1936 could sell blocked marks to foreigners at a discount of 65 percent. German corporations took advantage of that discount by soliciting thirteen-year loans comprised of emigrants' blocked marks, which the corporations agreed to repay at about twice the market rate for blocked marks. In theory, through such loans Jews could realize twice the amount offered by buyers of blocked marks, and in practice corporations definitely financed their operations more cheaply than by using a bank. Jews of modest means could pool their blocked marks together to make such loans. This was yet another way in which German business profited from the Holocaust. After Crystal Night, however, Jewish emigrants who wanted to liquidate their accounts normally had to sell blocked marks to a government bank at a discount below the already dismal market value. Even so they probably did better than Jews who participated in the loan scheme; one doubts that many Nazi corporations bothered to continue loan repayments past 1939 (*NYT*, Nov. 20, 1938, sec. 3, p. 6; *NYT*, Jan. 27, 1936, p. 11).

116. NMT 1816-PS (Red IV, 447).

117. See Goering's "3 1/2%" comments in NMT 1816-PS (Red IV, 449, 453).

118. For pointing out the shift in purpose, I am indebted to Hilberg, *Destruction* [1967], 90 (an area of text where details of the tax can be found); for the same theme see also *NYT*, Sept. 15, 1938, p. 9. The preceding account of the flight tax relies upon Hilberg. Strauss, 343–44 differs slightly.

119. Mayer to Hull, Sept. 12, 1936, in Dept. State, *Foreign*, 1936 v. 2, 202–3; *NYT*: May 19, 1937, p. 5; Oct. 25, 1938, p. 16.

120. *NYT*, Sept. 8, 1936, p. 1.

121. *NYT*, June 29, 1935, p. 6.

122. *NYT*, Sept. 15, 1938, p. 9.

123. Hans Heinrich Schulz testimony, Green III, 1072.

124. *NYT*, Feb. 26, 1939, p. 23.

125. Fay, "Germany's," 428; *TT*, May 31, 1939, p. 15; Hilberg, *Destruction* [1967], 94–96. Personal goods typically approved included wedding rings, watches, "clothes purchased to replace outworn clothing," and "two silver knives, forks, spoons, and teaspoons per person" (*NYT*, April 26, 1939, p. 10). Although emigrants could take some goods, a tax assessed at 100 percent of the property's value might have to be paid (*TT*, Aug. 4, 1938, p. 9; *NYT*: Feb. 26, 1939, p. 23; April 26, p. 10). Upon assuming power Nazis allowed Jews to take no more than RM 200 when emigrating, and allowed them to collect no more than RM 200 a month from investments left behind in Germany (*NYT*, June 20, 1933, p. 4), but those rules were later toughened. Most wealth of Jewish emigrants was left behind in blocked bank accounts (*TT*, July 6, 1938, p. 15). Limitations on deposits' liquidity were profitable for banks, and gave Germany's banks good reason to support the war on Jews. The Dresdner Bank, for example, hosted all blocked accounts for proceeds from sales of assets owned by Jews who were expelled to Poland in late 1938 (Milton, 172).

126. *TT*, Aug. 4, 1938, p. 9.

127. Milton, 175 n. 20.

128. *NYT*, May 29, 1937, p. 5.

129. *TT*, May 31, 1939, p. 15.

130. *TT*, Aug. 4, 1938, p. 9.

131. *NYT*, May 19, 1937, p. 5.

132. *NYT*, June 17, 1938, p. 3; July 28, p 7; Sept. 15, p. 9.

133. *NYT*, Nov. 20, 1938, p. 1.

134. *TT*, June 18, 1938, p. 15.

135. Quoted in *NYT*, Nov. 27, 1935, p. 11.

136. *NYT*, March 21, 1939, p. 8.

137. Sommer v. Mathews, 49 Lloyd's List L. Rep. 154 (1934); *TT*: May 10, 1934, p. 4; May 11, p. 4; May 12, p. 4; May 15, p. 4; May 16, p. 4.

138. *TT*, Feb. 10, 1939, p. 13.

139. *TT*, March 6, 1939, p. 10.

140. *TT*, March 18, 1939, p. 8.

141. NMT 3951-PS (Red A, 679).

142. NMT 3951-PS (Red A, 679–80).

143. NMT 342-PS, par. 7.

144. NMT 2237-PS. In contrast to their inability to determine the identity of Jewish owners of merchandise, even if it had store labels, Nazi officials tried to be fastidious about returning property seized from Aryan merchants in the heat of the moment (NMT D-183).

145. Diary June 28, 1938, Fromm, 275.

146. *NYT*, April 24, 1938, p. 36.

147. Wilson to Dept. State, Aug. 30, 1938, in Dept. State, *Foreign*, 1938 v. 2, 389–90; *NYT*: Aug. 21, 1938, p. 30; Aug. 24, p. 1.

148. Diary Aug. 23, 1938, Fromm, 279.

149. NMT 2682-PS.

150. *NYT*, Jan. 25, 1938, p. 13.

151. *NYT*, Aug. 17, 1935, p. 2.

152. Quoted in Barkai, 129.

153. Barkai, 48–49.

154. Ibid.

155. Ibid.

156. Schleunes, 147.

157. Ibid.

158. *NYT*, Feb. 2, 1936, sec. 7, p. 5.

159. *NYT*, July 28, 1938, p. 7.

160. *NYT*, Dec. 29, 1938, p. 6.

161. *NYT*, Nov. 19, 1938, p. 3; TT, Nov. 19, 1938, p. 11.

162. *NYT*, Aug. 13, 1938, p. 9.

163. Barkai, 108.

164. Quoted in Henry, 83.

165. NMT 1757-PS (Red IV, 285).

166. Grunberger, 102.

167. *NYT*, July 22, 1938, p. 7.

168. *NYT*, July 23, 1938, p. 3.

169. *TT*, Nov. 15, 1938, p. 14.

170. Barkai, 107.

171. Matchmaking might be aided by newspaper ads from Jewish business owners seeking Aryan buyers. Such ads from *Frankfurter Zeitung*, Oct. 20, 1935 are quoted in *Yellow*, 114.

172. Hilberg, *Destruction* [1967], 64.

173. Schleunes, 223; Burleigh and Wippermann, 327 n. 53; Marcus, 14, 269; *NYT*, Dec. 28, 1937, p. 16.

174. Bernstein, 729.

175. *TT*, July 23, 1938, p. 11.

176. *NYT*, Nov. 21, 1935, p. 15.

177. *NYT*, July 23, 1938, p. 3.

178. *NYT*, Oct. 5, 1938, p. 11.

179. Pozner, 34.

180. *NYT*, Feb. 20, 1938, p. 2.

181. *NYT*, July 11, 1938, p. 25.

182. *TT*, June 1, 1938, p. 13.

183. *NYT*: Sept. 24, 1935, p. 1; Nov. 21, p. 15.

184. *NYT*, Oct. 8, 1935, p. 13.

185. NMT 1816-PS (Red IV, 445); 1938 RGBl. I, 1580, quoted in NMT 1662-PS.

186. *Ostjüdische Zeitung*, Aug. 20, 1933, quoted in *Yellow*, 177.

187. 1933 RGBl. I, 175, quoted in NMT 1397-PS.

188. *Yellow*, 134; Hilberg, *Destruction* [1967], 56–57; NMT 841-PS; 1938 RGBl. I, 1751, cited in Burleigh and Wippermann, 93; *TT*, Dec. 15, 1938, p. 15.

189. Raymond H. Geist, NMT 1759-PS (Red IV, 303).

190. *NYT*, Aug. 23, 1933, p. 13.

191. NMT 1759-PS (Red IV, 303–4); *NYT*, March 10, 1933, p. 1. The next year the victim entered a nursing home to recover from injuries suffered in a subsequent attack after he demanded back rent (*TT*, Jan. 17, 1934, p. 11).

192. Marx, *Government*, 96.

193. Bernays, 523.

194. *TT*, April 15, 1933, p. 9.

195. NMT 1816-PS (Red IV, 449–50).

196. *NYT*, Nov. 13, 1938, p. 38.

197. *Yellow*, 192.

198. Allen, 213; Zeller, 87–88.

199. *TT*, Aug. 20, 1937, p. 9; *NYT*, Aug. 20, 1937, p. 4; Gilbert to Dept. State, Sept. 4, 1937, in Dept. State, *Foreign*, 1937 v. 2, 324.

200. *NYT*, July 26, 1938, p. 10; *TT*, July 26, 1938, p. 12.

201. *NYT*, June 20, 1933, p. 4.

202. *TT*, Dec. 28, 1934, p. 9.

203. *NYT*, Aug. 17, 1935, p. 2.

204. NMT 1757-PS (Red IV, 288).

205. 1938 RGBl. I, 415, cited in Hilberg, *Destruction* [1967], 65, 82.

206. Order cited in NMT 1757-PS (Red IV, 283).

207. NMT 1757-PS (Red IV, 285).

208. NMT 1759-PS (Red IV, 302–3).

209. Red Supp. A, 74; Grunberger, 93–94.

210. Pozner, 33.

211. Ibid.

212. Gross, 124–25.

213. Lore, "Little," 145.

214. Heiden, 39–40.

215. *TT*, April 25, 1938, p. 13.

216. *TT*, March 15, 1933, p. 14.

217. Barkai, 71–72.

218. *TT*, Aug. 23, 1933, p. 10.

219. *NYT*: July 21, 1933, p. 1; Dec. 24, sec. 4, p. 2. *TT*: July 21, 1933, p. 15; Aug. 1, p. 11; Sept. 4, p. 9.

220. *NYT*, July 21, 1933, p. 1.

221. *NYT*, July 31, 1933, p. 6.

222. *TT*, March 17, 1938, p. 14.

223. *TT*, June 18, 1938, pp. 15–16; July 1, p. 15.

224. *TT*, June 2, 1938, p. 13; June 21, p. 15.

225. Reck-Malleczewen, 70–71; Gellately, 145.

226. Quoted in Kershaw, *Popular*, 258.

227. Wilson to Hull, June 22, 1938, in Dept. State, *Foreign*, 1938 v. 2, 382.

228. Warburg, 120.

229. Dodd, "Germany," 178.

230. *NYT*: Sept. 25, 1936, p. 15; Oct. 4, p. 34.

231. *NYT*, May 1, 1937, p. 2.

232. *NYT*, March 16, 1938, p. 8.

233. *NYT*, April 24, 1938, p 36.

234. *NYT*, Dec. 8, 1938, p. 17.

235. Quoted in Fraenkel, 31.

236. Deutsch, "Disfranchisement," in Van Paassen and Wise, 52.

237. *NYT*: Dec. 22, 1935, p. 20; Dec. 23, p. 8. *TT*, Dec. 24, 1935, p. 9.

238. *TT*, Nov. 21, 1934, p. 13.

239. Barkai, 72.

240. Hilberg, *Destruction* [1967], 86.

241. Gürtner, "Administration," in *Germany Speaks*, 88.

242. Dickinson, 229, 231.

243. NMT 1816-PS (Red IV, 432).

244. *NYT*, June 13, 1938, p. 2.

245. Marcus, 14, 269.

246. *NYT*, Dec. 30, 1937, p. 4.

247. *TT*, March 29, 1933, p. 14.

248. NMT 3577-PS; Marcus, 15.

249. Quoted in diary June 28, 1938, Fromm, 274–75.

250. *Yellow*, 161.

251. *NYT*, Dec. 14, 1935, p. 10.

252. *Yellow*, 117.

253. *NYT*, July 28, 1938, p. 7.

254. *TT*, Dec. 31, 1938, p. 9.

255. Ibid.

256. "Jews," 22. The same information can could be found in *TT*: Dec. 31, 1938, p. 9; Jan. 25, 1939, p. 11; and *NYT*, Jan. 25, 1939, p. 7. The latter, in turn, cited the *Journal of the Association of Berlin Merchants and Industrialists*. Information classified as a war secret by the U.S. government in 1944 was published by the Nazis, *The Times* of London, and the *New York Times* in the 1930s.

257. Burleigh and Wippermann, 86.

258. *TT*, Nov. 22, 1938, p. 14.

259. *NYT*, Jan. 1, 1939, p. 17.

260. *TT*, Aug. 13, 1938, p. 9.

261. See Ribbentrop's comments in NMT L-205; Hilberg, *Destruction* [1967], 93.

262. NMT NO-724 (Green IV, 960).

263. NMT 1816-PS (Red IV, 427).

264. NMT 1816-PS (Red IV, 431). Here Goering was speaking of Jews with non-German citizenship who lived in Germany, but the technique was used with all Aryanizations.

265. Dickinson, 200.

266. Blue IX, 276–78.

267. NMT 1816-PS (Red IV, 434, 438, 455).

268. 1938 RGBl. I, 1579, quoted in NMT 1412-PS.

269. *NYT*, Nov. 24, 1938, p. 8.

270. *NYT*, Nov. 27, 1938, p. 46.

271. Ibid.

272. *NYT*, Dec. 5, 1938, p. 31; *TT*, Dec. 15, 1938, p. 15.

273. *NYT*: Dec. 6, 1938, p. 13; Jan. 18, 1939, p. 12. *TT*, Dec. 6, 1938, p. 13.

274. *TT*, Dec. 13, 1938, p. 16.

275. *TT*, Feb. 16, 1939, p. 13.

276. *NYT*: Dec. 1, 1938, p. 10; Dec. 15, p. 23.

277. *NYT*, Dec. 16, 1938, p. 18.

278. *NYT*, Dec. 16, 1938, p. 22.

279. Gilbert to Hull, Nov. 23, 1938, in Dept. State, *Foreign*, 1938 v. 2, 406; *TT*, Nov 24, 1938, p. 14. That reversed an initial policy disallowing such crediting (*TT*, Nov. 17, 1938, p. 14).

280. *TT*, Nov. 28, 1938, p. 16; *NYT*, Dec. 1, 1938, p. 10.

281. *TT*, Feb. 16, 1939, p. 13.

282. *NYT*, Nov. 27, 1938, p. 46.

283. Hilberg, *Destruction* [1967], 91–93.

284. *TT*, Nov. 24, 1938, p. 14.

285. Ibid.; *NYT*, Dec. 15, 1938, p. 23.

286. *TT*, Dec. 6, 1938, p. 13.

287. *NYT*, Nov. 14, 1938, p. 6.

288. 1938 RGBl. I, 1580, quoted in NMT 1662-PS. The 1662-PS version mistakenly puts the effective date as January 1, 1938 (compare with 2875-PS version). See also discussion of the decree among Nazi leadership in NMT 1816-PS (Red IV, 445–46).

289. Kulka, 139.

290. NMT 1816-PS (Red IV, 446).

291. Neumann, 120.

292. Ebenstein, 103–4.

293. *NYT*, Nov. 30, 1938, p. 14.

294. *TT*, Nov. 14, 1938, p. 12.

295. NMT 1816-PS (Red IV, 438).

296. 1938 RGBl. I, 1938, 1581, quoted in Green III, 1071; Burleigh and Wippermann, 93; Heiden, 140–41; *NYT*, Nov. 12, 1938, p. 4. The decree was anticipated by Bavaria's Minister of the Interior Adolf Wagner, who said all Jewish shops would be Aryanized after Jewish owners repaired them (*TT*, Nov. 12, 1938, p. 12). Wealthy Jews were ordered to pay into a fund for repairing damages that other Jews could not afford to repair (*TT*, Nov. 15, 1938, p. 14).

297. *NYT*, Dec. 23, 1935, p. 8; *TT*, Dec. 24, 1935, p. 9.

298. Grunberger, 461–62.

299. Dickinson, 304.

300. Kestenberg, 382.

301. Quoted in Milton, 195–96.

302. Grunberger, 103.

303. Police Sgt. Fritz Jacob, May 5, 1942, quoted in Hilberg, *Destruction* [1967], 653.

304. Grunberger, 103–4.

305. Fredborg, 200.

306. NMT 3661-PS.

307. Weinreich, 200–202; Hilberg, *Destruction* [1967], 305–6; NMT 2819-PS.

308. NMT NO-724 (Green IV, 961).

309. Weinreich, 201 n. 415.

310. NMT NO-724 (Green IV, 961).

311. Hilberg, *Destruction* [1967], 612.

312. NMT NO-5395 (Green IV, 972).

313. NMT NO-724 (Green IV, 962).

314. Hilberg, *Destruction* [1967], 613.

315. Ibid., 615 n. 30.

316. Weinreich, 200–202; NMT 4024-PS (Red A, 751).

317. Quoted in Kershaw, "Persecution," 283–84.

318. Grunberger, 107.

319. Smith, 190–91. See also Gross, 51.

320. Weiss, 73–75.

321. *NYT*, July 21, 1933, p. 1.

322. NMT 1919-PS (Red, 568); Alexander, 561.

323. *TT*, July 17, 1937, p. 12.

324. Ibid.

325. *TT*, March 17, 1939, p. 17. In a lecture I attended at Rockhurst College in 1994, Zev Kedem (who was included in the famed Schindler's list) recalled dental gold being removed from Jewish corpses dug up from the cemetery where Commandant Amon Göth's notorious Plaszów camp was erected.

326. *NYT*, Oct. 10, 1935, p. 13. A total between RM 10 billion and RM 12 billion has been given for 1933 (Barkai, 114).

327. *NYT*, Dec. 9, 1935, p. 13.

328. *NYT*, Nov. 13, 1938, p. 38.

329. NMT 1759-PS (Red IV, 304–5).

330. Wilson to Hull, April 30, 1938, Dept. State, *Foreign*, 1938 v. 2, 366.

331. Heiden, 130–31.

332. NMT 3545-PS.

333. *TT*, Nov. 26, 1938, p. 8.

334. Heiden, 140.

335. *NYT*, Nov. 30, 1938, p. 14.

336. *NYT*, Nov. 13, 1938, p. 38.

337. *TT*, Nov. 15, 1938, p. 14.

338. *TT*, Nov. 14, 1938, p. 12.

339. *TT*, Nov. 26, 1938, p. 8. The following two examples of capitalization are from this source.

340. That "wealth" also subjected him to the property registration decree; one wonders how many persons in such circumstances failed to register and thereby found themselves in custody.

341. *NYT*, Dec. 16, 1938, p. 18.

342. Before Crystal Night, the fiscal 1938 flight tax total was already far higher than revenue from the previous year because Jews fleeing Austria had to start paying the tax (*NYT*, Oct. 25, 1938, p. 16).

343. Hilberg, *Destruction* [1967], 90–91.

344. Weinreich, 201.

345. Green III, 25.

346. Green VI, 437; Green XIII, 76, 117.

347. Green VI, 1214.

348. Green XIII, 117.

Chapter 4: CONCENTRATION

1. *Yellow*, 22.

2. *NYT*, May 15, 1938, p. 29.

3. I am indebted to Kershaw, "Persecution," 263, for that insight.

4. Hilberg, *Destruction* [1967], 106.

5. *NYT*, Nov. 1, 1936, sec. 2, p. 9.

6. *NYT*, May 15, 1938, p. 29.

7. Hilberg, *Destruction* [1967], 106.

8. Barkai, 131.

9. *TT*, June 16, 1933, p. 13.

10. *NYT*, Oct. 10, 1935, p. 13.

11. Ibid.; *NYT*, Nov. 14, 1935, p. 10.

12. *TT*, Nov. 15, 1935, p. 15.

13. *NYT*, July 4, 1938, p. 7.

14. *NYT*, Nov. 14, 1935, p. 10.

15. *NYT*, Dec. 31, 1935, p. 7.

16. Dodd, "Germany," 177. Simultaneously the closing of B'nai B'rith lodges brought the regime RM 2 million in lodge real estate and RM 1.5 million in liquid assets (Dodd to Hull, April 29, 1937, in Dept. State, *Foreign*, 1937 v. 2, 321; *NYT*, April 20, 1937, p. 8).

17. *NYT*, July 6, 1938, p. 11; *TT*, July 6, 1938, p. 15.

18. *TT*, Nov. 8, 1935, p. 16.

19. *TT*, Oct. 7, 1938, p. 13.

20. *TT*, Aug. 4, 1938, p. 9.

21. *TT*, July 6, 1938, p. 15.

22. *NYT*, Aug. 2, 1938, p. 12.

23. *TT*, Aug. 8, 1935, p. 11.

24. *TT*, Nov. 8, 1935, p. 16.

25. *TT*, Aug. 4, 1938, p. 9. The Berlin League of Land and House Owners guaranteed that it would find tenants to replace all the Jewish doctors; the Berlin medical guild agreed to help in that task (*TT*, Aug. 13, 1938, p. 9).

26. Ilse Warburg, quoted in *NYT*, Feb. 14, 1936, p. 20.

27. *NYT*, Aug. 2, 1938, p. 12.

28. *TT*, May 5, 1939, p. 13.

29. Ibid.

30. *TT*, May 26, 1939, p. 14.

31. Barkai, 129.

32. Fraenkel, 93.

33. Ibid.

34. *NYT*, Sept. 2, 1938, p. 2.

35. *TT*, Jan 17, 1939, p. 8.

36. *TT*, Nov. 11, 1938, p. 14. *NYT*: Nov. 11, 1938, p. 3; Nov. 12, p. 4.

37. *TT*, Nov. 12, 1938, p. 12.

38. NMT 1757-PS (Red IV, 284).

39. Heiden, 133–34. Heiden speaks of Aryanizations involving the *Deutsche Arbeitsfront* rather than the *Gau*, but we may presume that techniques differed little among Franconia agencies controlled by Streicher's associates.

40. NMT 1757-PS (Red IV, 284). "Nominal value" in this instance seems to have been the tax assessment value (Grunberger, 102; Heiden, 133–34), which was below "exchange value" (the price that property would fetch in normal circumstances). Tax assessment value can be far below exchange value, meaning that victims may have received 10 percent of a pittance. The difference between nominal and exchange values in the Franconia post-Crystal Night instance, however, may have been less drastic, perhaps closer to 15 percent (see NMT 1757-PS [Red IV, 285]). Either way, Aryan buyers

received a bargain from Jewish sellers after Crystal Night, a fact well known around the world at the time (e.g., see Callender, 24).

41. NMT 1816-PS (Red IV, 428).
42. Grunberger, 97.
43. See an early example in *Kölnische Zeitung*, Oct. 13, 1935, quoted in *Yellow*, 116.
44. *TT*, Jan. 17, 1938, p. 8.
45. Quoted in *TT*, Nov. 18, 1938, p. 16.
46. *TT*, Dec. 12, 1938, p. 13.
47. *NYT*, Nov. 19, 1938, p. 2.
48. *NYT*, Nov. 27, 1938, p. 46.
49. *NYT*, Nov. 28, 1938, p. 6.
50. Hilberg, *Destruction* [1985], 476–77.
51. *NYT*, Nov. 30, 1938, p. 18.
52. Quoted in Kulka, 35.
53. Grunberger, 218.
54. Quoted in Hilberg, *Destruction* [1967], 86.
55. 1938 RGBl. I, 1580, quoted in NMT 1662-PS.
56. *TT*, Nov. 17, 1938, p. 14.
57. Fraenkel, 93.
58. Goering's explanation of Hitler's order in NMT 069-PS.
59. NMT 1816-PS (Red IV, 453).
60. MMT 1816-PS (Red IV, 452).
61. 1939 RGBl. I, 864, quoted in NMT 1419-PS.
62. *TT*: Nov. 17, 1938, p. 14; Nov. 18, p. 16.
63. *NYT*: May 26, 1939, p. 10; July 21, p. 10.
64. *NYT*, May 5, 1939, p. 13.
65. *NYT*, June 17, 1938, p. 1.
66. *TT*, Dec. 13, 1938, p. 16.
67. NMT 1816-PS (Red IV, 454).
68. *NYT*, May 26, 1939, p. 10.
69. *TT*, Dec. 1, 1938, p. 13.
70. NMT 2682-PS.
71. *NYT*, Dec. 4, 1938, p. 1; *TT*, Dec. 5, 1938, p. 11.
72. *TT*, Sept. 11, 1933, p. 8.
73. NMT L-205.
74. NMT 1816-PS (Red IV, 453).
75. NMT 1816-PS (Red IV, 452–53).
76. NMT 1816-PS (Red IV, 452, 454).
77. Barkai, 168.
78. Burleigh and Wippermann, 89.
79. NMT 374-PS; NMT 3051-PS (Red V, 800).
80. Fay, "Is," 746.
81. Marx, "Germany's," 882.
82. Kirk to Hull, June 6, 1939, in Dept. State, *Foreign*, 1939 v. 2, 585-86.
83. Kulka, 35.
84. *NYT*, Feb. 11, 1939, p. 4.
85. Hecht, 15.
86. Huttenbach, 26–32.

Chapter 5: ANNIHILATION

1. Zeller, 106.

2. April 7, 1933, supplemental decree to Law for the Restoration of a Professional Civil Service, cited in Deutsch, "Disfranchisement," in Van Paassen and Wise, 47–48.

3. *TT*, Nov. 22, 1935, p. 13.

4. *NYT*, Aug. 13, 1935, p. 6; *TT*, Sept. 7, 1936, p. 11.

5. *NYT*, April 6, 1936, p. 10.

6. *TT*: April 14, 1937, p. 13; Aug. 4, p. 12.

7. *TT*, July 9, 1938, p. 11.

8. Theilhaber, 59.

9. *Yellow*, 23.

10. Strauss, 318.

11. *NYT*, Jan. 14, 1934, p. 3.

12. Strauss, 320; *NYT*: April 26, 1936, p. 27; Oct. 19, p. 7.

13. *NYT*, Oct. 19, 1936, p. 7.

14. *NYT*: July 29, 1938, p. 5; Feb. 26, 1939, p. 23.

15. *NYT*, May 16, 1939, p. 7; July 21, p. 10.

16. *NYT*, April 26, 1936, p. 27; Oct. 19, p. 7; Jan. 25, 1938, p. 13.

17. *TT*, May 5, 1933, p. 13.

18. For details see Noakes, 311–12; *TT*: Nov. 16, 1935, p. 11; Oct. 17, 1936, p. 13.

19. Neumann, 114–15.

20. *NYT*, May 30, 1936, p. 5.

21. Schleunes, 118.

22. *NYT*, April 4, 1933, p. 12.

23. *NYT*, Sept. 30, 1933, p. 7; *TT*, Sept. 30, 1933, p. 12.

24. Marcus, 21.

25. Court decision quoted by *Frankfurter Volksblatt*, no. 113, 1934, as given in *Yellow*, 218.

26. *TT*, March 15, 1934, p. 13; *NYT*, March 21, 1934, p. 10.

27. *NYT*, Feb. 27, 1935, p. 12.

28. *TT*, July 2, 1935, p. 16; *NYT*, July 2, 1935, p. 6.

29. *NYT*, July 26, 1935, p. 8; Aug. 5, p. 1. *TT*, Aug. 6, 1935, p. 9; "It," 12; Büttner, 275 n. 24; Noakes 307.

30. *NYT*, July 13, 1935, p. 6.

31. Dodd to Hull, July 17, 1935 in Dept. State, *Foreign*, 1935, v. 2, pp. 401–2; *NYT*: June 30, 1935, sec. 2, p. 2; Aug. 12, p. 1.

32. 1935 RGBl. I, 609, quoted in NMT 2984-PS; *NYT*, June 2, 1935, p. 34.

33. 1935 RGBl. I, 1146, quoted in NMT 3179-PS.

34. Bielenberg, 127-29.

35. *NYT*, Aug. 6, 1933, sec. 4, p. 3.

36. *TT*, July 31, 1933, p. 12.

37. Quoted in Kühl, 36.

38. Quoted in Weinreich, 30.

39. *TT*, Sept. 30, 1933, p. 12.

40. *NYT*, June 2, 1934, p. 9.

41. *NYT*, Dec. 4, 1934, p. 12.

42. For example *TT*: March 13, 1937, p 11; Dec. 5, 1935, p. 15.

43. Quoted in *Yellow*, 85.

44. *NYT*, Feb. 27, 1935, p. 12.

45. *NYT*, Aug. 25, 1935, p. 7.

46. *NYT*, Aug 17, 1935, p. 2.

47. *NYT*, July 16, 1935, p. 1; July 23, p. 1; July 25, p. 9; Aug. 1, p. 6; Aug. 12, p. 1. Kulka 131.

48. Deuel, 211.

49. Ibid., 215.

50. *Yellow*, 85.

51. Gellately, 143.

52. Ibid., 143, 148–49.

53. *TT*, Dec. 5, 1935, p. 15.

54. Neumann, 115.

55. *NYT*, Dec. 14, 1935, p. 10.

56. Deuel, 212.

57. *NYT*, Feb. 26, 1936, p. 11.

58. *NYT*, May 7, 1936, p. 17.

59. *Yellow*, 233.

60. Gütt, "Population," in *Germany Speaks*, 61.

61. *TT*, Sept. 30, 1933, p. 12.

62. Dodd to Hull, June 18, 1934, in Dept. State, *Foreign*, 1934 v. 2, p. 297.

63. Quoted in *Yellow*, 216; *TT*, March 8, 1934, p. 11.

64. *TT*, July 13, 1934, p. 13.

65. *NYT*, May 21, 1934, p. 7; *TT*, May 19, 1934, p. 11.

66. *TT*, Jan. 28, 1937, p. 13; April 14, 1938, p. 11.

67. *NYT*, Aug. 14, 1934, p. 7.

68. Ibid.

69. *NYT*, July 13, 1934, p. 3.

70. *NYT*, Jan. 23, 1936, p. 17.

71. *NYT*, April 8, 1933, p. 8.

72. Diary June 23, 1933, Fromm, 117.

73. Quoted in Engelmann, 68. Not all Aryans took that approach. Some Aryan husbands chose suicide over divorce. "One famous instance was the triple suicide of the well-known author, Jochen Klepper, his Jewish wife and her daughter by an earlier marriage" (Fredborg, 200). Another was movie star Joachim Gottschalk who, Berlin correspondent Howard K. Smith noted, "repeatedly refused suggestions from the Nazis to divorce his wife and enjoy a smoother rise. . . . On the appointed evening, the Gestapo invaded the Gottschalk home to put an end to this unbearable *Rassenschande*. They found the family there waiting, but it was dead. Ten minutes before they came, Gottschalk had killed his child, his wife and himself. The incident was a hideous one, and the story spread over Berlin like wildfire." (Smith, 202–3.)

74. Wolfgang Preiss, quoted in Steinhoff, Pechel, and Showalter, 84.

75. Gross, 90.

76. *TT*, July 18, 1939, p. 13.

77. NMT-069.

78. Grunberger, 461.

79. Deutsch, "Disfranchisement," in Van Paassen and Wise, 54.

80. *TT*, July 9, 1938, p. 11.

81. *Frankfurter Zeitung*, Jan. 30, 1937, cited by Grunberger, 238.

82. *NYT*, Jan. 23, 1936, p. 17.

83. *TT*, Jan. 29, 1936, p. 9.

84. *NYT*, Nov. 21, 1936, p. 3.

85. *TT*: May 2, 1935, p. 14; May 9, p. 15.

86. Deutsch, "Disfranchisement," in Van Paassen and Wise, 55.

87. Fraenkel, 87, 225 n. 264 (quotation).

88. *Yellow*, 251.

89. *Juristische Wochenschrift* (June 16, 1934): 1516, quoted in *Yellow*, 217.

90. Quoted in Fay, "Nazi 'Totalitarian,'" 615.

91. Quoted in Deuel, 147; *NYT*, Nov. 30, 1937, p. 6.

92. Fraenkel, 56.

93. NMT D-229.

94. NMT D-897.

95. Grunberger, 242.

96. Quoted in Fraenkel, 55.

97. Ibid.

98. Quoted in ibid.

99. Ebenstein, 93.

100. Ibid.

101. Deuel, 148.

102. Weyrauch, 562.

103. Heiden, 181 n. 13.

104. Zeller, 25.

105. Quoted in Henry, 60–61.

106. Quoted in Hecht, 31.

107. Bielenberg, 59–60.

108. Ibid., 127.

109. Quoted in Gellately, 146 n. 76.

110. *NYT*: Dec. 21, 1934, p. 10; Dec. 22, p. 5; Dec. 23, p. 10.

111. *NYT*, Jan. 17, 1936, p. 3.

112. Diary Sept. 15, 1934, Fromm, 182.

113. Dodd, *Through*, 270.

114. Zeller, 87.

115. Heck, 83.

116. Heiden, 73–74.

117. Koehler, *Inside Information*, 201.

118. Reck-Malleczewen, 22.

119. Quoted in Fischer, 176.

120. Waln, 76–77.

121. Bernstein, 729.

122. Gellately, 195.

123. Quoted in Ziemer, 75–76.

124. *NYT*: June 3, 1933, p. 3; June 24, p. 6. *TT*: Aug. 1, 1934, p. 11; Aug. 4, 1937, p. 12. Marcus, 13; *Jews*, 89.

125. Dodd, *Through*, 286.

126. *TT*, Feb. 25, 1939, p. 11.

127. *TT*, Feb. 8, 1938, p. 13; *NYT*, Feb. 5, 1938, p. 3.

128. *NYT*, Nov. 6, 1938, p. 28.

129. Hilberg, *Destruction* [1967], 100; Neumann, 120.

130. Schleunes, 129.

131. *TT*, Dec. 12, 1935, p. 15; *NYT*, Aug. 6, 1933, sec. 4, p. 3.

132. *TT*, Oct. 19, 1935, p. 11; Deuel, 237.

133. Quoted in Deuel, 237.

134. Löhr, "Physician," in Mosse, 234.

135. Burleigh and Wipperman, 290.

136. Ibid.

137. *TT*, March 7, 1939, p. 13.

138. *TT*, April 8, 1939, p. 11.

139. Ebenstein, 86.

140. Burleigh and Wipperman, 289.

141. *TT*, Aug. 18, 1933, p. 9.

142. Quoted in *TT*, Aug. 21, 1933, p. 9.

143. *TT*, Sept. 27, 1933, p. 9.

144. *TT*, July 14, 1939, p. 13.

145. Quoted in *TT*, Nov. 21, 1938, p. 12.

146. Grunberger, 273 n.

147. Ibid., 273.

148. Deuel, 151.

149. Grunberger, 120.

150. Gross, "National," in *Germany Speaks*, 70–71.

151. Quoted in Weinreich, 30.

152. Castration was a criminal sanction applied to male habitual criminals (Kühl, 51), but Nazi spokesmen emphasized that male sterilization was not castration (Gütt, "Population," in *Germany Speaks*, 53).

153. Marcus, 299.

154. Quoted in Noakes, "Nazism," in Bullen, 87.

155. Gross, "National," in *Germany Speaks*, 71.

156. *NYT*, Jan. 14, 1934, p. 3.

157. *TT*, May 5, 1933, p. 13.

158. 1933 RGBl. I, 529, quoted in NMT 3067-PS.

159. Deuel, 222.

160. Fay, "Two," 745.

161. *TT*, July 25, 1934, p. 11. Loopholes did exist. Goebbels, for instance, was never sterilized despite his physical deformity. Also a diagnosis of mental retardation could be invalidated if military records showed the person had been promoted while serving in World War I. Rank was irrelevant; the guiding element here was promotion (Marx, *Government*, 118).

162. 1933 RGBl. I, 529, quoted in NMT 3067-PS; 1933 RGBl. I, 1021, quoted in NMT NG-715; *NYT*, Jan. 4, 1934, p. 10; Löhr, "Physician," in Mosse, 233; Waln, 174; Marx, *Government*, 117.

163. NMT L-305.

164. Fay, "Two," 745.

165. Ziemer, 26–28 (quotation on 28).

166. Weinreich, 32–33.
167. Gütt, "Population," in *Germany Speaks*, 53.
168. Quoted in Proctor, 296.
169. Quoted in Burleigh and Wippermann, 139–40.
170. Quoted in Deuel, 224–25.
171. Burleigh and Wippermann, 168.
172. NMT D-181.
173. Quoted in Proctor, 209.
174. Kühl, 49, 125 n. 53.
175. Quoted in ibid., 60.
176. Dodd, *Through*, 307–8.
177. Grunberger, 225.
178. Löhr, "Physician," in Mosse, 232.
179. 1935 RGBl. I, 289, quoted in NMT NG-715.
180. Marx, *Government*, 117.
181. Gross, "National," in *Germany Speaks*, 71.
182. Ibid., 72.
183. Deuel, 227.
184. Pommerin, 315.
185. 1933 RGBl. I, 529, quoted in NMT 3067-PS.
186. Proctor, 107.
187. Green III, 1076.
188. Green III, 21 #15 and 24 #27.
189. *TT*, July 9, 1938, p. 11.
190. *NYT*, Oct. 22, 1933, sec. 4, p. 3.
191. 1933 RGBl. I, 529, quoted in NMT 3067-PS.
192. Gütt, "Population," in *Germany Speaks*, 52–53.
193. Kühl, 30.
194. Proctor, 108.
195. *Frankfurter Zeitung*, Nov. 13, 1938, cited by Grunberger, 238.
196. *TT*, Nov. 22, 1938, p. 14.
197. NMT 654-PS.
198. Grunberger, 122; Ebenstein, 85; Neumann, 453; Picton, 440.
199. Neumann, 457.
200. Quoted in *Frankfurter Zeitung*, June 29, 1938, given in Grunberger, 122.
201. Bennett, 374–75.
202. Neumann, 453; Ebenstein, 85; Grunberger, 122.
203. Deuel, 213.
204. Huttenbach, 34 n. 6.
205. Marx, *Government*, 85–86.
206. *NYT*, April 27, 1938, p. 13.
207. Callender, 24; Huttenbach, 29–30.
208. Kwiet, 150.
209. NMT 1816-PS (Red IV, 454).
210. Huttenbach, 30.
211. Quoted in *Yellow*, 240.
212. NMT L-202 (Red VII, 1041).
213. *NYT*: Aug. 11, 1935, p. 19; Aug. 25, p. 1; Aug. 25, p. 7.

214. "Jews," 13.

215. *Yellow*, 283. Reportedly some small town Jews found ways to obtain food through mail and freight shipments from Berlin (*NYT*, Aug. 25, 1935, p. 7).

216. NMT 1816-PS (Red IV, 453).

217. *TT*: Nov. 14, 1938, p. 12; Nov. 15, p. 14.

218. *TT*, Nov. 17, 1938, p. 14.

219. *TT*, Dec. 16, 1938, p. 15.

220. Gross, 62.

221. *NYT*, Dec. 1, 1938, p. 10.

222. Koehler, *Inside Gestapo*, 82.

223. *NYT*: April 5, 1933, p. 10; April 16, p. 22; June 16, p. 5; July 11, p. 12; July 10, 1936, p 13; Aug. 21, p. 4; April 24, 1938, p. 36; May 18, p. 4; July 10, p. 20; Dec. 1, p. 10. *TT*: April 29, 1933, p. 13; Nov. 8, 1935, p. 16; March 22, 1938, p. 16; June 18, p. 15; July 30, p. 11; Aug. 9, p. 11; Jan. 17, 1939, p. 8. Bernays, 526–27.

224. Messersmith to Hull, Nov. 1, 1933, in Dept. State, *Foreign*, 1933 v. 2, 363.

225. Heiden, 36.

226. Ibid.

227. Quoted in ibid.

228. Fay, "Nazi Rally," 299; *TT*, April 29, 1933, p. 13; Dickinson, 146; Heiden, 36.

229. Dickinson 74–75, 155.

230. *Yellow*, 205.

231. Ibid., 208–9.

232. Diary June 28, 1938, Fromm, 274–75.

233. Diary July 28, 1938, ibid., 277.

234. Rabbi Dr. Max Eschenbacher quoted in Burleigh and Wippermann, 91.

235. Jarausch, 187; *Yellow*, 147.

236. Dorothea Schlösser, quoted in Steinhoff, Pechel, and Showalter, 46.

237. Quoted in Weinreich, 42.

238. Quoted in Lifton, 50.

239. NMT D-906 (Red A, 1052).

240. Proctor, 193.

241. NMT D-906 (Red A, 1053).

242. Quoted in Burleigh and Wippermann, 161–62.

243. Henry, 86.

244. For example Bettleheim, *Informed*, 261–62.

245. Mitscherlich and Mielke, 152.

246. *Germany: Twilight*, 164.

247. Marcus, 275–76; 300.

248. Zeller, 106.

249. Henry, 119.

250. Quoted in Weinreich, 30–31.

251. Quoted in ibid., 207.

252. NMT 1816-PS (Red IV, 425, 450–51, 455–56).

253. NMT 3358-PS.

254. Quoted in *TT*, Feb. 16, 1939, p. 13.

255. Burleigh and Wippermann, 57.

256. Ibid., 54.

257. Mitscherlich and Mielke, 152.

258. Naumann, xxvi.
259. NMT 2841-PS.
260. Poliakov, 457.
261. Gross, 72.
262. Poliakov, 457.
263. Stokes, 175.
264. Kershaw, *Popular*, 277.
265. Gellately, 185.
266. Gilbert, "Mentality," 39–40.
267. Schleunes, 224.
268. Kershaw, "Persecution," 289.
269. Kershaw, *Popular*, 277.

Coda: THE NEVERENDING STORY

1. Quoted in *TT*, Aug. 24, 1935, p. 9.
2. Quoted in Fay, "Nazi 'Totalitarian,'" 615.

SOURCES

Alexander, Leo. "Destructive and Self-Destructive Trends in Criminalized Society: A Study of Totalitarianism." *Journal of Criminal Law and Criminology* 39 (1949): 553–64.

——. "War Crimes and Their Motivation: The Socio-Psychological Structure of the SS and the Criminalization of a Society." *Journal of Criminal Law and Criminology* 39 (1948): 298–326.

Allen, William Sheridan. *The Nazi Seizure of Power: The Experience of a Single German Town 1930-1935*. Chicago: Quadrangle Books, 1965.

Arad, Yitzhak, Yisrael Gutman, and Abraham Margaliot, eds. *Documents of the Holocaust: Selected Sources on the Destruction of the Jews of Germany and Austria, Poland, and the Soviet Union*. Jerusalem: Yad Vashem, 1981.

Bach, Julian, Jr. "Death of a Killer: Case History on the Nazi Mind." *Commentary* 2 (1946): 317–19.

Ball-Kaduri, K. J. "Berlin Is 'Purged' of Jews." *Yad Vashem Studies on the Jewish Catastrophe and Resistance* 5 (1963): 271–316.

Barkai, Avraham. *From Boycott to Annihilation: The Economic Struggle of German Jews, 1933-1943*. Translated by William Templer. Hanover, New Hampshire: University Press of New England, 1989.

Bein, Alex. "The Jewish Parasite—Notes on the Semantics of the Jewish Problem, with Special Reference to Germany." *Leo Baeck Institute Year Book* 9 (1964): 3–40.

Bennett, James V. "Notes on the German Legal and Penal System." *Journal of Criminal Law and Criminology* 37 (1947): 368–74.

Bernays, Robert. "The Nazis and the Jews." *Contemporary Review* 144 (1933): 523–31.

Bernstein, Philip S. "Can Hitler Be Trusted?" *Nation* 137 (1933): 728–30.

Bettelheim, Bruno. "Individual and Mass Behavior in Extreme Situations." *Journal of Abnormal and Social Psychology* 38 (1943): 417–52.

——. *The Informed Heart: Autonomy in a Mass Age*. New York: The Free Press, 1960.

Bielenberg, Christabel. *Ride Out the Dark*. New York: W. W. Norton & Company, Inc., 1971.

Binion, Rudolph. *Hitler Among the Germans*. New York: Elsevier, 1976.

Blumenthal, Nachman. "On the Nazi Vocabulary." *Yad Washem Studies on the Jewish Catastrophe and Resistance* 1 (1957): 53–56.

Boas, Jacob. "The Shrinking World of German Jewry, 1933-1938," *Leo Baeck Institute*

Year Book 31 (1986): 241–66.

Boder, David P. "Nazi Science." *Chicago Jewish Forum* 1 (Fall 1942): 23–29.

Bolitho, Gordon. *The Other Germany*. London: Lovat Dickson Limited, 1934.

Bullen, R. J., et al., eds. *Ideas Into Politics: Aspects of European History 1880-1950*. Totowa, New Jersey: Barnes & Noble Books, 1984.

Burleigh, Michael, "Scholarship and the Swastika: The Politics of Research in Occupied Poland." *History Today* 38 (September 1988): 12–16.

Burleigh, Michael, and Wolfgang Wippermann. *The Racial State: Germany 1933–1945*. Cambridge: Cambridge University Press, 1991.

Büttner, Ursula. "The Persecution of Christian-Jewish Families in the Third Reich." *Leo Baeck Institute Year Book* 34 (1989): 267–89.

Callender, Harold. "The Germans in Germany." *Current History* 49 (February 1939): 22–24.

Cohn, Werner. "Bearers of a Common Fate? The 'Non-Aryan' Christian 'Fate-Comrades' of the Paulus-Bund, 1933–1939." *Leo Baeck Institute Year Book* 33 (1988): 327–66.

Dell, Robert. "The German Nightmare." *Nation* 137 (1933): 433–35.

——. *Germany Unmasked*. London: Martin Hopkinson Ltd., 1934.

Department of State. *Foreign Relations of the United States*, 1933-1939. Washington: Government Printing Office, 1949-1955. [SuDocs S1.1:1933-1939]

Deuel, Wallace R. *People Under Hitler*. New York: Harcourt, Brace and Company, 1942.

Dickinson, John K. *German & Jew (The Life and Death of Sigmund Stein)*. Chicago: Quadrangle Books, 1967.

Dicks, Henry V. *Licensed Mass Murder: A Socio-Psychological Study of Some SS Killers*. The Columbus Centre Series. Studies in the Dynamics of Persecution and Extermination. General editor Norman Cohn. New York: Basic Books, Inc., 1972.

Dodd, Martha. *Through Embassy Eyes*. New York: Garden City Publishing Co., Inc., 1939.

Dodd, William E. *Ambassador Dodd's Diary 1933–1938*. Edited by William E. Dodd, Jr., and Martha Dodd. New York: Harcourt, Brace and Company, 1941.

——. "Germany Shocked Me." *Nation* 147 (1938): 176–78.

Ebenstein, William. *The Nazi State*. New York: Farrar & Rinehart, 1943.

Engelmann, Bernt. *In Hitler's Germany: Everyday Life in the Third Reich*. Translated by Krishna Winston. New York: Schocken Books, 1986.

Esh, Shaul. "Between Discrimination and Extermination (The Fateful Year 1938)." *Yad Washem Studies on the Jewish Catastrophe and Resistance* 2 (1958): 79–93.

Fay, Sidney B. "Germany's Economic Plight." *Current History* 43 (1936): 424–28.

——. "The Hitler Dictatorship." *Current History* 38 (1933): 230–34.

——. "Is the Nazi Revolution Ended?" *Current History* 38 (1933): 741–47.

——. "The Nazi Rally at Nuremberg." *Current History* 43 (1935): 205–08.

——. "The Nazi 'Totalitarian' State." *Current History* 38 (1933): 610–18.

——. "Nazi Treatment of the Jews." *Current History* 38 (1933): 295–300.

——. "The Nazis' Birthday Party." *Current History* 40 (1934): 99–103.

——. "Two Years of Nazi Rule." *Current History* 41 (1935): 741–46.

Fearnside, W. Ward. "Three Innovations of National Socialist Jurisprudence." *Journal of Central European Affairs* 16 (1956): 146–55.

Fischer, Louis. "What I Saw in Germany." *Nation* 142 (1936): 176–78.

Fraenkel, Ernst. *The Dual State: A Contribution to the Theory of Dictatorship*. Translated by E. A. Shils, Edith Lowenstein, and Klaus Knorr. New York: Oxford University Press, 1941.

Fredborg, Arvid. *Behind the Steel Wall: A Swedish Journalist in Berlin 1941–43*. New York: The Viking Press, 1944.

Friedlander, Henry, and Sybil Milton, eds. *The Holocaust: Ideology, Bureaucracy, and Genocide*. Millwood, New York: Kraus International Publications, 1980.

Friedman, Philip. *Roads to Extinction: Essays on the Holocaust*. New York: Conference on Jewish Social Studies and the Jewish Publication Society of America, 1980.

Fromm, Bela. *Blood and Banquets: A Berlin Social Diary*. 1943. Reprint. A Birch Lane Press Book. New York: Carol Publishing Group, 1990.

Fuchs, Richard. "The 'Hochschule für die Wissenschaft des Judentums' in the Period of Nazi Rule: Personal Recollections." *Leo Baeck Institute Year Book* 12 (1967): 3–31.

Gaertner, Hans. "Problems of Jewish Schools in Germany during the Hitler Regime (with special reference to the Theodor Herzl Schule in Berlin)." *Leo Baeck Institute Year Book* 1 (1956): 123–41.

Garner, James Wilford. "Recent German Nationality Legislation." *American Journal of International Law* 30 (1936): 96–99.

Gellately, Robert. *The Gestapo and German Society: Enforcing Racial Policy 1933–1945*. Oxford: Oxford University Press, 1990.

Germany Speaks. London: T. Butterworth, Ltd., 1938.

Germany: Twilight Or New Dawn. New York: McGraw-Hill Book Company, Inc., 1933.

Gilbert, G. M. "The Mentality of SS Murderous Robots." *Yad Vashem Studies on the Jewish Catastrophe and Resistance* 5 (1963): 35–41.

———. *The Psychology of Dictatorship: Based on an Examination of the Leaders of Nazi Germany*. New York: The Ronald Press Company, 1950.

Gisevius, Hans Bernd. *To the Bitter End*. Translated by Richard Winston and Clara Winston. Boston: Houghton Mifflin Company, 1947.

Gordon, Sarah. *Hitler, Germans, and the "Jewish Question."* Princeton: Princeton University Press, 1984.

Gross, Leonard. *The Last Jews in Berlin*. New York: Simon and Schuster, 1982.

Grunberger, Richard. *The 12-Year Reich: A Social History of Nazi Germany 1933–1945*. New York: Holt, Rinehart and Winston, 1971.

Gutman, Israel, editor-in-chief. *Encyclopedia of the Holocaust*. New York: Macmillan, 1990.

Haffner, Sebastian. *The Meaning of Hitler*. Translated by Ewald Osers. New York: Macmillan, 1979.

Hamilton, Alice. "The Plight of the German Intellectuals." *Harper's* 168 (1934): 159–69.

Hammen, Oscar J. "German Historians and the Advent of the National Socialist State." *Journal of Modern History* 13 (1941): 161–88.

Hartshorne, Edward Yarnall, Jr. *The German Universities and National Socialism*. Cambridge: Harvard University Press, 1937.

Hausheer, Herman. "The Socio-Economic Background of Nazi Antisemitism." *Social Forces* 14 (1936): 341–54.

Hecht, Ingeborg. *Invisible Walls: A German Family under the Nuremberg Laws*. Translated by J. Maxwell Brownjohn. San Diego: Harcourt Brace Jovanovich, 1984.

Heck, Alfons. *The Burden of Hitler's Legacy*. Frederick, Colorado: Renaissance House Publishers, 1988.

Heiden, Konrad. *The New Inquisition*. Translated by Heinz Norden. New York: Modern Age Books, Inc., 1939.

Heifetz, Julie. *Too Young to Remember*. Detroit: Wayne State University Press, 1989.

Heneman, Harlow J. "German Social Honor Courts." *Michigan Law Review* 37 (1939): 725–44.

Henry, Frances. *Victims and Neighbors: A Small Town in Nazi Germany Remembered*. South Hadley, Massachusetts: Bergin & Garvey Publishers, Inc., 1984.

Herz, John H. "German Administration Under the Nazi Regime." *American Political Science Review* 40 (1946): 682–702.

Herzstein, Robert Edwin. "The Jew in Wartime Nazi Film: An Interpretation of Goebbels' Role in the Holocaust." *Holocaust Studies Annual* 3 (1985): 177–88.

Heymann, Curt L. "German Laws Against the Jews." *Current History* 48 (1938): 38–43.

High, Stanley. "The German Program of Anti-Semitism." *Literary Digest* 116 (Nov. 11, 1933): 13, 26–27.

Hilberg, Raul. *The Destruction of the European Jews*. 1961. Reprint. Chicago: Quadrangle Books, 1967.

——. *The Destruction of the European Jews*. Revised and definitive edition. New York: Holmes and Meier, 1985.

——, ed. *Documents of Destruction: Germany and Jewry 1933–1945*. Chicago: Quadrangle Books, 1971.

Hitler, Adolf. *Mein Kampf*. New York: Stackpole Sons Publishers, 1939.

——. *My New Order*. Edited by Raoul de Rossy de Sales. New York: Renal & Hitchcock, 1941.

Hoefer, Frederick. "The Nazi Penal System—II." *Journal of Criminal Law, Criminology, and Police Science* 36 (1945): 30–38.

Hull, David Steward. *Film in the Third Reich: Art and Propaganda in Nazi Germany*. 1969. Reprint. A Touchstone Book. New York: Simon and Schuster, 1973.

Huttenbach, Henry R. *The Destruction of the Jewish Community of Worms 1933–1945: A Study of the Holocaust Experience in Germany*. New York: Memorial Committee of Jewish Victims of Nazism from Worms, 1981.

"It All Happened in a Nazi Week." *Literary Digest* 120 (Aug. 3, 1935): 12.

Jäckel, Eberhard. *Hitler's Weltanschauung: A Blueprint for Power*. Translated by Herbert Arnold. Middletown, Connecticut: Wesleyan University Press, 1972.

Jarausch, Konrad H. "Jewish Lawyers in Germany, 1848-1938: The Disintegration of a Profession." *Leo Baeck Institute Year Book* 36 (1991): 171–90.

The Jews in Nazi Germany: A Handbook of Facts Regarding Their Present Situation. 1935. Reprint. New York: Howard Fertig, 1982.

"Jews of Germany." *Studies of Migration and Settlement*. Report R-73, Oct. 4, 1944. United States government document.

Kamenetsky, Christa. *Children's Literature in Hitler's Germany: The Cultural Policy of National Socialism*. Athens, Ohio: Ohio University Press, 1984.

Kershaw, Ian. "The Persecution of the Jews and German Popular Opinion in the Third Reich." *Leo Baeck Institute Year Book* 26 (1981): 261–89.

——. *Popular Opinion and Political Dissent in the Third Reich: Bavaria 1933–1945.* Oxford: Clarendon Press, 1983.

Kersten, Felix. *The Kersten Memoirs 1940–1945.* Translated by Constantine Fitzgibbon and James Oliver. London: Hutchinson, 1956.

Kestenberg, Milton. "Legal Aspects of Child Persecution During the Holocaust." *Journal of the American Academy of Child Psychiatry* 24 (1985): 381–84.

Kirchheimer, Otto. "Criminal Law in National-Socialist Germany," *Studies in Philosophy and Social Science* 8 (1939–1940): 444–63.

Koch, H. W. *In the Name of the Volk: Political Justice in Hitler's Germany.* New York: St. Martin's Press, 1989.

——, ed. *Aspects of the Third Reich.* New York: St. Martin's Press, 1985.

Koehler, Hansjürgen. *Inside Information.* London: Pallas Publishing Co., Ltd., 1940.

——. *Inside the Gestapo: Hitler's Shadow Over the World.* London: Pallas Publishing Co., Ltd., 1940.

Kühl, Stefan. *The Nazi Connection: Eugenics, American Racism, and German National Socialism.* New York: Oxford University Press, 1994.

Kulka, Otto Dov. "'Public Opinion' in Nazi Germany and the 'Jewish Question.'" *Jerusalem Quarterly* (no. 25, 1982): 121–44.

——. "'Public Opinion' in Nazi Germany; The Final Solution." *Jerusalem Quarterly* (no. 26, 1983): 34–35.

Kwiet, Konrad. "Forced Labour of German Jews in Nazi Germany." *Leo Baeck Institute Year Book* 36 (1991): 389–410.

Leiser, Erwin. *Nazi Cinema.* Translated by Gertrud Mander and David Wilson. New York: Macmillan, 1974.

Lifton, Robert. *The Nazi Doctors: Medical Killing and the Psychology of Genocide.* New York: Basic Books, Inc., 1986.

Loewenstein, Karl. "Law in the Third Reich." *Yale Law Journal* 45 (1936): 779–815.

——. "Reconstruction of the Administration of Justice in American-Occupied Germany." *Harvard Law Review* 61 (1948): 419–67.

Lorch, Jacob. "The Nazi Misuse of Mendel." *Wiener Library Bulletin* 23 (Winter 1968/1969): 29–33.

Lore, Ludwig. "The Little Man's Fate in Germany." *Current History* 39 (1933): 143–50.

——. "The Nazi Revolution at Work." *Nation* 136 (1933): 440–43.

Marcus, Jacob R. *The Rise and Destiny of the German Jew.* Cincinnati: Union of American Hebrew Congregations, 1934.

Marx, Fritz Morstein. "German Bureaucracy in Transition." *American Political Science Review* 28 (1934): 467–80.

——. "Germany's New Civil Service Act." *American Political Science Review* 31 (1937): 878–83.

——. *Government in the Third Reich.* Second edition, revised and enlarged. McGraw-Hill Studies in Political Science, edited by Fritz Morstein Marx. New York: McGraw-Hill Book Company, Inc., 1937.

Massing, Paul W. *Rehearsal for Destruction: A Study of Political Anti-Semitism in Imperial Germany.* Studies in Prejudice, edited by Max Horkheimer and Samuel H. Flowerman. American Jewish Committee Social Studies Series, Publication No. 11. New York: Harper & Brothers, 1949.

Mayer, Milton. *They Thought They Were Free: The Germans 1933–45*. Chicago: University of Chicago Press, 1955.

Mendelsohn, John, ed. *The Holocaust: Selected Documents in Eighteen Volumes*. Vol. 13, *The Judicial System and the Jews in Nazi Germany*. New York: Garland Publishing, 1982.

Meyer, Michael. "The Nazi Musicologist as Myth Maker in the Third Reich." *Journal of Contemporary History* 10 (1975): 649–66.

Milton, Sybil. "The Expulsion of Polish Jews from Germany: October 1938 to July 1939." *Leo Baeck Institute Year Book* 29 (1984): 169–99.

Mitscherlich, Alexander, and Fred Mielke. *Doctors of Infamy: The Story of the Nazi Medical Crimes*. Translated by Heinz Norden. New York: Henry Schuman, 1949.

Mosse, George L., ed. *Nazi Culture: Intellectual, Cultural and Social Life in the Third Reich*. Translated by Salvator Attansio, et al. New York: Grosset & Dunlap, 1966.

Müller, Ingo. *Hitler's Justice: The Courts of the Third Reich*. Translated by Deborah Lucas Schneider. Cambridge: Harvard University Press, 1991.

Naumann, Bernd. *Auschwitz: A Report on the Proceedings Against Robert Karl Ludwig Mulka and Others Before the Court at Frankfurt*. New York: Frederick A. Praeger, Publishers, 1966.

Neumann, Franz. *Behemoth: The Structure and Practice of National Socialism 1933–1944*. 1944, second edition with new Appendix. Reprint. New York: Octagon Books, Inc., 1963.

Noakes, Jeremy. "The Development of Nazi Policy Towards the German-Jewish 'Mischlinge' 1933–1945." *Leo Baeck Institute Year Book* 34 (1989): 291–354.

Office of United States Chief of Counsel for Prosecution of Axis Criminality, International Military Trials. *Nazi Conspiracy and Aggression*. 8 vols. and 3 supplements. Washington: Government Printing Office, 1946, (Red series).

Opler, Morris Edward. "The Bio-Social Basis of Thought in the Third Reich." *American Sociological Review* 10 (1945): 776–86.

Picton, Harold. "Justice in Nazi Germany." *Contemporary Review* 156 (1939): 437–46.

Poliakov, L. "The Mind of the Mass Murderer: The Nazi Executioners—and Those Who Stood By." *Commentary* 12 (1951): 451–59.

Pommerin, Reiner. "The Fate of Mixed Blood Children in Germany." *German Studies Review* 5 (1982): 315–23.

Posner, Gerald. "Secrets of the Files." *New Yorker* 70 (March 14, 1994): 39–47.

Pozner, Vladimir. "Pogroms for Profit." *Nation* 148 (1939): 33–35.

Preuss, Lawrence. "Germanic Law Versus Roman Law in National Socialist Legal Theory." *Journal of Comparative Legislation and International Law*, 3rd ser., 16 (no. 1 and 4, 1939): 269–80.

——. "Racial Theory and National Socialist Political Thought." *Southwestern Social Science Quarterly* 15 (1934): 103–18.

Proctor, Robert N. *Racial Hygiene: Medicine Under the Nazis*. Cambridge: Harvard University Press, 1988.

"Protected by Hitler: An Unbiased Account of a Real Experience." *Current History* (June 1936): 83–90.

Reck-Malleczewen, Friedrich Percyval. *Diary of a Man in Despair*. Translated by Paul Rubens. New York: Macmillan, 1970.

Rheinstein, Max. "Comparative Law and Conflict of Laws in Germany." *University of Chicago Law Review* 2 (1935): 232–69.

Roberts, Stephen H. *The House That Hitler Built*. New York: Harper & Brothers, 1938.

Rusche, Georg, and Otto Kirchheimer. *Punishment and Social Structure*. New York: Columbia University Press, 1939.

Schleunes, Karl A. *The Twisted Road to Auschwitz: Nazi Policy Toward German Jews 1933–1939*. Urbana: University of Illinois Press, 1970.

Schuman, Frederick L. "The Political Theory of German Fascism." *American Political Science Review* 28 (1934): 210–32.

Shirer, William L. *Berlin Diary: The Journal of a Foreign Correspondent 1934–1941*. New York: Alfred A. Knopf, 1941.

Showalter, Dennis E. *Little Man, What Now?: Der Stürmer in the Weimar Republic*. Hamden, Connecticut: Archon Books, 1982.

Shuster, George Nayman. *Strong Man Rules: An Interpretation of Germany Today*. New York: D. Appleton-Century Company, 1934.

Smith, Howard K. *Last Train from Berlin*. New York: Alfred A. Knopf, 1943.

Steinhoff, Johannes, Peter Pechel, and Dennis Showalter, eds. *Voices from the Third Reich: An Oral History*. Washington, D.C.: Regnery Gateway, 1989.

Stokes, Lawrence D. "The German People and the Destruction of the European Jews." *Central European History* 6 (1973): 167–91.

Strauss, Herbert A. "Jewish Emigration from Germany: Nazi Policies and Jewish Responses (I)." *Leo Baeck Institute Year Book* 25 (1980): 313–61.

Tal, Uriel. "The Nazi Legal System and the Jews in Germany." *Studies in Contemporary Jewry* 1 (1984): 386–96.

Tenenbaum, Joseph. "The Crucial Year 1938." *Yad Washem Studies on the Jewish Catastrophe and Resistance* 2 (1958): 53–56.

Theilhaber, Felix A. "Decline of the German Jews." *Living Age* 349 (1935): 58–60.

Trial of the Major War Criminals Before the International Military Tribunal: Nuremberg, 14 November 1945–1 October 1946. 42 vols. Nuremberg, Germany: Secretariat of the Tribunal, 1947–1949, (Blue series).

Trials of War Criminals Before the Nuernberg Military Tribunals Under Control Council Law No. 10: Nuremberg, October 1946–April 1949. 15 vols. Washington: Government Printing Office, 1949–1953, (Green series).

Van Paassen, Pierre, and James Waterman Wise, eds. *Nazism: An Assault on Civilization*. New York: Harrison Smith and Robert Haas, 1934.

Waln, Nora. *Reaching for the Stars*. Boston: Little, Brown and Company, 1939.

Warburg, Gustav Otto. *Six Years of Hitler: The Jews Under the Nazi Regime*. London: Allen & Unwin, Ltd., 1939.

Weinreich, Max. *Hitler's Professors: The Part of Scholarship in Germany's Crimes against the Jewish People*. New York: Yiddish Scientific Institute—YIVO, 1946.

Weinryb, Bernard D. "Nazification of Science and Research in Nazi Germany." *Journal of Central European Affairs* 3 (1944): 373–400.

Weiss, Winfried. *A Nazi Childhood*. Santa Barbara, California: Capra Press, 1983.

Wertheimer, Mildred S. "The Jews in the Third Reich." *Foreign Policy Reports* 9 (1933): 174–84.

Weyrauch, Walter Otto. "Gestapo Informants: Facts and Theory of Undercover

Operations." *Columbia Journal of Transnational Law* 24 (1986): 553–96.

Wistrich, Robert. *Who's Who in Nazi Germany*. New York: Macmillan, 1982.

Wolff, Hans Julius. "Criminal Justice in Germany." *Michigan Law Review* 42 (1944): 1067–68.

Wunderlich, Frieda. "Education in Nazi Germany." *Social Research* 4 (1937): 347–60.

The Yellow Spot: The Outlawing of Half a Million Human Beings: A Collection of Facts and Documents Relating to Three Years' Persecution of German Jews, Derived Chiefly from National Socialist Sources, Very Carefully Assembled by a Group of Investigators. New York: Knight Publications, 1936.

Zeller, Frederic. *When Time Ran Out: Coming of Age in the Third Reich*. Sag Harbor, New York: The Permanent Press, 1989.

Zeman, Z.A.B. *Nazi Propaganda*. 2d ed. New York: Oxford University Press: 1973.

Ziemer, Gregor Athalwin. *Education for Death: The Making of the Nazi*. New York: Oxford University Press, 1941.

INDEX

About the Author

RICHARD LAWRENCE MILLER is an independent scholar. He was trained as a broadcaster and historian. He is the author of *Truman* (1985) and *The Case for Legalizing Drugs* (Praeger, 1991).